M000166216

Preacher Woman

Preacher Woman

A Critical Look at Sexism Without Sexists

KATIE LAUVE-MOON

OXFORD
UNIVERSITY PRESS

OXFORD
UNIVERSITY PRESS

Oxford University Press is a department of the University of Oxford. It furthers
the University's objective of excellence in research, scholarship, and education
by publishing worldwide. Oxford is a registered trade mark of Oxford University
Press in the UK and certain other countries.

Published in the United States of America by Oxford University Press
198 Madison Avenue, New York, NY 10016, United States of America.

© Oxford University Press 2021

All rights reserved. No part of this publication may be reproduced, stored in
a retrieval system, or transmitted, in any form or by any means, without the
prior permission in writing of Oxford University Press, or as expressly permitted
by law, by license, or under terms agreed with the appropriate reproduction
rights organization. Inquiries concerning reproduction outside the scope of the
above should be sent to the Rights Department, Oxford University Press, at the
address above.

You must not circulate this work in any other form
and you must impose this same condition on any acquirer.

Library of Congress Cataloging-in-Publication Data
Names: Lauve-Moon, Katie, author.
Title: Preacher woman : a critical look at sexism without sexists /
Katie Lauve-Moon.
Description: New York, NY, United States of America : Oxford University
Press, [2021] | Includes bibliographical references and index.
Identifiers: LCCN 2020049120 (print) | LCCN 2020049121 (ebook) |
ISBN 9780197527542 (hardback) | ISBN 9780197527559 (paperback) |
ISBN 9780197527573 (epub)
Subjects: LCSH: Women clergy. | Sex discrimination against women. |
Women in Christianity. | Baptists—Doctrines.
Classification: LCC BV676.L38 2021 (print) | LCC BV676 (ebook) |
DDC 262.14/613—dc23
LC record available at https://lccn.loc.gov/2020049120
LC ebook record available at https://lccn.loc.gov/2020049121

DOI: 10.1093/oso/9780197527542.001.0001

1 3 5 7 9 8 6 4 2

Paperback printed by Marquis, Canada
Hardback printed by Bridgeport National Bindery, Inc., United States of America

For the little girls whose minds and souls are being formed from within church pews. May they see themselves in the leaders they encounter.

Contents

Preface

When people are committed to gender equality, what gets in their way of achieving it? Why do *well-intentioned* people reinforce sexist outcomes? In a country with (some) workplace equity laws in place and the vast majority of residents opposed to sexism, why do sexist outcomes persist? These questions are being asked in various workplaces, organizations, and institutions across the world with responses emerging in the form of diversity, equity, and inclusion initiatives. I became particularly interested in the answers to these questions after learning that women occupied only about 5% of solo senior pastor positions in congregations affiliated with the Cooperative Baptist Fellowship (CBF). Women pastors' vast underrepresentation in these organizations was particularly surprising because the CBF had been established 30 years ago in part to explicitly *support* women's equal leadership in the church. In light of this, I wanted to know why these sexist outcomes persist today.

Congregations affiliated with the CBF have established a theology that supports gender equality and women's equal leadership in the church. Unlike Southern Baptist congregations, which explicitly bar women from leadership positions, most CBF congregations additionally maintain organizational goals supporting the pastoral callings of men and women equally. Given the stated values of gender equality of these congregations, one hypothesis I carried into this research was that members and leaders of these congregations were well intentioned in relation to issues of sexism and gender inequality. After 18 months in the field and visiting seven different congregations, I found this to be true. To varying degrees, every congregation in this study wanted to learn more in order to reach their established goals of gender equality. I never met anyone who was explicitly resistant to my presence nor did I ever have trouble finding people to interview. Most study participants were deeply interested in my findings and insisted I share my conclusions.

Informed by these experiences, I drew on Dr. Eduardo Bonilla-Silva's theoretical frame, *racism without racists*, to develop this book's title, *Preacher Woman: A Critical Look at Sexism Without Sexists*. This book goes beyond the inclusive theologies and good intentions of CBF congregations to identify gendered processes that undergird the established inequitable gender outcomes of these organizations. The purpose of this book is not to reveal ill intent in these congregations, but rather to examine critically congregational processes with the purpose of building on established organizational goals of gender equity and inclusion and identify strategies to reach these intended outcomes more effectively. The findings of this book shed light on implicitly sexist organizational processes within moderate-progressive religious congregations, but the implications extend well beyond religious life to any workplace seeking outcomes of equity and inclusion. Each chapter includes action steps for working toward transformational organizational change as well as a list of discussion questions and supplementary readings that pursue similar inquiries at the intersections of race, sexuality, and class within different workplace contexts.

Acknowledgments

I am incredibly grateful to so many people who made this project possible. I want to first thank the congregants and church staff who agreed to be a part of this study. In every congregation I visited, I was overwhelmed by the level of generosity, warmth, and support. Thank you for your openness and allowing me to be a part of your community.

I owe a great deal of gratitude, particularly to the women pastors who shared deeply personal and difficult details of their journeys with me. Thank you for trusting me with your stories. My hope is that this work further elevates your voices of determination, hope, and justice.

I am deeply thankful for the mentorship of Dr. Mimi Schippers and Dr. Sally Kenney. Mimi, thank you for giving me new eyes and pushing me in this endeavor. When we first met, I had never taken a single course in gender—and here we are. I quite literally could not have initiated this work without your guidance, insight, and expertise. Sally, thank you for helping me find my voice and believing in me. I could have never written this book without your incredibly high standards for writing! I am so grateful for all of the knowledge and wisdom you have imparted to me over these last few years.

I want to thank the academic departments to which I have belonged during the development of this project. I am thankful for the continued support of the faculty, students, and staff of the City, Culture, & Community doctoral program at Tulane University. I especially want to thank the members of my cohort as well as the PhDivas and all of their affiliates for their positivity and encouragement. I am grateful to the Department of Social Work and Harris College of Nursing and Health Sciences at Texas Christian University (TCU). I am especially thankful for the active support of my colleagues in the TCU Women & Gender Studies Department and the ongoing conversations pertaining to gender and inequality. I would like to express my gratitude for my time spent in the Diana R. Garland School of Social Work at Baylor University. I am particularly grateful to the late Dean Diana Garland for generously sharing her story with me, which ultimately led to the development of this project.

I am grateful to the editors and production team at Oxford University Press. Thank you for taking a chance on this first-time author and allowing my voice to be heard throughout the process. I am also incredibly fortunate to those who helped copyedit and format the pages of this book prior to submission: Megan Pleshek, Ryan Lauve, and Tim Lauve-Moon. And I am thankful to Megan Morris and Shelby Enman, who helped organize survey data. I am also indebted to the talented artist and scholar, Dr. Amanda Wilson Harper, who repurposed the *stained-glass labyrinth* graphic in the conclusion of this book.

I am forever grateful for my grandparents and parents who have always supported and given me the tools to chase my goals. I am very thankful for the encouragement I consistently find in my in-laws. I am also incredibly grateful for the love and support of my siblings as well as my nieces and nephews, who are constant sources of light and joy.

I also must acknowledge the people in my life who have gone over and beyond to offer love, warmth, and encouragement at various stages of this endeavor: Merry, Rosemarie, Hannah, Mary Katherine, Laurie, Carly, Sam, Tee, Karina, Amy, Melissa, Mom, and Ryan—I am deeply grateful.

I am forever thankful for the unconditional love of Britain, Hobie, and Bil. Britain, your companionship carried me through!

Finally, Timmy. I am overcome by your constant flow of love, patience, generosity, and encouragement. There are not enough pages in this book to include all of the ways you have supported me in this endeavor. I could not ask for a better friend and partner. Thank you for all of it.

Introduction

The sanctuary was dim, quiet, empty. I arrived a little early and found a spot in one of the darker corners of the large room. I sat silently, still and alert. After a few minutes, I realized I had been holding my breath so as not to disturb the molecules of air around me. The air invited me to breathe. It was crisp, thin, and filled with anticipation. Something was about to happen here—something important, something sacred. And it was going to happen in approximately 42 minutes. Although, I suspected that it had already begun.

A few minutes later, I heard a door crack open. Two women walked in from a side entrance and a light flipped on over the stage at the front of the room revealing a full set of band instruments, microphones, and a couple of podiums. The women brought an excited, focused energy with them. One pointed at the stage as they talked and walked toward it. She used the three steps at the side of the stage to approach it. The other woman walked around to the front of the stage and jumped onto it from the floor of the sanctuary. Her landing interrupted the quiet of the room with a small bang. She stood up. The two continued to discuss various logistical details and positioned the podiums in different corners of the stage to see what worked best. At first the podiums were side by side to the far left of the stage, and the first woman moved one of them to the opposite end saying, "I think we should fill up the whole stage." "Yes, I agree," the other responded.

Three more women entered from the back of the sanctuary and made their ways down the center aisle to the front of the stage. It seemed like one of these women was making her first appearance of the day because the two at the front were delighted to see her and knelt at the front of the stage to embrace her. All five women began discussing. Two were on the stage, and three on the sanctuary floor, but they were all standing in the light now.

One of the women held a clipboard with what appeared to be the program for the ensuing event. She began working her way through it. On her cue, the women took turns taking the lead and explaining how they would go about their parts while the others listened. The women nodded in affirmation and offered the occasional suggestion.

A few minutes later their circle dispersed. The woman with the clipboard walked back down the aisle to sit in one of the many empty chairs front and center of the stage. She sat and observed the scene in front of her. The other two newcomers joined the other women on stage. One of them hopped to sit at the

Preacher Woman. Katie Lauve-Moon, Oxford University Press (2021). © Oxford University Press.
DOI: 10.1093/oso/9780197527542.003.0001

front edge of the stage, swung her legs around, and stood up. The fourth woman was given a hand up from one of the others. They began to work individually. One placed some papers on the podium at stage right and began reading over them. Another looked at the team in the sound booth situated above the chairs at the back of the sanctuary and began checking the microphones. The other two began tuning and setting up their instruments. The strum of a guitar came barreling through the room's speakers. The drums followed shortly as one of the women checked the foot drum and the cymbals one after the other. The space slowly became a living, breathing organism full of intention and energy.

As the space developed a heartbeat, my mind filled with memories of so many other church rooms transformed by women of the congregation. I thought of women repurposing bare fellowship halls into warm spaces for dining, socializing, and celebrating with full place settings, elaborate flower arrangements, and homemade casseroles and desserts—all of which they had made themselves. I thought of how divine sanctuaries smelled after churchwomen had filled the aisles with roses, gardenias, and lilies for weddings; this was actually equally true in the occasions of funerals. I remembered how warm I felt filling paper cups with coffee and orange Tang before and after Sunday school. This was all the often invisible work of women church workers. They'd come in before anyone else to put everything in place and disappear before anyone arrived. Women have served as the heartbeat of so many churches for a very long time now. This was no different.

The women wrapped up and exited through a door to the left of the sanctuary. Shortly after, people began to trickle in—just a few here and there at first. Then dozens of people began entering from all sides of the room and filling the seats. Some sat silently with a gaze of apprehension or introspect, others anxiously looked around to see if they recognized anyone, and some enthusiastically whispered in groups of two or three, smiling and laughing. But none of them spoke in their full voices yet.

The room was full now. It looked similar to any given sanctuary in the United States, mostly women and some men. In addition to the spotlight on the stage, glass globes were dimly lit along the walls, and the whispered chatter gained more and more power with every new person who entered. The sanctuary felt warm and alive.

As people continued to make their ways to their seats, the women from earlier returned along with a few others. Those in the band silently moved toward the stage and picked up their instruments. The others took a seat in the front row. This happened so swiftly and quietly that very few of the attendees noticed.

Moments later, the strum of a chord soared across the room and the bandleader's voice floated over our heads drawing us in. As she sang, the body language of the attendees relaxed a little. The band continued to play and many attendees stood up but some remained seated. After a song or two, one of the women from earlier walked to a microphone on the stage. The room quieted. In a strong, soft voice she opened:

> *Sister, you are welcome here. Your body, your person, your presence is welcome, your gender is welcome here, your voice is welcome here, your calling, your gifts, your radiance are welcome here. Your opinion is welcome here, your experience, your expertise are welcome here. Your truth is welcome here, your questions are welcome here. Your intellect is welcome here, your heart is welcome here.*
>
> *Your brain gets a seat at the table.* (The women in the crowd began to perk up and snap their fingers.) *Your perspective gets a place on the platform, your preaching gets a pulpit, and your fire is encouraged to burn. Sister, you are welcome here.*
>
> *There are no limits on your growth here, no interruptions to your speech here* (clapping), *no hesitations to affirm you here. We don't require your shrinking or your curtsying. And please, for the love of God, don't apologize for being here.* (The crowd let out a knowing laugh.)
>
> *Sister, I said you are welcome here. Your strength is welcome here. Your wounds, your tears, your struggles are welcome here. Your badass-ery is welcome here.* (The crowd began clapping louder and cheering). *Your awakeness, your intuitiveness, your curiosity are all welcome here. Did I mention your feelings are welcome here? Your sorrow, your joy, your anger, your exuberance are welcome here.*
>
> *Your skirt, your pants, your style is welcome here. Your soft voice, your loud voice, your high-pitched voice, your deep voice, your authoritative voice is welcome here.*
>
> *Brothers, did you think I left you out? You are welcome here! Your presence is welcome in this place. Your learning, your listening, your support, your partnership, your gifts, your time are welcome in this place. Sisters and brothers and every delightful gender in between, you are welcome in this place. So bring it. Don't sit back like an unwanted intruder afraid to engage, you are welcome and wanted in this place.*[1]

Another woman joined her on the opposite end of the stage, and they offered each other reassuring looks. She stood tall, composed, and resolute, but her face was soft and peaceful. The first woman began again:

> *Let's continue with an old and ancient story. Once upon a time, she was warned. She was given an explanation.*

The second woman responded, "But nevertheless, she preached," and continued, "She was told she was too bossy, her brazen exterior too fly, too flossy." The first woman raised her open-palmed hand up and to the front of her, and then she and the crowd responded, "But nevertheless, she preached." The two women continued the call and responsive reading alternating every other one with the crowd responding in between each time:

She was told she was too soft, too weak, too passive. She didn't have the stuff of a leader.

But nevertheless, she preached.

She was told she was too timid, her caution mistaken as indifference.

But nevertheless, she preached.

She was told she was too confident, her calling mistaken as arrogance. Her gift is her shame, her vocation a mere power grab.

But nevertheless, she preached.

She was told she was too loud, she had too much to say, too alive, too proud.

But nevertheless, she preached.

She was told she was too quiet. I can't hear you. I won't hear you. Did you say something?

But nevertheless, she preached.

She was told emotion clouded her clarity, that nothing good comes from when we are undone.

But nevertheless, she preached.

She was told she was too radical, too extreme. She really ought to calm herself down. Be more moderate, ride the fence. Whatever you do, don't upset anyone. Ever.

But nevertheless, she preached.[2]

After the crowd responded the final time, they cheered, laughed, cried, and held each other. They held hope in their eyes. Their bodies were now open. They moved around like humans feeling seen and heard and known for the first time in a long time. I quickly realized that what I was witnessing was distinctly different than my previous observations of women working in the church. Women were not invisible here, their jobs not thankless. They were front and center. They made up the majority of the band. They were the organizers. They were the preachers. They were the prayers, the poets, and the announcers. They weren't the token Scripture readers or soloists or pianists. They weren't only in charge of the flowers or refreshments or children or administrative tasks. They led the service in every way. I had never before experienced this in a sanctuary. It occurred to me that this must be how so many men feel every time they attend a church service! Or, perhaps they take it for granted?

This worship service marked the opening night of the inaugural *Nevertheless, She Preached* conference. *Nevertheless, She Preached* was first breathed into life by a group of women ministers who were met with the news that the seminary from which they graduated would be hosting a lecture given by a religious leader known for his opposition to women's leadership in the church. Their Baptist seminary was founded as a safe place for women to prepare for vocational ministry in response to the Conservative Takeover within the Southern Baptist Convention (SBC) that doctrinally barred women's ministerial leadership across the SBC. Their seminary had officially educated and affirmed the calling of women ministers since its inception and, therefore, it pained and frustrated many of its women graduates when it agreed to endorse this particular religious leader. In response, many of these women pastors organized a counterevent "aimed at fully empowering and encouraging the clergy women who felt sidelined by the very institution that had loved and supported them into being."[3]

The seminary eventually canceled their involvement in this religious leader's lecture but plans for *Nevertheless, She Preached* carried on. One of the organizers, Reverend Kyndall Rae Rothaus, wrote:

> Our plans grew into a two-day preaching event designed and led by women. Men were welcome in the space, but for once, women held the stage. We named it, "Unauthorized: Nevertheless She Preached," a title that resonated with women across the nation and across denominations. We saw it as an outward sign and symbol that women desperately needed a place to be fully seen and heard, and that we were not getting that support out in the world—not consistently, not enough, not in our churches, not even in our seminaries. It wasn't an act of hostility but an act of truth-telling.[4]

These women's frustrations with being denied a voice are further corroborated by statistics that extend beyond the seminary and into Baptist churches. Their seminary is primarily affiliated with two Baptist denominational entities. One of its affiliations is a statewide denominational entity, the Baptist General Convention of Texas (BGCT); only a half percent of this organization's churches employ women as senior pastors (25 out of 5,318).[5] Their seminary is also affiliated with the Cooperative Baptist Fellowship (CBF). The CBF is a national denominational entity with only 5% of its churches employing women as solo senior pastors despite women enrolling in almost equal rates as men (46.7%) at CBF-affiliated seminaries.[6] Rothaus continued:

> We created our preaching event out of the sense that we were not the only women who felt unheard and unseen, who needed a word of sincere and unmitigated acknowledgment. We weren't the only denomination still struggling to give women a place at the table.

The underrepresentation of women pastors in most non–Southern Baptist Baptist denominations mirrors distinctly low national trends in other religions and Christian denominations with women representing only 13.5% of head clergy[7] and 20.7% of all clergy across all religious traditions in the United States;[8] these statistics have remained about the same for the last 20 years. When Roman Catholic (2.6% women leaders), white conservative, evangelical, fundamentalist such as the Southern Baptist Convention (2.4% women leaders), and non-Christian (32.6% women leaders) religious congregations are removed from the figure, women still only constitute 16.2% and 29.8% of religious leaders in Black Protestant and white liberal/moderate congregations, respectively. These statistics are particularly telling, given that women represent at least 60% of membership in the vast majority of congregations of all religious traditions and Christian denominations in the United States.[9]

Women ministers' underrepresentation in religious congregations reflects similar trends in leadership positions in the United States. For instance, women represent only about a fourth of U.S. Senators and Representatives and 7% of Fortune 500 company chief executive officers. Even in the field of education in the United States, which is predominately female, only 67.7% of education administrators are women.[10] Moreover, in the predominately female field of social work, a profession inherently committed to the pursuit of social justice and gender equality, men disproportionately hold leadership positions.[11] These patterns raise an important question: In a country with at least some workplace equity laws in place and the vast majority of residents opposed to sexism, why do sexist outcomes persist? And more specifically, why do congregations affiliated with the CBF, a denominational entity founded by Baptists who separated from the fundamentalist SBC in part *to support* women in leadership, continue to produce sexist outcomes almost 30 years later? I argue that investigating explanations to the second question moves us closer to a more comprehensive answer to the first question.

Following the women's liberation movement of the 1970s, there was a significant increase in the number of women pursuing official ministerial positions. A couple of decades later, religion and gender scholars began investigating the development of what is now commonly referred to as the "stained-glass ceiling" or the underrepresentation of women in top leadership positions in religious organizations.[12] In the context of American Christianity, one study shows that the conservative or fundamentalist theological belief in the inerrancy of biblical Scripture functions as the strongest organizational barrier to women in leadership positions.[13] However, only a few studies investigate why the stained-glass ceiling persists in moderate-liberal Christian congregations that interpret biblical Scripture in ways that affirm women's leadership in the church and, therefore, explanations remain limited in scope.

Mark Chaves's study on the ordination of women reveals that denominational characteristics are often generated by organizational responses to external, institutional pressures that may only tenuously reflect actual congregational pragmatic activity, thereby resulting in a *loose coupling* between doctrine and actualized practices. In other words, the women's liberation movement in the United States may have resulted in subsequent doctrinal shifts toward the formal theological and organizational affirmation of women's leadership in the church; however, "a denomination's policy allowing (or prohibiting) women's ordination is better understood as a symbolic display of support for gender equality (or of resistance to gender equality) than as a policy either motivated by or intended to regulate the everyday reality of women inside the organization."[14] This study further demonstrates that specifically in more moderate-progressive denominations, congregations are more likely to create gender-inclusive leadership policies in response to external, secular pressures than as a result of overarching organizational progressive attitudes.

So we find that even within these more progressive denominations, women clergy are more likely to hold part-time ministerial positions, work in precarious situations, pastor the smallest congregations, and make smaller salaries than men.[15] Studies also show that women pastors are less likely to progress to the same professional positions as their male counterparts and the number of women clergy decreases drastically as one climbs the religious ladder.[16] Moreover, it takes significantly longer for women to receive their first ministerial position than their male counterparts.[17] While this work effectively establishes a disconnect between organizational goals and outcomes in moderate-progressive congregations, questions remain as to what types of organizational processes actually reinforce this loose coupling between organizational goals and women's equal leadership in the church.

The few available studies examining the specific congregational processes that contribute to the stained-glass ceiling show that women pastors' dual expectations of family and work responsibilities, traditional masculinized conceptions of the role of pastor, and congregants' gendered assumptions and hiring practices reinforce inequality between men and women pastors.[18] This small, valuable collection of research represents the initial step in understanding specific organizational barriers faced by women pastors, but it proves limited in scope. First, most of these studies investigate the experiences and perceived expectations of clergy, thus leaving the assumptions and behaviors of congregants and hiring entities largely underexplored. Secondly, many of these studies investigate one particular organizational process within a particular congregation. To date, almost no research provides in-depth analyses of multiple gendered organizational processes across multiple congregations. Also, most of these studies were conducted at least a decade if not two decades ago. Today, significantly more women are graduating from seminaries and more congregations have taken intentional steps toward affirming women's leadership, yet women's underrepresentation in pastoral positions remains largely unchanged. Therefore, investigation into *why* these trends persist, particularly within congregations morally committed to supporting women's equal leadership, proves even more relevant and important.

In addition to research studies, a new wave of literature has emerged illustrating women's significant underrepresentation in pastoral positions. This emerging body of literature includes newspaper editorials and magazine articles demonstrating the persistence of the stained-glass ceiling as well as blogs and books written by women pastors that present ways to best maneuver through sexist barriers within congregations.[19] These contributions are important because they raise the voices of women pastors working in the trenches, highlight the persisting issue of women's unequal leadership in the church, and provide strategies for negotiating ways to push through gendered organizational barriers. Much like the aforementioned research studies, much of this literature does not adequately address *why* these gendered barriers persist within these congregations. Moreover, these works primarily help women pastors succeed *despite* congregational barriers rather than identifying the organizational processes that underlie these barriers and strategizing about how to change the organizations themselves. This book centralizes structural change by investigating ways in which well-intending congregational actors reinforce sexism within churches that affirm the equal leadership of women.

The Theoretical Framework

The concept of gender and its relationship to structural inequality proves key to understanding the ways in which gendered organizational processes reinforce sexist outcomes despite the good intentions of individual actors. At the emergence of formal scientific research on sex and gender in the early twentieth century, researchers argued that there were essential differences between men and women that extended well beyond our physical bodies. Medical experts in the production and regulation of hormones initially believed that the embodiment of masculinity (e.g., rationality) and femininity (e.g., emotionality) resulted from different sex hormones, and these biological differences produced gendered and, therefore, different personalities.[20] At the time, this research was often cited in opposition to women securing the right to vote, moving into the workforce, and enrolling in higher education. However, as this vein of study progressed, it became apparent rather quickly that estrogen and testosterone to varying degrees existed in *both* sexes. Moreover, in some cases, levels of estrogen were found to be higher in males than females.[21] Therefore, sex hormones failed to sufficiently distinguish between males and females.[22]

Later Young et al. (1965) presented the *brain organization theory*, which proposed that men and women have different brains, which predispose them to complementary sexual attractions and gendered behaviors.[23] Specifically, Young et al. suggested that different levels of estrogen and testosterone in gestation resulted in differences in male and female brains, thereby creating personality differences between men and women understood as fixed. Through this study as well as dozens of subsequent studies, sexual differentiation, sexual orientation, and gendered behavior became understood as a result of differences between men's and women's brains.[24] While more recent medical research generally acknowledges at least some influence of the social environment on gendered personalities and behaviors, there has been a resurgence of medical research centralizing brain organization theory and supporting the notion of a rigid gender binary,[25] and therefore, many medical professionals argue that brains function as the connection between gendered personalities and sex hormones.

Even a casual observer may notice, however, that there is often overlap in the gendered personalities and behaviors of men and women. The position of *gender essentialism*, the idea that behavioral differences between men and women are biologically natural and fixed, fails to address why, for example, some women often act more rationally than some men and other women, or why some men are more nurturing than some women and other men. In an effort to address these conclusive gaps, sex and gender researchers investigated the various assumptions made in brain organization studies and found that overall this research fails to pass the basic indicative test for scientific research.[26] By and large this collection of work consists of quasi-experimental studies with most conducting tests on animals with assumed transferability to humans. Moreover, this collective research relies on inconsistent understandings of sex, gender, and/or hormones; is rarely replicated; and is often methodologically flawed.[27] In fact, one recent analysis of 1,400 human brains actually revealed extensive overlap in the characteristics of female and male brains and determined that human brains cannot be divided into the two distinct categories of male brains and female brains.[28] For more extensive information about this study, refer to *Gender Mosaic: Beyond the Myth of the Male and Female Brain* by Dr. Daphna Joel and Luba Vikhanski (2019). Despite more recent findings and major critiques of brain organization research, the prevailing sex and gender medical discourse largely remains situated in essentialism with considerably less emphasis on the social environment as it relates to the development of gendered personalities. For a comprehensive overview and critique of brain organization research, refer to *Brain Storm: The Flaws in the Sciences of Sex Differences* by Dr. Rebecca Jordan-Young (2010) as well as *Testosterone Rex: Myths of Sex, Science, and Society* by Dr. Cordelia Fine (2017).

Sex Roles

Into the 1970s, psychologists began utilizing established personality and employment tests to measure personality attributes defined by sex roles.[29] These instruments implicitly positioned masculinity (e.g., leadership, assertive, agency, efficacy, rational) as opposite to femininity (e.g., submissive, passive, dependent, nurturing, emotional). For example, a woman who tested high on femininity was automatically understood as low on masculinity. Subsequent studies found that these measurements produced results that failed to accurately reflect the personalities of participants.[30] These critiques led to a conceptual framework that serves as the foundation for all gender theory today. Subsequent empirical studies illustrate that masculinity and femininity should not be understood as opposite ends of a spectrum but rather two different personality dimensions; the two are not mutually exclusive.[31] A person could test both high on masculinity *and* femininity or low on both and so on. For example, depending on the context, an assertive, agentic leader may *also* be nurturing and empathetic and, therefore, would likely test as both high masculinity and high femininity, a category referred to as *androgyny*.

While the conception of sex roles and gendered personality dimensions served as more dynamic perspectives than purely biological ones, these conceptualizations of sex and gender eventually proved limited as well. Researchers argued that the very use of the term "role" suggests that the ways women and men lived their lives were fixed and constant across contexts and life stages.[32] It did not allow for gendered tasks and behaviors to be understood as activities men and women may both come in and out of depending on the time and place. The notion of sex roles also suggests a fixed complementarity between men and women and fails to address the inherent structure of power and subordination between traditional male roles and traditional female roles. In the same way that the notion of "race roles" is insufficient for legitimizing different roles for people of different races, the idea of sex roles should be understood in this way as well. Finally, more recent scholarship argues that the use of feminine and masculine labels in personality tests is unhelpful and reinforces the gender binary.[33] Instead, the scale labeled "masculine" should be represented by personality traits such as leadership, assertiveness, and agency and the "feminine" scale should instead be understood as personality traits such as nurturance, empathy, and compassion. While these critiques are a positive step forward in the conceptual development of gender, the distinction between masculinity and femininity remains necessary for describing gendered processes and will be utilized throughout this book.

Socialization and Doing Gender

In the mid-twentieth century, social scientists began investigating how the interaction between sex and cultural experiences exacerbate, reduce, or eliminate sex differences (with the exception of reproductive capabilities). This research drew on the scholarly traditions of *social constructionism*, which maintains that knowledge and meaning are created through interactions with others rather than as separate phenomena within individuals, and *social constructivism*, which argues that humans' social contexts (including interactions) influence their learning and development. Building on this vein of research as well as psychologists' theory of socialization, sociologists developed *sex role socialization theory*, which states that children are encouraged to perform *gender-appropriate* behaviors and rewarded when they do so (or face consequences when they fail to do so). This theory posits that sex role socialization shapes children's personalities, influences psychological development, and shapes their abilities and desires.[34] The pervasiveness of sex role socialization forms the illusion that gendered behaviors are innate and naturally occurring. For example, some studies show that children with a same-sex primary caregiver are more likely to develop the ability to nurture. Since mothers are most often the primary caregivers, girls are more likely to be nurturing than boys.[35] Other research found that mothers often coalesce identities with their daughters and relate to their sons as distinct and separate individuals, which increases men's ability to develop autonomous identities.[36]

The impact of sex socialization extends well beyond the parent–child relationship. Until recently, women in children's stories and movies were largely portrayed as beautiful princesses who were trapped in towers or in comas until a strong, agentic prince saved them. Or they were the wicked witches responsible for these unfortunate situations. Additionally, boys are most often dressed in clothes that allow for rough and active play while girls usually wear dresses or delicate fabrics fit for sitting still or being small, disciplined, and "lady-like."[37] Girls are more likely to be disciplined for speaking loudly, not following instructions, and engaging in physical play than boys.[38] However, boys' rough or disruptive behavior is overlooked for longer and understood as "boys being boys." Boys, often regardless of athletic ability, are registered for sports, which offers opportunities to build leadership skills and make independent decisions on the court or field, while girls are enrolled in ballet classes that often follow rigid choreography, rarely promoting free thinking. Boys are given bats and balls while girls, even as babies themselves, are given baby dolls to care for and kitchens in which to cook, serve, and clean.[39] Consequently, "we get nurturant women and independent men in a society dominated by men and which values independence."[40]

While girls have recently been given more opportunities to participate in traditional boys' activities and a wider range of toys, boys are still most often encouraged to play with masculine toys and enrolled in *boyish* activities.[41] In fact, when boys engage in girlish activities, they are often called derogatory names such as fairy or tink or fag (an assumption of sexuality based on gendered acts). Or if boys fail to perform at high levels in traditional boys activities, they are often referred to as girls (e.g., throwing like a girl); this is usually not considered to be a positive attribute. However, when girls perform boyish activities with excellence and competence, it is considered a step up. Girls are called studs, bad asses, or tom-boys, because an athletic girl who is competitive in sports *must* be part-boy. As long as girls are still able to maintain a socially expected level of femininity, it is often perceived positively when girls are viewed as *exceptions to their sex*. Critical perspectives of socialization reveal how female socialization disadvantages girls, particularly in Western societies, and shows the structural inequality that persists between masculinity and femininity, girls and boys, men and women.

Although gendered personality development and socialization research proves more illustrative than biological explanations of gendered behaviors, it is limited in its explanatory power. First, gender socialization assumes the continuity of behaviors and gendered personalities throughout the entire life course. For instance, socialization theories fail to explain why women become more career oriented after their children go to school. Second, they fail to show why men and women display qualities of femininity (e.g., passivity) in some situations and embody qualities of masculinity (e.g., assertiveness) in other contexts. For example, men are found to be nurturing when there is no woman present to do the job.[42] Third, these explanations of gender fail to show why some women embody forms of masculinity more often than other women or some men and why some men embody femininity more often than some women. While socialization remains a key part in explaining gendered patterns, it is limited in scope.

Due to discrepancies found in gender personality and socialization theories, sex and gender researchers and scholars built on this social constructionist framework to demonstrate how gender is something *we do* rather than something *we are*.[43] Different from *sex*, which is usually assigned at birth and determined by "socially agreed-upon biological criteria," or *sex category*, the social category in which one is assigned based on sex and the "socially required identificatory displays," *gender*, understood in terms of masculinity and femininity, is something we are held morally accountable to perform in relation to normative conceptions of behaviors appropriate for one's assigned sex category[44] (i.e., men should behave in a masculine manner; women should behave in a feminine manner). In other words, gender is a constructed script we perform; masculinity and femininity are behaviors we move in and out of in every interaction, vary depending on the context and actors involved, and are created, regulated, constrained, or enforced through dominant expectations and social consequences. Gendered interactions, then, act as a legitimating force for one of the most significant divisions of society and underlie gender inequality. "Doing gender" remains the dominant conceptual framework in sociology with several thousand subsequent empirical studies presenting evidence of how men and women do gender.[45]

Gender as a Social Structure

Building on new structuralists' notion that gender inequality can be attributed to the structure of organizations and women predominately occupying lower positions in the workplace,[46] Joan Acker[47] broadened the "doing gender" framework from the interactional level to the organizational level. Specifically, Acker shifts the understanding of organizations as gender-neutral to actual gendered or masculinized structures.[48] Gendered organizations are understood as gendered when "advantage and disadvantage, exploitation and control, action and emotion, meaning and identity are patterned through and in terms of a distinction between male and female, masculine and feminine."[49] Here, gendered organizations are conceptualized as part of socially constructed institutions.[50] Acker writes, "The term 'gendered institutions' means that gender is present in the processes, practices, images, and ideologies, and distribution of power in the various sectors of social life."[51] Acker argues further and empirical research shows that gender is embedded in five interactive organizational processes: (1) organizational logic and culture;[52] (2) symbols and images;[53] (3) division of labor;[54] (4) interactions;[55] and (5) construction of individual identities.[56]

The aforementioned empirical studies and hundreds of others utilize Acker's theoretical framework to illustrate how embedded organizational processes contribute to and reinforce the *glass ceiling* across a variety of professions and workplaces. Drawing on Acker's notion of sexism being embedded at different organizational levels, some gender researchers further refine the concept of the glass ceiling, which suggests that women face only one barrier in their paths to positions of leadership, and instead show how women more accurately face a labyrinth of sexist barriers in most workplaces.[57] Therefore, women may successfully enter the workplace, but sexist barriers negatively influence their abilities to climb the organizational hierarchy. Today, the framework of gendered organizations remains the predominant analytical tool for investigating gender inequality as well as other inequalities in workplaces and organizations.[58]

About a decade after the theoretical frameworks of *doing gender* and *gendered organizations* were established, sociologist Barbara Risman pulled these frameworks together to illustrate how rigid conceptions of a gender binary are reflected at every level of society, including the individual, interactional, organizational, and institutional levels.[59] In the same way that societies construct political and economic structures, they also construct gender structures, which vary by place and time. In other words, like economics and politics, gender is always at play.

On the individual level, we are socialized to act in particular ways, so much so that these socialized behaviors are often perceived as naturally occurring. We also internalize gendered expectations and often judge ourselves and others by these standards. We may also make life choices based on the same-sex role models around us and the choices they made. On the interactional level, our internalized lessons of gender are often created, reinforced, and regulated through our interactions with others, and we interact with each other based on socially agreed-upon gendered scripts. On the institutional level, the gender binary is further reflected through cultural images such as portrayals of men and women in labor, social media, television, advertising, and literature. Dominant gender structure shapes our belief systems, religious teachings, dating practices, and forms our stereotypes. It often manifests in the policies and cultures of organizations and workplaces, the division of labor, and the representation of same-sex role models in positions of power (or lack thereof).

Dominant gender structure proves so pervasive that it is assumed to be a natural way of organizing the world. Here, we see that gender emerges as a ubiquitous fixture of society that is cyclical as a social influence, always active, always relevant, often taken for granted, and ultimately unequal. Risman argues that "as long as women and men see themselves as different kinds of people, then women will be unlikely to compare their life options to those of men . . . the social structure is not experienced as oppressive if men and women do not see themselves as similarly situated."[60] Gender, then, understood as a *social stratification structure* assumes a dualism between an idealized, normative, or dominant gender structure serving as a constraint *and* individuals functioning as free actors. Whether individuals behave in ways that reinforce dominant gendered expectations or disrupt (resist) them, gender remains at play.

For instance, in Western societies, idealized images of authority and power are often conflated with images of straight, white, cisgender men. Therefore, it remains difficult to imagine that anyone who fails to fit this mold is capable of such leadership. In fact, research shows that the presence of women role models is vital to the development of women's identities as professionals and leaders as well as the reconceptualization of idealized images of leadership.[61] In religious denominations like the SBC, the lack of women role models in positions of leadership may negatively influence girls' decisions to pursue the role of pastor. This message may be reinforced by the exclusionary theological doctrine taught in religious services and Sunday school classes, which suggests that God created men to be leaders and women to be complementary assistants. This notion may be further reinforced through girls' interactions with pastors, parents, or other church members and their lack of opportunities to preach and lead in youth group. Even if girls engage more inclusive beliefs later in life, they may continue to wrestle internally with the exclusionary beliefs they encountered in their formative years or feel they lack the leadership tools to pursue being a pastor. Here, we see how gendered processes at all levels may mutually reinforce each other and hold the potential to result in inequitable outcomes between men and women.

Gender structure not only forms individuals' conscious gendered opinions and behaviors, it also shapes our unconscious or implicit biases. In other words, people are consistently formed and influenced on unconscious levels by the images, systems, and processes that form dominant gender structure thereby resulting in what researchers refer to as an *unconscious* or *implicit gender bias*.[62] Specifically, unconscious gender bias is defined as unintentional and automatic mental associations based on gender deriving from norms, traditions, values, culture, policies, institutions, interactions, images, and/or experiences, which we are all consciously and unconsciously engaging and processing all the time.[63] This means that people can reinforce inequitable outcomes between men and women even when consciously opposing sexism.[64] For example, even in moderate-progressive churches that promote the leadership of women, unchecked implicit biases and organizational processes formed by dominant gender structure may result in sexist hurdles faced by women pastors, thereby reinforcing the underrepresentation of women pastors in these congregations. This book utilizes the theoretical lens of gender structure and gendered organizations to reveal implicit gender biases and organizational processes that persist within moderate-progressive congregations *despite* the good intentions of gender equality by congregants and church staff.

Sample and Methods

I conducted a critical mixed-methods study examining the ways in which congregations committed to gender equality reinforced sexist outcomes as well as their strategies for achieving gender equity. Specifically, I utilized a purposive, snowball sampling method to investigate seven Baptist congregations affiliated with the CBF; four of the more progressive of these congregations were dually aligned with the Alliance of Baptists. While a snowball sampling method runs the risk of creating a homogenous sample, I was purposeful in selecting congregations of various ages, leadership structures, and theological perspectives. Female pastors served as senior pastors for three of the churches, male pastors served as senior pastors for three of the churches, and a male/female pastoral team led the seventh church. While all congregations in the sample theologically support the equal leadership of women, the sample includes congregations across the spectrum of conservative-moderate to liberal ideologies, theologies, and political views. All of the congregations included in the study were located in the southern United States (Texas, Louisiana, Mississippi, Tennessee, Alabama, Georgia) or what is commonly referred to as the "Bible Belt," a prominent Baptist churchgoing region in the United States. The sample is also predominantly cisgender, white, middle-upper class, and heteronormative, which represents the majority of congregants attending these congregations. I interviewed a few congregants who identified as gay or lesbian, including a couple of ordained ministers, but none were currently serving in official roles of congregations included in the study.

In each of the congregations, I sought to examine all five of Acker's gendered organizational processes (i.e., individual identities, interactions, organizational logic, symbols or organizational culture, division of labor) as well as how these processes interacted with and reinforced each other. I utilized multiple methods of research, which both increased validity and controlled for reflexivity through the triangulation of data. In the first stage, I built a database presenting the male-to-female ratio of every church position for all CBF-affiliated congregations in 2016–2017 ($N = 656$). Ranging from senior pastor to secretary, this offered a snapshot of the types of church staff positions men and women occupy within CBF congregations as a whole. I determined the sex of each church staff member through pronouns used in their personal bios listed on the church websites. If there were no bios available, I called the church offices for clarification. Churches with no website were not included in the study (<5%).

In the second stage, I emailed a congregational survey to each senior (lead) pastor of the seven congregations and asked that they email it to all of their congregants as well as send three follow-up email reminders. The survey included text communicating that survey participation was completely voluntary and all participants (18+ years old) would remain anonymous. The congregational survey collected demographic data and inquired about congregants' conceptions of *ideal pastors* as well as common attributes of different types of pastors and church staff ($N = 189$).[65] This information is particularly relevant in the context of the Baptist tradition because Baptist congregations function autonomously from any denominational hierarchy and individual congregants vote on major hiring decisions; therefore, congregant preferences and biases play a key part in the church power structure.

In the third stage, I traveled to each congregation to conduct interviews, observe, and participate in church events, activities, classes, meetings, and so on. Interviews typically lasted between 60 and 90 minutes. I first conducted semistructured interviews with church staff members ($N = 24$). During church staff interviews, I inquired about life histories particularly within the context of their families and churches as well as various professional experiences. Additionally, I conducted interviews with key congregants who had previously or currently held leadership roles within their congregations ($N = 32$). For instance, I typically interviewed deacons, members of pastoral search committees, and other lay leaders in the church, most of whom had been members for at least a decade and some for a few decades. These congregants offered insight into the congregations' histories, hiring processes, personnel decisions, and congregational expectations as well as other organizational processes.

In most of the congregations, I also engaged church members and leaders more casually at various church events and activities such as worship services, Wednesday night programs, committee meetings, volunteer activities, staff meetings, church dinners, weddings, and other social gatherings. Therefore, some of the data included in this study come from conversations within these contexts as well as my observations of interactions between congregants and church staff. I utilized a critical ethnographic approach in my observations, which seeks to reveal underlying and inequitable power structures within particular settings. However, my observations for all of the congregations except one cannot be classified as ethnography, given the truncated amount of time I spent in each congregation (10–20 hours per congregation). Most of my ethnographic observations were derived from my experiences in the seventh church, a female-led congregation of about 125 members and dually aligned with the CBF and the Alliance of Baptists. Here, I engaged in about 80 hours of participant observation over the course of 18 months. Given the number of church members and opportunities per week to observe (1–4 hours), I was able to hit my saturation point in this amount of time. Generally, participation observation provided additional opportunities to examine individuals' unconscious biases, expectations, and behaviors in informal settings. Additionally, I critically examined congregational documents such as job descriptions and promotional materials.

Once I had completed data collection within the seven congregations included in the study, I distributed a separate survey to seminary graduates predominately from *non-Southern Baptist* Baptist seminaries. The survey was posted on seminary social media pages and filtered for only seminary graduates ($N = 159$). The survey inquired about salaries, ministerial job satisfaction, number of years searching for ministerial jobs, congregational policies, paid family leave policies, and other information related to employment. This data offered additional information about the gender structure in Baptist life overall. Finally, I also attended denominational conferences where I participated in various activities and conversed with additional Baptist ministers and congregants about their experiences within the Baptist context.

Overview of Book

This book is interdisciplinary in scope with potential appeal to a variety of different types of audiences, including those in academia, religious professionals, social workers, and churchgoers. Opinions around gender are often inherently moral, for example, slut shaming and mommy guilt. Therefore, although this study examines congregations affiliated with the CBF, it may serve as a critical lens for investigating why sexist outcomes persist in contexts without explicitly sexist actors such as other workplaces with diversity, inclusion, and equity initiatives.

It also covers a wide range of theories and concepts related to gender, and as such, it has the potential to serve as a textbook or supplementary text in introductory gender courses as well as those focusing on gender inequality in labor, the workplace, and organizations. It also may act as a useful resource for faculty and students of the seminary, pastors, and social justice–oriented congregants. Finally, I have included a list of supplementary readings, discussion questions, and action steps at the end of each chapter in the hope of furthering and enhancing conversations around implicit issues of gender and inequality in various types of settings, including congregations, classrooms, and other workplaces.

Chapter 1 first provides a historical account of events leading to the formation of the CBF. It also serves as the theoretical foundation of the book and offers an in-depth description of Acker's concept of gendered jobs. This chapter presents quantitative data illustrating the gendered division of labor across the entire CBF and utilizes survey and interview data to explore congregants' conceptions of the *ideal pastor* in relation to gender.

Chapters 2 and 3 are best read together. Chapter 2 presents the life histories of women pastors and reveals the gendered barriers they face from childhood to becoming a pastor within the context of Baptist life. Chapter 3 examines congregational hiring processes, which are most often perceived by congregants as "gender neutral." This chapter draws on interview data to reveal hiring committees' aversion to an "affirmative action" approach and show that their failure to recognize the gendered hurdles faced by women prior to the job market actually results in masculinized hiring processes rather than gender-neutral ones, thereby reinforcing sexist hiring practices and outcomes. It also explores the conscious and unconscious gender biases of hiring committee members, which inevitably play a role in hiring decisions.

Chapter 4 illustrates how congregants' perceptions of women's bodies prove incongruent with their preferred conceptions of embodied authority and leadership. It then draws on interview data to show how women pastors are simultaneously expected to conceal and accentuate their femininity, are sexualized by male congregants as they engage in leadership tasks, and face organizational expectations about their weight and appearance that are often contradictory. Moreover, this chapter demonstrates how gendered congregational perceptions related to the body create near impossible and additional expectations for women pastors that are not applied in the evaluation of male pastors' performances. Chapter 4 additionally highlights how women maneuver through these organizational barriers in ways that are perhaps necessary to succeed but ultimately reinforce the inequitable gender structure of these congregations.

Chapter 5 presents dual congregational expectations placed on women pastors to engage in the responsibilities of the traditional wife and mother in addition to her role as a pastor.

It also shows ways in which organizational paid family leave policies reinforce traditional gender roles at home as well. Additionally, Chapter 5 provides an overview of the historical role of "pastor's wife" in congregations and ways in which congregants often expect women pastors to take on responsibilities of a pastor's wife, thus negatively impacting their job performance, causing burnout, and ultimately advantaging men. Given that women pastors are often expected to be the primary caregiver at home in addition to their professional duties, I refer to the additional expectation of filling the role of pastor's wife as the "third shift."

Chapter 6 surveys the historical relationship between feminization and devaluation, particularly as it relates to work. This chapter presents survey and interview data demonstrating the devaluation of feminized positions in churches (e.g., children's pastors, office managers) and the devaluation of leadership positions (e.g., associate pastor) when occupied by women.

Finally, Chapter 7 examines the particular standpoint of women pastors and how their experiences of exclusion and marginalization inform their social justice–oriented and more risky approaches to their jobs as compared to men pastors. It also shows how women pastors' male counterparts often, themselves, function as gendered barriers due to a lack of listening to and understanding the perspectives of their female colleagues. Each chapter highlights ways in which congregations have made progress in relation to gender equity and provides steps toward more equitable outcomes. The Conclusion provides a bird's-eye view of how the collection of inequitable organizational processes creates a structure in which women pastors face multiple barriers on their paths to the pulpit and in their congregations.

Discussion Questions

- What role has religion, family, media, and/or education played in shaping your personal ideas about gender?
- Explain the terms *gender essentialism* and *gender binary*. How are these related?
- Why is the theoretical concept of *sex roles* problematic?
- Explain the term *androgynous*.
- Explain the theoretical concept of *doing gender*. How does it differ from *essentialism*? Identify an empirical study that illustrates the process of *doing gender*.
- Explain the theoretical concepts of *gendered organizations* and *gender structure*. How are they related? What five organizational processes does Acker identify as gendered? Identify empirical studies that illustrate each of these.
- Do your perspectives of gender shift at the intersection of race, class, and sexuality? For example, do you perceive femininity differently when embodied by a Black woman? Do you perceive masculinity differently when embodied by a Black man? If so, how and why?

Supplemental Readings

Adams, Jimi. 2007. Stained glass makes the ceiling visible: Organizational opposition to women in congregational leadership. *Gender & Society*, 21(1), 80–105.

Bagilhole, Barbara. 2006. Not a glass ceiling, more a lead roof: Experiences of pioneer women priests in the Church of England. *Equal Opportunities International*, 25(2), 109–125.

Connell, R. W. 2005. *Masculinities*. Cambridge: Polity.

Fine, Cordelia. 2017. *Testosteronerex: Unmakingthemythsofourgenderedminds*. London: Icon Books.

Jordan-Young, R. M. 2011. *Brainstorm: The flaws in the science of sex differences*. Cambridge, MA: Harvard University Press.

Manville, Julie. 1997. The gendered organization of an Australian Anglican parish. *Sociology of Religion*, 58(1), 25–38.

Mountford, R. 2003. *The Gendered Pulpit*. Carbondale, IL: SIU Press.

Purvis, Sally B. 1995. *The stained-glass ceiling: Churches and their women pastors.* Louisville, KY: Westminster John Knox Press.

Risman, Barbara J., and Davis, Georgiann. 2013. From sex roles to gender structure. *Current Sociology, 61*(5–6), 733–755.

Risman, Barbara J. 2004. Gender as a social structure: Theory wrestling with activism. *Gender & Society, 18*(4), 429–450.

Sullins, Paul. 2000. The stained glass ceiling: Career attainment for women clergy. *Sociology of Religion, 61*(3), 243–266.

West, Candace, and Zimmerman, Don H. 1987. Doing gender. *Gender & Society, 1*(2), 125–151.

Zikmund, Barbara Brown, Lummis, Adair T., and Chang, Patricia M. Y. 1998. *Clergy women: An uphill calling.* Louisville, KY: Westminster John Knox Press.

1

The Gendered Pastor

The Southern Baptist Convention (SBC) is the largest Baptist denomination in the world. With 14.5 million members and 47,000 congregations throughout the United States,[1] it is second only to the Catholic Church as the largest Christian body in the United States. Since its establishment in 1845,[2] it has developed into a wide-reaching web of churches, associations, mission societies, and schools, particularly in the southern United States. As it continued to grow, Southern Baptists began to dominate Southern culture through revivals and cultivating an evangelical ethos characterized by authoritative, directive, hellfire-and-brimstone sermons; this ethos continues even today.[3] The Southern Baptists' evangelical approach contributed to a membership growth rate that was three times more than the region's population growth rate at the time. Nancy Ammerman, author of *Baptist Battles*, wrote, "With evangelicalism at the center of the culture, Baptists in the South began to proclaim theirs as the best possible way for a Christian to live, a model for humanity."[4] The SBC has historically intersected with the lives of prominent US leaders such as former US President Jimmy Carter, a well-known Southern Baptist who left the denomination "for equality" in the early 2000s when the SBC barred women from leadership positions.[5] Still, the SBC remains the denominational affiliation of prominent figures associated with conservative right-wing US politics such as Franklin Graham, Jimmy Draper, and Ted Cruz.

Historically, Baptist congregations have adhered to two distinct denominational components: *priesthood of the believer* and *autonomy of the local church*. The concept of *priesthood of the believer* refers to the idea that pastors' wills, desires, and beliefs *should not be* elevated above those of congregants. The *autonomy of the local church* refers to an autonomous democratic organizational structure that adheres to no centralized denominational hierarchy or doctrine, thereby theoretically allowing for various perspectives and approaches to biblical Scripture to exist within one denomination. Consequently, Baptist churches typically maintain a series of democratic organizational decision-making processes usually carried out through individual congregational committees and voting. However, shortly after the women's liberation movement of the 1960s and 1970s, conservative Southern Baptist leaders devised a plan that challenged these two fundamental elements of Baptist life and ultimately resulted in the

Preacher Woman. Katie Lauve-Moon, Oxford University Press (2021). © Oxford University Press.
DOI: 10.1093/oso/9780197527542.003.0002

official denominational barring of women in leadership positions. Moderate-liberal Baptists commonly refer to this shift in the SBC as the "Conservative *or* Fundamentalist Takeover," while fundamentalist Baptists refer to it as the "Conservative Resurgence."

Conservative, moderate, and liberal perspectives in Baptist life are largely determined by different approaches to interpreting biblical Scripture. For example, conservative and/or fundamentalist Baptists believe the Bible is an inerrant text given to people by the hand of God. Fundamentalist approaches to Scripture rarely consider the economic, cultural, social, and political contexts of the text and the impact of space and time in relation to overarching biblical themes. However, more moderate and progressive Baptists interpret the biblical text in relation to its social, political, and historical contexts and often understand absolute Truth in relation to overarching themes.

For example, conservative Baptists typically read the passage in Genesis 2 that refers to Eve, the first woman, as what is commonly translated as the "helper" or "helpmate" of Adam, the first man, to mean that it is by God's holy order that men are to be leaders and women to be supporters or assistants whether it be at home or at church. In fact, this interpretation of Scripture fueled much of the Conservative Takeover in Baptist life. However, the suggested subordination of women loses all power when one considers the historical and cultural context of the text. *Ezer*, which is the Hebrew word for *helper* used in the original version of this Genesis passage, holds no meaning of subordination and is originally derived from the phrases "to rescue, to save" or "to be strong."[6] In fact, the word *ezer* appears twenty-one times in the Old Testament. Twice it refers to women, three times it refers to people helping (or failing to help) in life-threatening situations, and sixteen times it refers to *God* as a great helper (in eight of these instances the word means "savior"). Moreover, in this passage the word *ezer* is directly followed by the word *kenegdo*, which means "in front of him" or "corresponding to him" like a mirror's image. Some scholars argue later that in the Mishnaic Hebrew language, the root of this word translated to mean "equal."[7]

And so by this, a moderate-liberal interpretation of this passage considers the original language of the text and consequently situates women as "as a power equal to man." This moderate-liberal interpretation of this passage ultimately reinforces (rather than contradicts) themes of social equality found throughout biblical Scripture, particularly in the Gospels. These types of more moderate-liberal approaches to biblical interpretation challenged the agenda of the Fundamentalist Takeover of the 1970s–1990s and still do today.

And so in 1976, former president of Southwestern Seminary and Southern Baptist leader Paige Patterson, then president of Criswell College in Dallas, and Paul Pressler, a judge in Houston, met to devise a political plan to elect a conservative president of the SBC who would subsequently ensure that all other leadership positions would be held by other conservative leaders from then on. Less than three years later and after months of campaigning, the first stage of this plan was achieved. In 1979, the SBC elected a conservative president, and conservative candidates have secured the presidency every year since. Shortly after, in 1984, the SBC met in Kansas City and adopted an emphatic proposition against the leadership of women in churches "because man was first in creation and the woman was first in the Edenic fall."[8]

In 1987, the board of trustees of Southeastern Baptist Seminary in Wake Forest, North Carolina, "whose majority was conservative, voted only to hire faculty members who followed and fully believed in the revised Baptist Faith and Message, which barred women from leadership."[9] With this decision, the SBC asked Randall Lolley, president of Southeastern Baptist Seminary, to resign because he did not fully agree with the revised Baptist Faith and Message. This was the first of dozens of forced resignations from moderate-liberal leaders of the SBC during this time.

Subsequently in 1992, the conservative majority board at Southwestern Seminary in Fort Worth, Texas abruptly fired Russell Dilday, the seminary's president for over 15 years. Despite the fact that trustees gave him a favorable annual job evaluation only 24 hours prior to the day he was fired, they released a statement claiming that Dilday failed to support the conservative agenda in the SBC and held liberal views of Scripture.[10] Although the majority of Southwestern Seminary faculty opposed these charges made against Dilday, the board of trustees "denied him access to his office by quickly changing the locks."[11] In the month of November 1992 alone, 159 employees of the SBC voluntarily or involuntarily retired.

In 1998, the Conservative Takeover came full circle with the election of Paige Patterson as president of the SBC. After his election, the SBC added a clause to the Baptist Faith and Message stating that a wife was to "submit herself graciously to the servant leadership of her husband."[12] Shortly after in 2000, the SBC officially adopted the new version of the Baptist Faith and Message as a creedal statement to be followed by SBC congregations, organizations, and institutions. This version forbade the leadership and ordination of women in the church and remains today.[13]

Moderate-liberal Baptists established the Cooperative Baptist Fellowship (CBF, 1991) and the Alliance of Baptists (1989) in response to the Fundamentalist Takeover. Given that these Baptists had experienced a realized threat to the Baptist ideals of the *priesthood of the believer* and *the autonomy of the local church* as well as to the leadership of women, CBF Baptists particularly emphasize a democratic congregational structure with most decisions voted on by congregant committees or the entire congregation and considers the equal leadership of women as a core component of its collective identity.

Today, over 700 Baptist congregations are affiliated with the CBF. Furthermore, women's enrollment in CBF-affiliated seminaries has steadily increased from 40.4% in 2010 to 46.7% in 2015. Despite the apparent intentionality pertaining to women's equal leadership and women's steady and almost equal enrollment in CBF-affiliated seminaries, today women still remain vastly underrepresented in leadership positions within these congregations. And so the question posed is, *why?*

The Concept of Gendered Jobs

Acker's theory of gendered organizations provides an analytical tool for investigating the inequitable gender outcomes within CBF congregations. A foundational component of Acker's theory of gendered organizations is that job positions themselves are gendered. Acker's conceptualization of gendered jobs includes the sex composition as defined by the ratio of males to females within particular occupations *and* the gendered expectations and tasks associated with particular jobs. By the latter definition, masculinized jobs are jobs that value qualities commonly associated with masculinity such as strength, leadership, authority, assertiveness, rationality, technical skills, taking risks, and power.[14] The common assumption that masculinity is the essential nature of men in conjunction with the widespread expectation of the *ideal worker* effectively embodying masculinity (i.e., male body, little to no connection with procreation or domestic responsibilities, effective embodiment of aforementioned masculine attributes) often contributes to men's dominance in masculinized professional roles such as business and finance officers,[15] lawyers,[16] doctors,[17] engineers,[18] judges,[19] academic professors,[20] and scientists[21] and to white, straight, cisgender men disproportionately occupying leadership positions such as managers, directors, partners, executives, supervisors, and political leaders, a phenomenon referred to as "the glass ceiling."

Meanwhile, feminized positions within masculinized occupations are typified by support roles such as secretaries or assistants and are predominately held by women.[22] Feminized occupations are typically characterized by feminine qualities such as being nurturing, supportive, emotional, helpful, and are often defined by roles related to domestic work, caring, and/or children (e.g., children's pastor/director, nurses, elementary school teachers, social workers, school librarians, housekeepers). Moreover, even within feminized professions, white, straight, cisgender men disproportionately ascend to top management positions (e.g., school principals, nursing supervisors) because attributes of authority, leadership, power, and status are conflated with masculinity, a phenomenon termed "the glass escalator."[23]

Although feminized and masculinized jobs are sometimes understood as "different but equal," their established relationships with status, power, authority, autonomy, and financial benefits show that these jobs are not equal at all. Women working in feminized jobs within both masculinized occupations (e.g., secretaries in law firms) and feminized occupations (e.g., teachers) often are overworked, underpaid, lack professional autonomy and opportunities for vertical advancement, and/or are overrepresented in part-time or temporary positions. Here we not only observe *differences* between masculinized and feminized jobs but a hierarchical relationship between masculinized and feminized jobs as well. To understand the underlying causes of women's underrepresentation in the church leadership positions in the CBF, we first must understand how church staff positions, particularly senior pastor positions, are gendered both in terms of sex composition and gendered expectations. The following sections present the sex composition of all church staff positions in CBF-affiliated congregations and demonstrate how congregants conceptualize the *ideal pastor* in terms of gender.

Sex Composition of Cooperative Baptist Fellowship Church Positions

To gain an initial understanding of the gendered division of labor within CBF-affiliated congregations on a structural level, I first investigated the sex composition of all pastoral and church staff positions in 656 CBF-affiliated congregations. Of all solo senior pastor positions ($N = 652$), 95.0% ($N = 619$) were held by men and 5.0% ($N = 33$) were held by women. After combining the number of solo senior pastors with co-senior pastors ($N = 675$), findings showed 631 (93.5%) male senior pastors and 44 (6.5%) female senior pastors. The clergy position typically next in status and authority to the senior pastor is the associate pastor. Results showed that of all associate pastor positions ($N = 288$), 67.0% were held by men ($N = 193$) and 33.0% were held by women ($N = 95$). Typically equal in status and authority to the associate pastor is the executive pastor, also referred to as the administrative pastor. The person in this role typically oversees human resource tasks, for example, evaluations, hiring, terminations, staff development, and logistical details. Results showed that of all executive pastor positions ($N = 54$), 41 (75.9%) were men and 13 (24.1%) were women.

Typically, the third tier of status and authority comprises of positions responsible for particular ministries or tasks (e.g., music ministry, education, spiritual formation, pastoral care). It is important to note, however, that the levels of status and authority vary depending on how many other staff members the

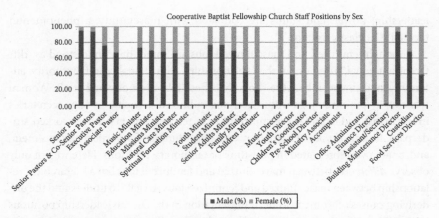

Figure 1.1 Sex composition of church positions on denominational level.

church employs, size of the congregation, and resources available. For instance, if a church does not employ an associate or executive pastor, a third-tier pastor may be considered second in authority and status. The fourth tier typically comprises positions responsible for engaging particular groups of people (e.g., youth, senior adults) and are often part-time positions. The fifth ministerial tier of status and authority typically comprises individuals who are responsible for particular ministries or groups but are not given a ministerial title and are typically subordinate to pastors or ministers of all levels. This group of church staff usually includes positions that are typically "ministers in training" or ministerial support roles (e.g., ministry associates, ministry residents, ministry assistants). Finally, all nonministerial positions are typically subordinate to all ministers and pastors. Of the nonministerial positions, also referred to as administrative positions, the office manager or administrator and the finance director (e.g., accountant) typically have the most status and authority with secretaries and assistants having the least. Of CBF congregations, women represent 95% of all secretarial positions. See Figure 1.1 for the sex composition of all pastoral and church staff positions.

Figure 1.1 reveals that generally as power, authority, and status decrease, the number of women increases; as power, authority, and status increase, the number of men increases. These results illustrate overall vertical job segregation between men and women workers within CBF congregations and, ultimately, a gendered hierarchy of labor. In other words, women are both *underrepresented* in the most powerful positions and *overrepresented* in the most subordinate positions. In an organization of well-intended actors committed to gender equality, the question remains, *why?*

Gendering the Role of Senior Pastor

In addition to conceptualizing occupations and jobs as gendered in terms of sex composition, jobs may also be gendered by symbolic significance, expectations, and tasks. To further investigate my question, I asked congregational survey participants to list two to three qualities or traits they associated with the position of senior (lead) pastor. Results showed that the vast majority of congregants listed traits associated with feminized jobs such as caring for people (e.g., empathetic, compassionate, kind, nurturing, loving, giving, understanding, patient). In fact, this category accounted for almost one fourth of all responses (24.2%, $n = 67$). Secondly, congregants associated lead pastors with being intelligent, well educated, and knowledgeable (11.6%). While 5.4% of responses referred to strong leadership, an attribute typically associated with masculinity, as an ideal trait of pastors. See Table 1.1 for comprehensive findings.

The survey then asked participants to list two to three qualities or traits they *value most* in a senior pastor. These responses proved similar to those of the previous question. A little more than one fourth of descriptors referred to pastors' ability to care for people (25.9%). The second most reported category was "Collaborator-Listener" (14.2%). This category referred to senior pastors' ability to work alongside and listen to congregants rather than

Table 1.1 Qualities Most Associated with Senior Pastors

	Total	%
Cares for people	67	24.2
Knowledge/intelligence	32	11.6
Moral/ethical	27	9.7
Relational/personable	23	8.3
Charismatic	23	8.3
Administrator	21	7.6
Accessibility/servant leader	17	6.1
Visionary/prophetic	15	5.4
Effective public speaker	15	5.4
Strong leader	15	5.4
Other	12	4.3
Open/listening skills	11	3.9
Total	277	100

authoritatively or unilaterally make decisions—another feminized trait. The categories of "Leadership" and "Administration" only made up 3.6% and 3.3% of reported qualities, respectively, while "Humility" constituted 4.3% of responses. Furthermore, congregants' expectations of senior pastors being available, accessible, and helpful to congregants accounted for 5.3% of responses.

For good measure, congregants were then asked to list two to three *skills* they would look for in a senior pastor if they were serving on a pastoral hiring committee. The most valued skill in a pastor was preaching and public speaking (18.7%). Other findings mirrored responses to the previous questions showing that over one third of skills were related to caring for people and being relational, moral/ethical, or available, while 5.5% of congregants indicated that they valued strong leadership skills in their pastors. See Table 1.2 for more details.

Finally, congregants were asked to list two to three traits or qualities they valued *least* in senior pastors. The highest reported category pertained to being prideful or egotistical (26.2%). The second and third highest showed congregants' dislike for pastors to act authoritatively or dictatorially (13.9%) and not working collaboratively or listening to congregants (13.9%). See Table 1.3 for comprehensive findings.

Table 1.2 Skills Most Valued in a Senior Pastor

	N	%
Preaching	44	18.7
Caring for people	34	14.5
Intellectual	31	13.2
Relational	26	11.1
Administrator	16	6.8
Visionary	14	5.9
Moral	14	5.6
Collaborator	13	5.5
Strong leader	13	5.5
Available	13	5.5
Wise	11	4.7
X-Factor (charismatic)	3	1.3
Brave	3	1.3
Total	235	100

Table 1.3 Skills Valued Least in a Senior Pastor

	N	%
Prideful	49	26.2
Authoritative/dictatorial	26	13.9
Not inclusive or collaborative	26	13.9
Uninvolved	24	12.8
Judgmental or merciless	12	6.4
Unethical	12	6.4
Not relational	10	5.3
Insecure	9	4.8
Indecisive	4	2.1
Not a good communicator/preacher	3	1.6
Immature	3	1.6
Not educated or thoughtful	1	0.5
Other	8	4.2
Total	187	100

These findings suggest that congregants' primary expectations of lead pastors are similar to the expectations commonly associated with feminized jobs (e.g., nursing, social work, childcare). In addition to congregants' ideal pastoral qualities being largely understood in terms of femininity, congregants' least desirable qualities were most often characterized by masculinity. Consequently, congregants' feminized expectations of senior pastors fail to fit squarely into the conclusions of other empirical studies, which suggest that expectations of masculinity typically function as barriers for women who are often perceived as incapable of masculine qualities, thereby resulting in the glass ceiling effect within masculinized professions. Therefore, congregants' overall feminized expectations of senior pastors present an additional question: *If congregants maintain feminized expectations of lead pastor positions, then why do women, often assumed to innately possess feminine qualities, remain significantly underrepresented in these positions?*

The Authority of Pastor

In interviews, I asked congregants to describe each senior pastor that had served at their church since they became a member. Many of the congregants had been at their churches since their inceptions, sometimes for 20–30 years. As they spoke about the qualities and leadership of past pastors, the narratives often intersected with the Fundamentalist Takeover as well as their experiences of breaking away from the SBC and becoming affiliated with the CBF. Many of the congregants recalled friends and connections they lost as a result of this denominational split and grieved the SBC's aggressive threat to the Baptist ideals of the *autonomy of the local church* and the *priesthood of the believer*. In fact, congregants' pastoral expectations of collaboration and a nonauthoritative leadership style were often recalled in direct relation to these experiences. Most congregants expressed that they never wanted to be in a situation where the voices of the congregants were powerless and the pastor retained the power to lead the congregation in a direction with which they felt uncomfortable or disagreed. For instance, one congregant who had served on his church's pastoral search committee stated:

> Yeh, we didn't want to go there again. We didn't want someone telling us what to do or what to believe. You know, we didn't want a dictator. . . . You see Southern Baptists weren't always the way they are now. They weren't just conservative. They used to have all different types of people—conservatives, liberals, you name it! We just really just didn't want a pastor who dictates to us what we are supposed to believe. That's how we got here to begin with [breaking from the SBC]. We wanted to get away from that.

Like other congregants, this congregant's reaction to the Fundamentalist Takeover influenced his understanding of the role of pastor and resulted in the desire for a pastor who was *not* authoritative or dictatorial but rather respected and complemented Baptists' democratic ideals. His conception of the ideal pastor proved less masculinized than previous images of pastors. This finding proved salient among congregants.

Conversations with congregants further reinforced survey findings, which suggested that congregants perceive the act of preaching as one of the primary ways pastors establish authority. When asked about preferred preaching styles, congregants' responses were often stated in comparison to the traditional authoritative Southern Baptist preaching styles. For instance, congregants of different congregations stated:

> Congregant: Well, for me personally, it's someone who speaks to, appeals to my intellect as opposed to my fear of hellfire and brimstone. Since I was influential

in the selection of our next pastor that's in my view [current pastor's] preaching style. Not someone who is shouting from the pulpit for dramatic effect or beating... [Sermons should be] researched, logical, connected thoughts, a message that makes sense in light of the biblical passage that is the focus of the message.

Congregant: What do I mean by good preaching? I can tell you we didn't want someone who had one way of preaching the Bible and expected us to believe that way, too. I personally don't want overemotional preaching where pastors try to scare you into believing a certain way. I prefer sermons that make you think, are researched, that connect Scripture with today and aren't divisive.

Congregant: We always look for excellent preachers. [This church] has a lot of highly educated folks. [laughs] They have to be pretty intelligent preachers; well read. Pastoral but challenging, well read, educated, and probably not evangelistic.

Consistent with congregational survey findings, congregants disliked preaching styles that were authoritative and determined, preferring sermons that created room for varying perspectives. Additionally, congregants desired sermons that were grounded in intellect and research rather than emotions, a preaching approach that had historically been used to ensue fear in congregants so that they would believe a particular way. These expectations were usually cited as reactions to fundamentalist understandings of Scripture that often proved to be uninformed by or not situated in the cultural, historical, political, and social contexts of biblical Scripture; such approaches to biblical Scripture have historically excluded marginalized people groups from leadership and full participation in the Christian faith. While the emotional realm is typically understood as decidedly feminine, here we see that a shift from emotionalism is conflated with a shift away from authoritative and directive preaching, characteristics typically associated with masculinity. Moreover, a shift toward intellectualism and rationality, qualities typically understood as masculine, signals a shift toward the feminine qualities of inclusivity, collaboration, and passivity. It is through both demonstrating intellectual prowess *and* being pastoral (i.e. loving, inclusive, relational) that pastors meet the criteria of the ideal pastor as it relates to preaching and establishing their authority. Here we begin to see that congregants' gendered expectations of pastors, particularly preaching, ideally encompass both feminine and masculine traits.

Congregant interviews also revealed complex expectations pertaining to pastors' administrative skills. Congregants equally expected pastors to be *involved* and *strong leaders* as well as *hands-off administrators* who *did not micromanage*. For instance, after having a senior pastor who congregants described as *soft as a leader, uninvolved,* and *weak administratively,* congregants searched for and hired a more *take-charge* type pastor. However, congregants quickly discovered that this pastor was *too hands-on*:

> Congregant: David [current pastor] has done a lot more hands-on in administration [than the previous pastor], which interestingly I was on the transition committee. [Before hiring him] One of the things we did was a survey of the congregation, we said "Okay you had this kind of pastor for 35 years, what kind of pastor do you want?" We found out they didn't want somebody to stand up and tell us what to do. But they wanted somebody who is going to be a strong leader and be hands-on and all this stuff. Well, they were blowing smoke. They failed at what they want because that's not what they wanted. But they got what they asked for.
>
> Congregant: The one that does stick out for me is they said they wanted someone who was more hands-on, more outgoing, more socially comfortable, you know visiting with people in the hospital, visiting shut-ins, you know, pastoral. And David certainly is [comparatively]. . . But he [David] came into a congregation that was full of chiefs and not many Indians. There was a certain amount of head-butting that occurred because David wanted to do certain things his way and other people who were entrenched in their positions were used to doing it a different way. . . . It's taken a little longer, I think, for David to get used to us and for us to get used to David. All of which is to say that now, I think David better understands our dynamic and the necessity for asking permission rather than asking for forgiveness. He almost always gets what he asks for, but it seems to be important to this congregation that he ask before something is done. [It needs to go through the committee process.]

These findings suggest that congregants expect pastors to lead but not *take charge*. This finding parallels congregants' expectations of pastors leading through their preaching but not dictating what congregants should believe. They also suggest that congregants continue to prefer more feminine qualities (e.g. submissive, passive) to more masculine leadership qualities (e.g. take charge, authoritative, assertive). However, other parts of my conversations with congregants suggest being a senior pastor was conflated with being strong and assertive, masculine qualities commonly associated with leadership and authority.

> Congregant: I thought—I was on that committee—that she was too gentle and kind. I think we would have beat her up. You got to be tough here. It's not deliberate, but it's such a group of strong-willed people that you have to [be able to stand firm].
>
> Congregant: I think that was one thing the search committee was really looking for was someone who could be senior pastor [be assertive] regardless

of their age and regardless of their experience. This is not an easy staff to be senior pastor of because we have an associate pastor who's been here for 35 years or 30 years or whatever. Also, a lot of Baptist congregations serve a lot of different groups and different people who have different focuses on different things and different things matter to them and they all want their thing to matter the most.

These findings further illustrate that congregants expect pastors to lead and initiate change collaboratively while being able to stand firm in these decisions when some congregants disagree. The distinct expectation of senior pastors to be able to exhibit strong leadership separates them from congregants and other church staff; it is within this distinction that their authority resides. For instance, associate pastor Ben describes the relationship between senior pastor Olivia's authority and her accountability to congregants:

BEN: [As an associate pastor] I do not have to deal with conflicts, difficult personalities or that kind of thing. Olivia has to deal with petty personality differences as well as when people get really angry over theological, ideological, practical differences. I have to deal with plenty of nonglamorous stuff as well, but she as the [senior] pastor is the one who has to answer more directly to the congregation on all matters. I answer more directly to her.

INTERVIEWER: Do you think she has more authority or freedom than you do?

BEN: I would say Olivia absolutely has more authority than me. She has less freedom though because she has more direct consequences of her actions because she is on the front line of receiving the negative feedback. When I say something prophetic or uncomfortable in a sermon, people who disagree can say "Oh, well he's the associate pastor so we don't have to hear from him again for a couple of months." When Olivia says something prophetic, it becomes more personal because her words, in a sense, represent each member who chooses to attend the church.

INTERVIEWER: So what does her having more authority look like or mean?

BEN: Olivia has more authority because she is the senior pastor. While she fosters a more collaborative model where she genuinely values my opinion and the opinions of members, ultimately she makes the final decisions and deals with the positive and negative feedback that follows. From an institutional standpoint, the congregation has given her authority to make most decisions, although there are balances in place for the congregation to weigh in or have a majority vote for veto on big decisions. She is higher on the hierarchy than me. She is my boss and supervisor, whereas the church is her supervisor but also, she is the authority figure of the church. Everyone turns to her to lead and expects her to uphold that authority responsibly and with wisdom.

Similarly, Jane describes the differences between her role as associate pastor and Anna's role as senior pastor:

> I would say, I have more autonomy but she has more authority. She definitely has more authority in the congregation than I do . . . I think she as pastor speaks to and with the whole congregation and she carries the weight of that role, and the associate pastor has a lot more freedom.

Here we see that senior pastors' elevated level of authority and status signifies an increase in accountability to congregants and a decrease in autonomy. Therefore, pastors' power (not necessarily authority) is constrained by congregants' expectations and undergoes constant negotiation. Additionally, the process of accountability between pastors and congregants requires constant communication between congregants and pastors. It is within these interactional processes that pastors are expected to practice the idealized skills of listening, patience, understanding, and working collaboratively *and* it is through effectively practicing these skills that pastors are able to establish and maintain their authority. Moreover, it is through the effective embodiment of authority that the masculinized significance of the ideal senior pastor emerges.

I asked pastors to describe how they balanced the dual expectations of maintaining authority and leading *as well as* being relational, collaborative, and inclusive. Senior pastor Olivia recalled congregants' reactions to a sermon she preached about race that pushed the bounds of the normative congregational discourse and discussed how she negotiated these dual expectations:

> It's not easy . . . the first time I preached a sermon on race here that was pretty bold, there were people waiting to talk to me, and so I had a couple of weeks there where I had some really difficult, sometimes painful, conversations. There was one church member that, we cried together and held hands at the end and prayed for each other and just left it, knowing we don't see this in the same way, but we really respect each other and we want to hear what the other has to say, and we want to stay in a relationship. So maybe we're not going to understand it today, but we value staying in a relationship more than we value being right and feeling right. I try to be respectful of everybody who's there, as long as I feel like, [laughs] it's worthy of respect. If you're being cruel, then I'm not going to respect your position of cruelty and I'm going to part ways with you. But even then I'm going to try to do it with grace, if you'll let me. . . . But it's part of it. These relationships have to happen so that I'm trusted to take them to uncomfortable places.

Here, Olivia meets congregants' expectations of empathy, patience, and relationality as she interacts with congregants who disagreed or felt uncomfortable with her sermon on racial issues. Despite congregational discord, she did not recant her position or let congregants "push her around." It is both through establishing caring, trustworthy relationships with congregants *and* standing her ground that Olivia's authority is established and reinforced. In this way, the expected feminine qualities that were most reported by congregants (e.g., being relational, compassionate, accessible, collaborative) partially serve as the vehicle by which pastors establish and maintain their authority within their congregations.

Similarly, when the associate pastor, Ben, wants to lead the congregation through a perhaps uncomfortable change, he takes a relational and methodical approach:

> I would say, if I'm wanting to change something on the committee level, it's really preparing people so that when you share this big change, or this new book, or a big set of information that may or may not be well received, doing it in little bits and preparing them over time. If I wanted to invite the church as part of following the ways of Jesus to participate in Black Lives Matter protest, I might plan six months or a year out even, because, in my time as a minister I've realized that things usually move way slower, than maybe, I would like— but, I think that's part of walking alongside people.
>
> I would maybe mention Black Lives Matter in a sermon just briefly, or maybe mention it in a business meeting where I talk about how I heard a talk about Black Lives Matter—to just get them to thinking about it. Then, maybe, having a Wednesday Night Program that talked about race and starting to draw parallels between the civil rights movements in the '50s and '60s in connection to where we are now. At some point, I would have to preach a sermon that became more open about my beliefs and that would be the one. Eventually, you're going to have to do something that might get a lot of pushback and hopefully, you have spent enough time having individual conversations with people and what you have done up until that point lessens that pushback or at least creates a little more open-mindedness and space for discussion. After doing some of that preparation, then invite people into maybe a protest or being more actively involved in Black Lives Matter. You're ultimately not going to get everyone to agree with you and that is just anytime in you're in an organization, you're not going to typically have complete agreement. But as a pastor, it's also my responsibility to lead.

Like Olivia, Ben exhibits care for people and consideration for varying perspectives as he establishes his authority in his pastoral position, which is tasked with leading community outreach and education around social justice issues. Many congregants described this relationship between pastors and church members by using the metaphor of a shepherd leading (his) sheep. The shepherd must establish the trust of his sheep, tend to them, and ensure that none have been left behind. However, the shepherd ultimately leads the sheep and is, therefore, distinctly different from the sheep in relation to status and authority. The metaphor is limited because sheep do not have a valued and organized voice in the same way that congregants in Baptist churches do and shepherds were historically men, but it helps explain the unique ways that pastors utilize feminine qualities to lead and establish their positions of authority. While congregants expect pastors to exhibit more feminine attributes like empathy, compassion, relationality, collaboration, and inclusion than did many Southern Baptist pastors of the past, the role of pastor remains conflated with authority and leadership and, therefore, is ultimately masculinized.

Understanding Pastor as Masculinized

While these data provide a more nuanced understanding of congregants' gendered expectations of senior pastors, these findings remain in an uncertain relationship with existing research on the glass ceiling. First, these findings fail to demonstrate a traditional hierarchical structure that culminates with senior pastors occupying the top position *and* maintaining the most power. Although senior pastors typically have ultimate power over other church staff, democratic organizational processes and congregants' expectations constrain pastors' ultimate power over organizational processes and goals. Secondly, although pastoral positions have historically and are currently predominately occupied by men, these jobs are primarily characterized in terms of femininity. The combination of these findings proves different from other research on the glass ceiling effect within more masculinized male-dominated professions where stakeholders most often value masculinized attributes.

In fact, men's overrepresentation in senior pastor positions seems to closely parallel the "glass escalator effect," which disproportionately pushes white, straight, cisgender men to top authority positions in feminized professions.[24] However, the vocational ministry also proves different from other feminized professions because *all* pastoral roles, with the exception of children's pastors and family pastors, have historically and are currently predominantly occupied by men. Additionally, survey results suggest that with the exception of the most feminized pastoral position of children's minister, congregants associate all pastoral positions with varying levels of authority and leadership. This means that different from other feminized professions, the vocational ministry as a whole is conflated with authority and authority is conflated with masculinized positions not feminized ones. Finally, feminized professions are typically intrinsically linked with processes of deskilling and deprofessionalization and, therefore, devalued in comparison to masculinized professions. In contrast, the role of pastor proves to be highly revered and valued by congregants as evident by their expectations of skilled preaching as well as pastoral authority and leadership. For these reasons, the glass escalator effect also proves limited in its explanatory power in relation to the masculinized position of senior pastor.

Congregants' conceptualizations of the ideal pastor are best understood in relation to a small body of research that examines a similar shift in patients' conceptualizations of the ideal doctor.[25] Similar to congregants' conceptual shift from authoritative and omnipotent senior pastors often characteristic of the SBC, relatively recent studies illustrate that in response to a medical profession that has become increasingly clinical, medically negligent, and *not* patient centered, patients' conceptions of the "ideal doctor" have become increasingly more feminized. Whereas historically patients commonly understood doctors as god-like, omnipotent medical authorities, more recently patients often describe the ideal professional behavior of doctors as being "able to draw patients out, to listen to their concerns and to translate medical jargon into terms that patients can easily understand."[26] Additionally, patients are beginning to characterize their ideal doctors as having attributes such as being good communicators, empathetic, understanding of patients' needs and perspectives, genuinely interested in people and their welfare, and able to cultivate collaborative relationships with patients. While "bad doctors" are best understood as being dishonest, failing to listen carefully and establish rapport, money driven, and one who "preaches to patients and has a prepared routine that they are forever giving to this patient and that patient."[27]

Similar to the expectations of pastors, this feminized shift in the medical field demonstrates that "doctors may have been removed from their pedestals to some extent, but they still find that at the individual and interpersonal levels patients often expect them to retain an air of authority and formality"[28] and effectively demonstrate their scientific knowledge and expertise. Despite this feminized shift, no research suggests that doctors' status and authority have diminished as a consequence.[29] Medical practitioners still receive the highest ranking of all occupations in terms of social status and public esteem.[30] Therefore, idealized conceptions of pastors and doctors both serve as atypical cases by which the integration of feminized skills into the profession fails to result in a subsequent devaluation of these positions overall, but rather contributes to pastors' and doctors' ability to establish their authority and status as professionals within their particular contexts. In other words, feminized skills valuably contribute to the overall authority of pastors and doctors and strengthen their ability to establish their authority rather than weaken it.

Despite the demonstrated value of feminized skills in establishing the authority of pastors, the ultimate significance of the senior pastor position lies in the symbolic and actual authority of the position itself. To continue the comparison to more contemporary idealizations of doctors, despite the integration of feminized skills and responsibilities into the position of doctor, in 2019 women still only made up 40% of all physicians and surgeons in the United States and in 2017 earned 77.3% of what male doctors made.[31] These statistics suggest and empirical research shows that images of the ideal doctor remain intertwined with the male body and are best understood in terms of masculinity.[32] Similarly, women's underrepresentation in pastoral positions overall and CBF-affiliated churches specifically suggests that with the exception of children's and family pastors, pastoral positions as positions of authority remain conflated with maleness and masculinity despite expectations of feminized attributes and tasks.

Given the established relationship between senior pastors and authority, I argue that pastoral positions are ultimately masculinized; therefore, the stained-glass ceiling effect offers some explanation for the underrepresentation of women in top leadership positions in the church. I also argue that the stained-glass ceiling proves to be a limited theoretical framework for conceptualizing women's underrepresentation in these positions because it suggests that women face only a single gendered barrier when pursuing top positions in the church. Instead, I draw on the concept of the gendered labyrinth to demonstrate all of the gendered barriers women face along the way to occupying the masculinized position of senior pastor.[33] The upcoming chapters illustrate how women face a variety of masculinized barriers prior, during, and after being hired as pastors and provide further insight into the persisting underrepresentation of women leaders in congregations seeking gender equality.

Discussion Questions

- Describe the concept of gendered jobs. Do you observe senior pastor positions (or the equivalent) to be gendered similarly or differently in your congregation or denomination?
- For students, how do you observe the role of professor to be gendered? Does it vary by subject? If so, why? How does it compare to elementary and secondary schoolteachers? Identify an empirical research study that illustrates ways in which the roles of teachers and professors are gendered.
- Describe the concepts of the glass ceiling and the glass escalator. What is the relationship between these concepts and the theoretical framework of

gendered jobs as well as gender inequality in the workplace? Identify an empirical research article illustrating Acker's concept of gendered jobs.

- Explain how the concepts of leadership and authority are related to masculinity.
- For social work educators and students, why is the concept of gendered jobs important to understand as social workers prepare for macro practice and develop skills for addressing inequalities on the organizational level? Why are findings of this chapter particularly relevant to church social workers?
- How may jobs also be racialized or sexualized? Identify a research study that demonstrates how jobs may be exclusionary at the intersections of gender with race, class, and/or sexuality. What about ability and age?

Supplemental Readings

Ammerman, N. T. 1990. *Baptist battles: Social change and religious conflict in the Southern Baptist Convention.* New Brunswick, NJ: Rutgers University Press.

Bagilhole, B. 2006. Not a glass ceiling more a lead roof: Experiences of pioneer women priests in the Church of England. *Equal Opportunities International, 25*(2), 109–125.

Giuffre, P., Dellinger, K., and Williams, C. L. 2008. "No retribution for being gay?": Inequality in gay-friendly workplaces. *Sociological Spectrum, 28*(3), 254–277.

Hatmaker, D. M. 2013. Engineering identity: Gender and professional identity negotiation among women engineers. *Gender, Work and Organization, 20*(4), 382–396.

Jones, L., and Green, J. 2006. Shifting discourses of professionalism: A case study of general practitioners in the United Kingdom. *Sociology of Health and Illness, 28*(7), 927–950.

Kelly, E. L., Ammons, S. K., Chermack, K., and Moen, P. 2010. Gendered challenge, gendered response: Confronting the ideal worker norm in a white-collar organization. *Gender and Society, 24*(3), 281–303.

Watkins-Hayes, C. 2009. Race-ing the bootstrap climb: Black and Latino bureaucrats in post-reform welfare offices. *Social Problems, 56*(2), 285–310.

Williams, Christine L. 1995. *Still a man's world: Men who do women's work.* Vol. 1. Berkeley: University of California Press.

Williams, Christine L. 2013. The glass escalator, revisited: Gender inequality in neoliberal times, SWS feminist lecturer. *Gender and Society, 27*(5), 609–629.

2
Women's Path to the Pulpit

Growing up, I went to a Southern Baptist Church. I was extraor-
dinarily involved in my youth group. In a typical week, of course,
I was there Sunday morning for Sunday school and for worship.
I was there for Sunday night training union. Sunday afternoon, I had
girls' ensemble rehearsal and youth choir rehearsal. I would come
to church on Monday afternoons for discipleship group. I would
come on Tuesdays for youth hand bells. Be there Wednesday for
youth group. If I could find an excuse to come on Thursday, I would
do that, too. I would just show up and volunteer, "What can I do
to help?" I would, you know, I have vacuumed sanctuaries, I have
swept stairwells. I just loved being there. Yet it never entered my
mind that I might be called to ministry. And I look back on that and
I think, you know, why did my youth minister or other people, who
observed me closely—why didn't they see that? Why didn't they call
it out? Because it's so clear to me now, looking back. But, you know, it
was just that my whole identity was wrapped up in my involvement
in the church. . . . But again, it didn't enter my mind that it might be
[a vocational call].

—Allie, associate pastor

There are approximately 46,800 Southern Baptist Convention (SBC)
congregations in the United States and only about 800 Baptist congregations affiliated with the Cooperative Baptist Fellowship (CBF) and/or the Alliance of
Baptists. This means that Baptist folks living in the southern United States are
significantly more likely to be raised in or attend Southern Baptist churches and
significantly less likely to be introduced to the idea of women in church leadership positions, much less engage an actual woman pastor. Given the timing of the
Conservative Takeover and the subsequent emergence of more moderate-liberal
Baptist denominations and congregations in the early 1990s, the vast majority of
pastors and church staff in this study were raised in a Southern Baptist congregation before or during the Conservative Takeover. Consequently, almost all of
the women in this study shared Allie's experience of being intensely involved in

Preacher Woman. Katie Lauve-Moon, Oxford University Press (2021). © Oxford University Press.
DOI: 10.1093/oso/9780197527542.003.0003

church activities and passionate about ministerial work from a very young age, but discouraged and excluded from the pursuit of ministry as a vocation.

Like many of the other women pastors who were denied access to ministerial leadership early on, Allie attended college to pursue a field unrelated to ministry; she received a business degree and was married soon after. Allie and her husband then returned to her home church:

> [After graduating college and getting married] When we came back, we went back to the same church that I had been a teenager and jumped right back in— my husband and I were teaching preschoolers in Sunday school, I was working with children's choir, I was singing in the adult choir, I was even working a few hours a week officially for the church, for the minister of music. I was teaching in Parents' Day Out. I was involved in WMU [Woman's Missionary Union] and all of it. Still, it is not on, you know, not on my mind [to go into the ministry] at all.
>
> Then we changed churches. We started going downtown to [First Baptist] when our son was almost four and we were there for 15 years. And it was at First Baptist where there were some women in the church who immediately—some older women who latched on to me and began to call out my gifts. Began to verbally affirm what they were seeing in me.
>
> Within a week of having joined that church, I found myself in a car with three senior adult women being driven to Birmingham to WMU [Woman's Missionary Union]. Very quickly they gave me an opportunity at the church to help lead. And then I began to have opportunities with WMU in our association and state to lead sessions—that's when I started writing for WMU. I really owe a debt to those women.

Even after returning to her home church in her thirties, Allie remained constrained by the dominant gender structure of Baptist life. Still, she had never engaged a woman pastor and had internalized the notion that women should not be called to be pastors. As a result, the thought to be one had still never occurred to her.

Although still within the confines of this gender structure, it was at this time that Allie was introduced to women members of the Woman's Missionary Union (WMU), which is an auxiliary organization of the SBC focused on creating *mission* opportunities for women. Women were permitted to lead in the WMU only because they were leading other women, not men; this suggests that the official barring of women's leadership in the church is less about a theological notion prohibiting women from leadership and more about women not having power over men. This created a loophole for Allie to explore her ministerial gifts and leadership skills and to be affirmed in these by others. Through these opportunities and interactions, Allie began to realize her leadership capabilities:

> Anyway, I began to have more a sense of my giftedness. I remember going to a young women's church retreat in Gatlinburg. They had a break out session called "Unwrapping Your Spiritual Gifts." I went and took an inventory and I remember being genuinely astonished that I had spiritual gifts. That was like I'd always heard of spiritual gifts. But the fact that I had them and that on my inventory I was kind of looking at other people's scores, and I was off the charts on some things.
>
> And then there was another conference that we went to and there was a session on leadership and there was a leadership inventory we took. And you would chart these different things and plot them on a graph. I was kind of looking at other people's stuff and they had these, you know, little shapes and I had this huge triangle—And I thought, "Oh my gosh. There's, there's something untapped there!"

All of Allie's previous church work had never been framed in relation to spiritual giftedness or leadership. Therefore, she was completely surprised to learn that she actually had spiritual gifts and leadership abilities. By finally being exposed to leadership development opportunities, Allie began to realize that her desire to work in the church was related not only to her willingness to help others, but to her ability and desire to lead as well. She recalled the moment she decided to become a pastor and how this calling came from an internal voice rather than an external one:

> I just continued to take advantage of, you know, whatever opportunities opened up. I was working with children at church. I was leading some big events for women. I was enjoying the writing that I was doing. But again, still, just not on my horizon because at that point, you know, I was fully entrenched as a young mom, I was involved in the PTO and all that stuff. But it was Holy Week of 1999 and we were in the mountains in a cabin on spring break and—this is my favorite part of the story. I was outside alone at night in the hot tub. No kidding. Looking at the moon, I had just this very clear sense that God was speaking to me and calling me go to seminary. I sat there and I said, "You know, this is—I'd always—I'm a lifelong learner, I love to learn new things, I enjoy writing papers, I enjoy reading." But I had not—after I became a mom, I thought, "If I've had to do anything like that, it will be after my son's graduation." It just didn't make sense. But it was such a strong impulse . . . I just had this sense of clarity that I was supposed to go to seminary. And I knew two things about [the named seminary]. I knew where it was and I knew one woman who I had met through

WMU. She was actually the elected [state] WMU president. And she, she's at least 15 years older than me. She was going as a student, she started seminary in her '50s. And I thought, "Well, I can do that."

In addition to exclusionary theology, a lack of female role models in church leadership positions, and little verbal affirmation of her gifts and skills, Allie also faced dominant societal pressures to align motherhood as her top priority until her child graduated from high school; only at this time should she freely pursue her professional goals and dreams. Allie said, "It just didn't make sense." Allie's perception of pursuing her professional goals as a mom only doesn't make sense in relation to a dominant gender structure that asserts that women's primary roles are acting as supporters and nurturers. Despite all of these gendered hurdles, Allie finally found her path to becoming a pastor in Baptist life. After Allie observed another woman with whom she shared some similarities enroll in seminary, she began to believe she actually could pursue vocational ministry as well. While it may be assumed that the exclusionary theology of Southern Baptist life contributed to Allie not connecting with a same-sex role model until later in life, it is important to note that with less than 5% of CBF churches being led by female pastors, the odds of engaging a woman in this top leadership position remain very low for girls growing up even in more theologically inclusive Baptist congregations.

In the end, Allie's final push to attend seminary came from a voice within rather than from the verbal affirmation of someone in her life, like the kind of affirmation many men in this study received implicitly or explicitly at various points in their lives. Allie's story proves indicative of the experiences and professional trajectories of many of the women in this study. The stories of women pastors presented in this chapter reveal the gendered hurdles they face on their paths to becoming pastors and demonstrate how they are constrained by a dominant gender structure at every stage of their professional development starting from childhood. Rather than investigating the "stained-glass ceiling,"[1] which suggests that women pastors face only one barrier on their paths to becoming senior pastors, this chapter examines the series of hurdles women face on their climbs to top leadership positions in churches; this is what gender researchers refer to as the gendered occupational labyrinth[2] or perhaps for this context, the *stained-glass labyrinth*.

The Gendered Path to the Pulpit

Although it was much later in life that many of the women in this study fully realized that they could pursue being a pastor without sinning or going to Hell, some felt called to the ministry as a child. I asked associate pastor Jane when she knew she wanted to go into the ministry, and she very quickly recalled this moment:

> I didn't realize until college . . . Now, when I was a kid, I definitely thought, "Maybe I'm supposed to be a missionary. Maybe I'm supposed to blah-blah-blah," and I said to my mom at some point when I was probably 10 or a little younger, "I think I'm going to be a preacher. I think I want to be a preacher," and she said, "Well, Baptists don't have women preachers. Maybe you should marry one." As a kid, I just thought, "Hmm—well, Hmm." And I probably thought, "Well, maybe I could be something else. Maybe I could be a different type [other than Baptist]." But probably in my young head, I couldn't really imagine that was possible.

Jane's interaction with her mother, someone she trusted, was deeply influenced by the exclusionary beliefs and policies of her Southern Baptist congregation. Whatever courage Jane had mustered to speak truthfully about her ministerial calling was quickly dismissed by the notion that this simply was prohibited and, perhaps, sinful. In fact, Jane wasn't just given a *different* option to pursue; her mother suggested that she pursue an unpaid support role instead, thereby situating men as having exclusive access to the role of pastor. Experiences like this not only teach girls that their aspirations of becoming pastors are morally wrong, they also cause girls to question and repress their personal intuitions, desires, and ambitions. As a child, who "couldn't really imagine" being a pastor was possible, Jane internalized these sexist beliefs and did not consider the possibility of becoming a pastor again until college.

Despite women being told early in life that they should not pursue ministry, I found that both men and women pastors were equally involved in youth and college groups as teenagers. They both led Bible studies, served as youth group leaders and interns, sang in the choir, and attended church camps. The distinct difference was primarily in how their involvement was framed by their youth pastors and other church leaders. Women's involvement in ministerial activities in high school and college was often interpreted as an extension of their faith, largely temporary, or constrained to nonleadership roles, whereas men's involvement was part of their leadership development, thus advancing the cultivation of their pastoral identities. Associate pastor Allie illustrated the disparate experiences of men and women once announcing their call to the vocational ministry:

> My pastor talked about when he was a senior in high school, one Sunday he had gone forward to tell the church that he felt called to the ministry. Within the week, other men in his church had taken him to the prison and gave him an

opportunity to preach. I said to him, "The door of opportunity does not swing open as quickly for women as it does for men." I've heard [women pastors] tell stories about having to be like "me me pick me, pick me!" whereas, you know they'd grab any ol' man and let him preach.

Allie explained that as soon as her pastor announced he felt called to the vocational ministry, it was only a week later that he received an opportunity to preach even as a high school senior. These types of opportunities build men's pastoral skills and help them feel more secure behind the pulpit. However, women were not offered these types of opportunities as often or at all. For instance, Laura, a co-senior pastor, described her calling experience in high school:

> See, I felt called to the ministry in youth group, but I didn't know what that was allowed to look like. So I made a profession of faith at youth camp, and I come to church the next Sunday and I have a card that's given to me that says, "So you've been called to be a missionary?" And never did I say that, but that's what the expectation was, that, "Oh, she's called to ministry. Clearly she's called to be a missionary." I think I still have it somewhere. . . . So then I put that on the back burner, because I didn't have a context for that, right? I mean the only women who served in my church served Wednesday night supper, and they served in the nursery, and cleaned up after, and they didn't have a real children's minster, so those were the women who were the ones who did it. So I had no model, I had no idea what it meant that I was called to ministry. I go to college and end up specializing in volunteer management, social work, sociology and psychology, because I'm like, "Well, I'll just go into the helping profession and live it out that way."

In Southern Baptist culture, women are not permitted to serve as ministers or pastors, but they are allowed to serve as missionaries, who are generally understood as humble and exist outside the religious organizational hierarchy. This distinction demonstrates that barring women from ordained positions in the church is not related to a belief that women engaging in ministerial activities is theologically unsound, but rather the belief that women maintaining ministerial positions of *authority* and *leadership* should not be permitted. As a result, Laura's call to the vocational ministry was immediately limited to the calling of a missionary by those with authority in the church, therefore denying her the freedom to determine her own ministerial path within the Southern Baptist gender structure.

Laura's story also suggests that the lack of women role models in official Baptist leadership positions offered her no imaginable path to becoming a pastor. Laura said, "I had no model, I had no idea what it meant that I was called to ministry."

In fact, the only positions that Laura had witnessed women occupying in the church were subordinate, unpaid, support roles. With no conceivable alternative, Laura internalized the exclusionary beliefs of Southern Baptist life, put her desire to become a pastor aside, and went to college to pursue other fields that would help her live out her ministerial calling, thereby delaying the development of her pastoral identity and skill set.

Although men, specifically white, straight, cisgender men, who grew up in Baptist congregations, never experienced this exclusion and constantly observed men in leadership positions, the most social justice–oriented male senior pastor in the study, Kyle, became aware of the effects of Southern Baptist gender structure on women's callings at an early age:

> My mother shared a very strong calling story from when she was 16, 17 at her Baptist church. She went to Union University—a Baptist school—wondering what that meant, fell in love with my father who was going to be a pastor. And thought, "Okay, this is how I will live out my calling." Because what else was there in Baptist life? What other models?

Kyle's mother, Anne, had no women role models or opportunities to pursue her calling as a pastor. Consequently, she turned to her only available option as a pastor's wife and began developing her identity within a supportive role, a role that existed only in relation to her husband's leadership position as pastor. As Kyle said, "Because what else was there in Baptist life? What other models?" After Kyle's father passed away, Anne went on to become a Methodist minister, a denomination historically more open to women ministers, particularly older women. However, that happened almost 40 years later! Similar to Laura, Jane, and Allie, the lack of role models and opportunities for women to lead in Baptist life delayed the development of Anne's pastoral identity and ultimately contributed to her becoming a minister in a completely different denomination years later.

While most congregations did not permit women to pursue pastoral positions, some made exceptions for women with whom they had close relationships. Heather, a part-time church office manager who had attended seminary and held two master's degrees in theology, communicated that she returned to her childhood church and requested that the congregation ordain her as a minister. Although leaders of her congregation eventually agreed to this idea, Heather remembered receiving mixed messages at her ordination service:

> At the church I grew up in, we didn't really have any women pastors, but I asked to be ordained at the church. They took a while to decide over it, but then finally decided yes, and with no stipulations, just full ordained kind of thing.

I was the first woman to be ordained at that church and a lot of people came to the ceremony. A couple people didn't like it, but then I had like one lady—old lady who was like 89, 90 kind of thing—who brought me a card, and she's like, "Well, I don't agree with women in ministry, but congratulations," and gave me a congratulations card. It's just a weird mix. Like "I'm not for this. I want you to know that, but here's a check for $25. Don't spend it all in one place." You just take it and whatever.

Here we see that despite Heather's personal certainty about being ordained, the possibility of her moving forward in her vocational calling was largely dependent on the permission of a group of men in her home congregation. This power structure ties Heather's ability to make her own professional decisions to the will of men and reinforces men's positions of power. Although Heather's woman-hood caused debate over her inherent value and status as an ordained minister, the church leaders ultimately allowed it. This decision demonstrates that the theological assertion that women should be barred from the ordained ministry on account of their sex may be lifted for only the exceptional women, thus communicating that Heather must not only be qualified but exceptional enough to be accepted *despite* being a woman. Furthermore, the church leaders' decision to make an exception for Heather suggests that the policy barring women from leadership is more about male pastors maintaining the authority to determine who deserves the power to lead rather than the belief that women's leadership is actually sinful.

Despite the temporary lift on the congregational policy barring women from ordination, some congregants in the church had never observed another woman being ordained in their congregation and internalized the conservative interpretations of biblical Scripture prohibiting women's ordination. Although the barring of women's leadership was challenged through the act of Heather's ordination and perhaps loosened this assertion, one congregant who had been taught that it was sinful for women to lead in the church all of her life, explicitly stated, "I don't agree with women in ministry, but congratulations," thereby characterizing Heather's ordination as immoral despite its approved status. Heather refers to this woman's comments as a "weird mix," illustrating that these mixed messages failed to offer Heather full affirmation of her ordination on account of her sex.

Although few women pastors engaged women role models in their youth, some encountered male pastors who taught more inclusive approaches to biblical Scripture. These experiences caused some women to question theological perspectives and policies that barred women's leadership. Grace, a part-time children's pastor, recalled her youth pastor being a major influence on her path to the vocational ministry:

As far as having an image of women in ministry, I didn't have that model. I grew up in a Southern Baptist Church. . . . But I did have a Truett [CBF-affiliated seminary] grad as a youth minister, an early Truett grad. He really kept that rebellious spirit. He had grown up in that type of church, so he came back and I think you had kind of this underground thing in the youth ministry, where he was more liberal in his ideas, definitely supported women in ministry . . . he really affected my interest in studying religion and in asking the follow-up questions in Sunday school. I think that is part of the reason why I ended up taking the path that I did, that eventually led me to seminary.

Although at this point Grace didn't have a *model* or *image* of women in ministry, her male youth pastor utilized the privilege of his position to offer an alternative way for approaching Scripture that supported the inclusion of women in leadership. Through this relationship and teachings, Grace experienced freedom from sinful notions of women's leadership in the church and, therefore, was able to imagine her possibilities as a minister as early as high school.

Only one woman pastor in the study actually had a woman as a minister when she was a teenager. Meg, an associate pastor, communicated the particular value of her youth minister who influenced her and other young women:

[I went to] First Baptist Church, so it's probably the most moderate in this small town that I grew up in and actually when I was in ninth grade, we had a female youth minister come, which was huge for me and she was a big influence on my life and on me coming into the ministry. She's had at least three females who have come through in her youth group and gone on to be ministers of churches. . . . Because you really don't know it's possible until you see.

Meg's opportunity to observe a woman *doing* and *embodying* a pastoral role offered her a more inclusive, alternative image of ministers that encompassed women as leaders rather than only helpers. Meg's consideration of pursing the vocational ministry earlier in life was greatly influenced by the presence of a woman role model. As a teenager, Meg was able to begin cultivating her ministerial identity and skill set. Meg went on to explain the limitations of even supportive male pastors:

Well, even if people tell you. Even men could tell you all they want to that you could be a minister, but when you're in churches and you only see men in leadership . . . [pause] We've been reading about feminist theology and the invisibility of women has just really stood out to me so much because that's what we see, invisibility in so many Southern Baptist churches because the women are working and they're keeping the church going all behind the scene. But heaven forbid we let them get up behind the pulpit and speak the Word of God.

Here, Meg communicated that the overrepresentation of women in supporting roles not only renders them subordinate but invisible as well. Therefore, normative images of men in leadership roles and women in invisible, undervalued support roles prove more influential than any verbal messages that men may offer affirming women's ability to become ministers. Consequently, women role models prove vital to women's pursuit of the vocational ministry, specifically pastoral positions. While CBF-affiliated congregations theologically support women's leadership, with only 5% of pastors being women, few opportunities are available for girls and women to engage women pastoral role models in Baptist life. This pattern further reinforces the dominant images of men in leadership and the underrepresentation of women in pastoral positions.

College

For most of the women pastors in the study, college offered an opportunity to engage peers, professors, and university groups who offered more inclusive views of women in ministry. But despite being freer from Southern Baptist sexist beliefs on their college campuses, several women still faced opposition and resistance in other contexts like their churches or families. Sophie, a senior pastor, recalled being encouraged to consider ministry by her college professors but found that her congregation disapproved:

Well, I started thinking about ministry in college. That was new to me because I had grown up in a Southern Baptist Church in [the Midwest] so I'd never met a female pastor. But I kept feeling this tug to it and my college—I went to a [different Christian denomination] college and they had women pastors for a while but I was like "I can't do that!" It was kind of this really slow process for me all through college and my professors were really supportive and peers in school but my church not so much. For example, one time I was—for a time I was helping lead the youth group because the youth pastor had resigned and so there was no one to do it. Then without talking to me they just canceled youth like there was no youth group anymore. Then one time they were doing something over the summer for Sunday school instead of their normal classes; they were going to do this different series. I think there were videos or something. Anyway, they were looking for people to guide the discussion and lead it. I volunteered and I think at that point as a junior in college I had more theological education than anyone in the church, including the pastor. I got a letter from an elder saying that like "Well, we can't have you teaching because there'll be men in the room and everything."

Sophie had never witnessed a woman pastor until college. At this point, new images of women pastors challenged Sophie's internalized Southern Baptist sexist beliefs, which excluded women from leadership. Moreover, her college community's affirmation and support of women's leadership initiated a process of *undoing* Sophie's internalized "I can't do that!" that proved residual of her religious upbringing. Once her exclusionary gender beliefs began to loosen, she was able to cultivate her intuitive tug toward the ministry. The exposure to more inclusive theology, women role models, and interactions with affirming peers and mentors disrupted her previously conceived notions of who could hold authority and lead in religious life and ultimately contributed to her pursuit of the pastoral ministry.

We also see that although Sophie began to believe that she could in fact be a leader in the church, she was not completely free of the constraining influence of normative Baptist beliefs around women's leadership. Even though she had more theological education than all of the congregational leaders, including the senior pastor, church leaders still told her that she couldn't teach classes. As a woman, Sophie was prohibited to teach classes at this Baptist church because women were supposed to serve as supporters to men, not as teachers of men. In fact, the issue did not seem to be that Sophie would be teaching, but that she would be teaching men rather than women and children. Sophie was restricted from leading Sunday school workshops not because she was unqualified, but simply because she was a woman. Therefore, Sophie's status as a woman superseded whatever gifts, knowledge, and skills she may offer as a church leader. This decision not only prevented Sophie from further developing her pastoral identity and skill set; it reinforced a gender structure that keeps men in positions of power over women. Despite Sophie being freed from sexist theological beliefs on a personal level, she remained structurally constrained by the exclusionary policies of her congregation, thus resulting in her lack of opportunities to gain experience in church leadership.

Co-senior pastor Laura continued to experience exclusion in college as well. Consequently, Laura sought out alternative forms of ministerial leadership in college and recalled that her fiancé and some of his friends voiced their sexist opinions about women leading in the church:

I started a Christian sorority while I was [in college], and so being able to minster to about 60 or 75 girls—I was able to be filled that way. But I was engaged at the time. I didn't know what that was going to look like. I secretly had been looking at seminary and all of that, but I didn't even really know what that was—no idea. I had no context for any of it. One day we were just driving in the car. He [fiancé] was with his college friend and I'm in the back seat, and his friend asked him, "Would you ever go to a church if a woman was the pastor?" And keep in mind we're getting married in three months. And he said, "Well, I mean, I think they could be ministers, but I wouldn't go if she was the senior pastor. I don't believe in that." And there's no part in me, in sitting in that car, that I thought I was going to be a senior pastor, but for whatever reason it just triggered something and I couldn't really tell you why. We broke up.

Laura wasn't allowed to pursue her calling to the pastoral ministry in high school, so she decided to start a Christian sorority in college. In so doing, she was able to bypass the existing gender structure of Baptist life by creating a space for ministering to other college women that existed outside of the authority of the church. While this loophole allowed her to begin exploring her professional identity as a minister during college, she remained constrained by the exclusionary beliefs of her friends and fiancé. Laura's interaction with her fiancé reinforced the belief system that undergirds the normative Baptist gender structure, which ultimately ensures men's power and women's subordination in Baptist congregations. This realization perhaps provided Laura a glimpse of how her marriage would be arranged in terms of power, with her subordination and his leadership. Laura breaking up with her fiancé after this interaction demonstrates that the dissonance she previously experienced between her status as a woman and her calling was beginning to diminish.

Although most had grown up in Southern Baptist congregations, all of the male pastors in this study supported the equal leadership of women in the church. Matt, a youth minister, spoke about how he and his wife both had planned to attend seminary upon graduating college. He recalled his feelings about one of his friends saying that she felt called to be a pastor's wife:

I remember one of [my wife's] friends, I can't remember who it was, we were talking about what they were going to do [after college], and she was like I really feel called to be a pastor's wife. I remember thinking at that point in time, "That's stupid." [Laughter] Not because we [he and his wife] knew we were going to be pastors, but why would you feel called to [be a pastor's wife]?

While Matt notably supports women in leadership and fully supports his wife's pursuit of pastoral roles, his dismissal of his friend's choices as "stupid" reveals two important issues. First, it reveals the *androcentric* assumption that the work of pastors' wives is insignificant, if not "stupid." Second, it reveals his lack of sociological understanding of the gendered hurdles women face. Clearly, he has never experienced exclusion or doubt about his own vocational calling precisely because he is a man. In other words, his calling had never been judged as sinful *because* he was a man. While it seems obvious to Matt that women should feel free to pursue leadership positions within the church, it is also reasonable to assume that this woman had never been exposed to a woman pastor or had been encouraged to freely engage more inclusive beliefs around women's leadership. Having never had his desire to pursue the vocational ministry questioned on the basis of sex, Matt is blind to the ways this woman's choices were likely constrained by conservative Baptist beliefs that bar women from pastoral positions and, perhaps, fear of the consequences related to pursuing a goal outside of the approved norm. This type of blind spot often leads people to perceive women's choices as a reflection of their individual capabilities and resolve (or lack thereof) rather than a reflection of how society is unequally structured in relation to gender.

Some women pastors who grew up in more moderate Baptist congregations attended college already approaching Scripture in a way that affirmed women's pastoral leadership. However, even those who were affirmed in their pastoral callings in high school encountered and experienced doubts about women's leadership in college. Olivia, a senior pastor, recalled feeling conflicted about women holding senior pastor positions when she was in college:

> I was a high schooler who knew I wanted to work in a church, and had done the whole Baptist walk the aisle and said I wanted to go into full-time Christian vocation. [I] grew up Southern Baptist, but in a congregation that was on the moderate side before the takeover thing was official. My pastor was on the first coordinating council of the CBF. . . . But still going into [college], even then, I still wasn't sure that women should be senior pastors, and I can remember my first year in college. Somebody was doing this senior thesis about this and asked, "Do you think women can work as a church secretary?" "Do you think women can work as youth ministers?" I remember checking "yes" on every single one until I got to senior pastor. And feeling like I should say yes to that, but I just really wasn't sure that it was okay for that one particular task.
>
> It was just like, I felt really conflicted about it. I had flirted with fundamentalism in high school, more out of adolescent anxiety asked what if I'm wrong? What if we need to have these rules? What if the Bible really is literal and my church is teaching the wrong thing? Because I had plenty of conservative friends telling me that my church was teaching the wrong thing. I know that I put "No" on that, but felt really disloyal and conflicted about it.

Despite her more inclusive beliefs related to women's leadership going into college, Olivia faced judgment and pressure from her peers to reconsider the role of women in the church. Olivia internalized this judgment and began to question the notion that women could actually be senior pastors. Here we see that even growing up in a more gender-equitable congregation doesn't preclude women from facing judgment and, subsequently, feeling conflicted in other more conservative contexts later in life. Consequently, Olivia continued to question the morality of women serving as senior pastors in college until she actually met a woman pastor who mentored her. She explained further:

> I worked in a church in college that had a female senior pastor and it was their first. And I watched that, and she really pushed me to preach and to lead some Wednesday nights. She constantly put me in leadership roles and would leave the room so that I couldn't turn to her for help [laughs]. We took a trip together to Atlanta one day. She was preaching at McAfee School of Theology. She really invited me to go with her just because it meant that we had a car ride alone together. On the way there, she was saying, "Do you understand that God has called you to preach?" I was like, "No, I like preaching but I want to be an associate pastor, because—then the responsibility is not on you for all things. You can preach sometimes, but not all the time." I just felt like that it was a way to do a lot of the work that I like to do, but not have the burden on me. She was just calling BS [bullshit] on that . . .[She finally said] You have to go to seminary. We can't keep you here forever. You have to go seminary.

Once Olivia got to witness a woman occupy the top position of leadership in the church, she became more confident in the idea of women serving as senior pastors. In addition to being a role model, this pastor mentored and affirmed Olivia in her giftedness as a preacher and minister. This experience offered Olivia meaningful opportunities to connect with and develop her pastoral identity in college and ultimately led to her enrollment in seminary.

Similarly, Meg, who previously had a woman youth minister as a role model, arrived at college more theologically confident in the idea of women pastors. However, even after experiencing a woman as youth minister, it still had not occurred to her that she could be a senior pastor. Meg recalled the first time the thought of pursuing a senior pastor position crossed her mind:

> When I went for my college visit and said something to them about having an idea that I wanted to go into ministry of some sort, [the college administrator] asked what I wanted to do and I don't know but I was talking about an associate type role and she said, "Well why wouldn't you want to be the senior pastor?" [After that interaction] I felt this is a good place for me. [laughter] I need to be in a place where that would be expected. . . . Or at least not a surprise and that doesn't necessarily mean that's for me but that it's an option. . . . I mean not every man is suited to be senior pastor. And it's almost expected that they are going to try to get there.

Interviewer: Like that's the course, that's their professional ladder?

Yes. Educational or associate or youth [pastor] or whatever for now, then senior pastor after that.

While Meg had never been explicitly discouraged from becoming a senior pastor, she had never been encouraged to pursue that position either; she had also never had an example of a woman in a senior pastor position. When she arrived at her college campus, the juxtaposition of the silence she had experienced previously with her college counselor's explicit encouragement to pursue the top position in the church got her attention, and she concluded that it was this type of voice and sentiment that had been missing in her life. After this, Meg pushed back on the status quo and surrounded herself with people who would actually expect her to pursue leadership roles that she may not have considered otherwise.

Meg also observed that most people in Baptist life generally expect men to eventually pursue senior pastor positions while women are not held to this same expectation. Here we see that although Meg believed women should be free to become pastors and engaged people in college who affirmed women's leadership, she continued to face expectations that propelled men to leadership positions and naturalized women in more subordinate roles. Even within the CBF, a denomination that affirms women's leadership, this pattern assumes that women will pursue less powerful positions or perhaps more flexible ones and reinforces the historically idealized masculine image of senior pastor.

Seminary

Some women attended seminary with the hope that they would finally be released from sexist theology, policies, and expectations related to their pastoral callings. Despite enrolling in seminaries that affirmed women's leadership, they sometimes discovered that their classmates remained unconvinced that women should hold senior pastor positions. Sophie recalled her experience at the CBF-affiliated seminary that she attended:

Once I got to seminary I thought like "I'm free!" and so I would just tell people [about wanting to be a senior pastor], assuming everybody was okay with it. I didn't learn until years later that several people have told me like "You are the first person I ever met that wanted to be a head pastor—you were the first female I'd ever met." One friend [from seminary] told me—this is like a couple years, several years after we graduated, she told me that I was the person who changed her mind [about women as senior pastors] and I was like "I didn't even know you ever changed your mind!"

Sophie attended seminary assuming that she would finally be *free* of a sexist gender structure. However, later on she found that some of her classmates were still opposed to women as senior pastors. Sophie's classmate, like many of the students attending this Baptist seminary, was raised in a Baptist church and had likely never encountered a woman pastor. On one hand, by pursuing the role of senior pastor, Sophie effectively changed the conservative opinions of some of her classmates, which is significant because this challenged the beliefs instilled in them by the SBC. On the other hand, this story shows that attending a more theologically inclusive seminary does not necessarily guarantee complete freedom and acceptance. Given the dearth of women in Baptist pastoral positions overall, it is likely that most Baptist seminary students have not actually interacted with or seen a woman Baptist pastor. Even though the seminary might support the leadership of women, it is not unreasonable to assume that the students will probably continue to (consciously or unconsciously) adhere to sexist beliefs about women's leadership abilities and question whether women can or should hold the top position in the church. In other words, though it is likely that women will, for the first time in their lives, be affirmed in their pastoral callings in seminary, it is also likely that many of those women will be around classmates who do not fully affirm their leadership or remain silent about it.

Some women experienced more overt forms of sexism despite being enrolled in seminaries that supported women's leadership. For example, Allie recalled an example in which Southern Baptist leader Paige Patterson once visited her seminary for a speaking engagement and interacted with one of her female classmates:

> They would tell me stories about some things that happened right before I got there, like when Paige Patterson came to speak and one of them went up to him afterwards and said, "You know, I've grown up as a Southern Baptist and I value my Baptist roots, but I feel called to be a pastor. What would you say to me?" He said, "Women were created last, first to fall and they're saved through childbearing and you shouldn't be a pastor."

Although this woman seminarian attended a seminary that affirmed her call, her seminary put her in a position to still receive these exclusionary messages by inviting a person who explicitly did not support women's leadership in the church to speak on campus. Allie continued:

> Then, they told me about [someone from the Presbyterian denomination], he was PCA, and spoke in the chapel service one day. A young woman went up to him and said, "What would you say to me if I told you that I felt called to be a pastor?" He said, "I would tell you to go back into your prayer closet, because

you have misunderstood the call of God." Some of those things have been said
directly to me [as well].

Despite working past gendered barriers they faced in their childhoods and early
adulthood, Allie and her colleagues continued to receive explicit messages of exclusion while in seminary. It is key to point out that such comments do not land
on a blank slate; rather, they land in an internalized pile of explicit and implicit
messages that these women have received regarding their pastoral callings their
entire lives. Allie explained further that she felt her calling as an adult had been
so strong and, therefore, these types of messages no longer deterred her pursuit
of becoming a pastor. It is important to acknowledge the high level of strength,
faith, self-assuredness, devotion, assertiveness, and courage it takes to be resolute and continue on in the face of such explicitly sexist interactions; such qualities often come from the consistent experience of exclusion and discrimination.
It is through these experiences of marginalization that many women pastors
developed the skills and confidence to effectively work through the subsequent
emotional, psychological, and social consequences of choosing paths that resist
the dominant power structures.

Other women pastors who eventually ignored the theological restrictions of
their youth faced gendered processes in seminary that sought to redirect their
vocational goals. Laura, unaware of moderate-liberal Baptist congregations' recent separation from the SBC, first planned to attend a Southern Baptist seminary. During her preregistration visit, Laura was urged by seminary professors to
switch to a more theologically sound professional path:

> I decide I'm going to go to Southwestern, but there's something in me that didn't
> feel right about it. And so as I make an appointment with the Dean's office and
> have to go talk to him before I can register, I go talk to them and they say, "Well,
> once you take hermeneutics courses and your theology courses, you'll under-
> stand why women shouldn't be in the M.Div. program, or women shouldn't be
> in—I was accepted into the M.Div. program. I was accepted into the graduate
> school for Southwestern, but they said that it would be better for me to do the
> Master of Christian Counseling or the Master of Christian Education. And
> once I took my hermeneutics courses I would understand why, you know, once
> I read Titus and First Timothy.

As expected in a Southern Baptist seminary, the staff urged Laura to pursue alternative ministerial paths that were more *theologically suitable* for women. The
biblical teachers further stated that she would understand why this was the case
once she was more familiar with biblical Scripture, suggesting that the issue was
that she was either ignorant of the Bible or misunderstood it rather than a sexist

gender structure. This interaction not only caused Laura to doubt her calling once again but also reinforced a gender structure that ensures men's power over women.

This experience did not deter Laura's pursuit of vocational ministry. Instead of giving up, Laura connected with a CBF-affiliated seminary that theologically supported her professional goals. She went on:

> So I leave the office and call [a representative from a moderate Baptist seminary] crying in the parking lot and told her that I made a horrible mistake. And I'm there by the end of the week for an orientation. Yes, showed up homeless. Just packed my little bag. [laughter] And I when I got to orientation and [the dean at the time] gets up and says, "All of you will take leadership, all of you will take preaching because who are we to say what you are called to do based on your gender?" So that right there, finally confirmed it.

For the first time, Laura was provided with an alternative theological perspective that offered her freedom to pursue the ministerial calling that she had connected with as a teenager. After a long road of being barred from leadership positions in the church or redirected to *more appropriate* roles, this experience "finally confirmed" her pastoral calling.

Despite overcoming the theological hurdle at seminary, Laura later discovered that there were few seminary professors who served as mentors or advocates to women in particular (there were only two women faculty at the time). Women's underrepresentation in seminary faculty positions resulted in a lack of women role models for students, particularly women students, who could offer insight into the persistent gendered barriers within Baptist life, teach biblical Scripture from a gender liberation or feminist perspective, and help foster the development of women's ministerial identities within the current gender structure. Despite experiencing more freedom to pursue the pastoral ministry in seminary, Laura remained constrained by a gendered division of labor. Laura and Michael, co-senior pastors, and Ben, an associate pastor, further explained the different and unequal messages they received in seminary.

LAURA: Did I have professors [while in seminary] saying "Yes, you're supposed to do this. Go do it, I'll help you do it."? No. That came from [my social work professors]. I had to go through [pauses]—this question's so loaded because I had to go through [tears up]. I mean they [men] get to start seminary knowing—[begins to cry] I can't talk about all of this. [pauses]

MICHAEL: We have the opportunity to know that there's something on our side . . . on the other side [of graduating]. It's a lot easier.

BEN: People were grooming us to do it. Lots of affirmation, lots of "Yes, you can do this."

LAURA: They got to start seminary knowing—not just men, maybe women who had been able to find someone to show them [what it looked like] earlier, but knowing what they get to do after graduation. . . . I think I had to spend a few years figuring out that, first, I was allowed to do it, but then (tears up) that I was capable of doing it.

The messages of exclusion that Laura had internalized for most of her life required her to spend a lot of time as an adult processing the devaluation of her calling, *undoing* these messages of exclusion, and replacing them with ones of affirmation. Laura said, "I had to spend a few years figuring out that, first, I was *allowed* to do it, but then that I was *capable* of doing it." While she spent most of her time in seminary building her pastoral identity from the ground up, Laura's male counterparts retained the privilege of starting seminary having received various forms of affirmation their entire lives, church leadership experience, and the security of knowing that *all* churches would be open to hiring them on the basis of their sex once they graduated, thereby increasing their chances of securing a job.

It is important to note that these two different narratives about men's and women's leadership abilities are *not* one of exclusion in the case of women and neutrality for men nor is it one of affirmation of men and neutrality for women. These narratives are about *both* excluding women *and* affirming men. Narratives and beliefs about male pastors never included moral or religious judgment about their desire to lead because of their maleness. As a result, none of the male pastors in this study ever questioned whether or not it was morally or theologically permissible on the basis of sex to pursue the vocational ministry at any points in their lives. In fact, most were the sons or grandsons of male pastors and, therefore, were probably cultivating pastoral skills through their same-sex role model since the moment they were born. The women pastors were not able to grow up with their mothers as pastoral role models. By the time male pastors arrived at seminary, most had experienced if not explicit affirmation from others, then implicit support in the form of male role models. Conversely, Laura was discouraged, questioned, and judged at every stage toward becoming a pastor. It is no wonder that it took much of her young adult life to develop her pastoral identity and only after attending a seminary that theologically affirmed her equal leadership as a woman.

Despite not connecting with a mentor in seminary, Laura connected with one of her social work professors, who was also an ordained minister and helped Laura cultivate her pastoral identity:

At dinner she said, "Look at you, you're worthy." I haven't thought about this in a long time. She told me, "You are your worst enemy—get out of your way because you're going to do it—you're limiting yourself." She still tells me that, she texted me that a month ago, or something because she wanted me to apply for the PhD program and I didn't do it. [laughs] I'm not going to be hurt ... I've heard "No" too many times. Because even in trying to find a job—there are more churches that are not open to a woman.

For fear of being excluded or hurt again, Laura initially did not go after some opportunities of which she was interested. But Laura's interactions with her mentor began to replace the messages of exclusion she had experienced since she became aware of her calling as a teenager. It is important to note that Laura eventually applied and was accepted to a PhD program while serving as a co-lead pastor. Although this process occurred much later than most male pastors, we see that largely through this mentorship Laura evolved from believing she was *allowed* to do it to believing she was *capable* of doing it and then *doing it.*

Similarly, when Anna first considered becoming a senior pastor, she had a conversation with a seminary professor who helped her connect with her ministerial calling and affirmed her desire to become a pastor:

I chose the perfect person to talk to about it—[name of seminary professor].... He was a peer to my parents.... I made an appointment and went by to talk with him and I said, "Dr. [name of professor], I'm finding that I appreciate my religious education classes. The trick was I wasn't learning anything different from what I had learned as an early childhood major [in undergrad]." I said, "Where I'm finding my greatest challenges are in my theology classes. I love New Testament and that's what I really want to study." He said, "Okay, so what does that mean to you?" I said, "Well, I really think that my call is changing." He just kind of leaned into me and said, "How do you think it's changing?" I said, "Well, I'm a little bit afraid to say it." He said, "Why are you afraid?" I said. "Because I've never seen it done before." Then he reached over to me and grabbed both of my hands and he said, "Or would you rather be a part of something? I know it's exciting to be a part of something that hasn't always been." I said, "I think I'm called to preach." He said, "Then you must go home and tell your family." [laughs] But I softened it. I went home and because I was still so—I was a little unsure and I softened it to them and said, "I think I want to stay and get another degree," and they said okay.

Before interacting with her seminary professor, Anna remained constrained by having never encountered the image of a woman *doing* the role of pastor. Although Anna was afraid initially, her interaction with her professor offered an alternative path to the one that had been constructed by exclusionary SBC beliefs and policies. Instead of encouraging her to continue pursuing "religious educa-tion," Anna's mentor encouraged her to pursue something she had never seen done before, that is, to become a woman senior pastor. Yet Anna said she was still a little unsure and "softened" her plans to become a pastor when she told her parents; her father was an SBC pastor, which impacted her in the exact opposite way that having a pastor as a father influenced the male pastors. Despite Anna's loosening beliefs about women's ability to lead as pastors, her freedom to em-brace her calling fully was constrained by her parents' Southern Baptist beliefs and her fear of their response to her wanting to become a pastor.

Unlike the women in my study who considered their experiences with mentors as vital to their career trajectory, male pastors rarely pointed toward a life-altering professor in seminary. When they did, they did not characterize them as crucial influences on their vocational paths so much as in admiration of their work. Moreover, when male pastors mentioned role models or mentors, they spoke of these relationships as enhancing their callings, not directing them toward their callings. For instance, Brett, a lead pastor, emphasized a need for a mentor that guided his personal development as a husband and father rather than his professional development. Brett's need for development in this way points toward the differential ways men and women are socialized that re-sult in few opportunities or role models for this type of development in men. Differently, women pastors' rare opportunity to connect with mentors relates to the gendered division of labor within Baptist life and negatively implicates their professional development, income, status, authority, and the ability to cul-tivate their ministerial callings. Brett's lack of mentors for personal development presented no noted bearing on his ability to become a pastor. In fact, he received a full-time preaching position upon graduating from seminary.

Becoming Pastors

While many women who want to be senior pastors have not yet attained these positions, the few women who were hired as senior pastors continue to face pro-cesses of exclusion and resistance within their congregations or community. In some cases, Baptist women ministers leave the Baptist denomination all to-gether to begin the ordination process over in more inclusive denominations. Given that the churches in this study were all congregationally led to varying degrees, those congregations that did hire a woman as a senior pastor rarely had very many congregants who held oppositional opinions about having a woman as lead pastor. Conversely, in a church that hired a husband and wife co-senior pastor team, some congregants refused to acknowledge Laura as their pastor.

I asked one congregant if he thought that if some of the people who were at first resistant to Laura becoming their co-lead pastor still primarily look to Michael as their pastor. He responded:

> Oh yes, they do. There's still people saying, "This is our preacher and here's our preacher's wife."
>
> It makes Laura so mad. [laughs] You know that's another thing, in this world, in this day and time, if you're going to do this, you got to understand reality. [laughs] These people ain't reality. So you can't let little stuff like that bother you. You just got to understand, thank God that we're as far as we are, don't be upset with these people.

Although Nate didn't seem to agree with the sexist behaviors of congregants who refuse to acknowledge Laura as their pastor, as a male, retired, Baptist pastor, Nate fails to understand that for most of Laura's life these types of exclusionary opinions have determined her reality and actually barred her from ministry opportunities in very real, concrete ways. Also, congregants' refusals to acknowledge Laura as their pastor undermine her authority and result in inequitable professional outcomes between her and Michael in terms of being able to effectively do their jobs. Laura cannot effectively lead as a pastor if congregants refuse to acknowledge her authority and only respond to the pastoral authority of her husband, Michael. Even in a CBF-affiliated congregation where she is officially a pastor, congregants' sexist beliefs and behaviors *are* her reality and reinforce the exclusionary system that has created barriers to her calling as a pastor her since high school.

Nate further states that if Laura's "going to do this" (be a woman pastor), then she can't let sexist behaviors bother her. Additionally, she should be grateful for how far society has come in relation to gender equity. This statement puts the responsibility on Laura to get over it or deal with it rather than on the congregation to change. Moreover, rather than comparing her experiences to those of men, he instead compares her current experiences to those of women who came before her and states that she should "thank God" that she has it as good as she has it. It also communicates that if Laura is going to choose this profession, she needs to be prepared for the negative consequences. Nate remains blind to how the organization itself is gendered, and he expects Laura to adjust her behavior and perspective instead of working to change the congregation itself. Nate, a retired Baptist pastor whose authority had never been called into question on account of his sex, fails to see how congregants' discriminatory attitudes and comments are not inconsequential; they collectively contribute to barriers faced by women pastors and ultimately result in structural inequality (e.g., unequal and gendered division of labor). Despite Laura successfully securing the position of pastor within a CBF-affiliated congregation, sexist beliefs about her ability to lead persist and undermine her authority as a pastor.

While upcoming chapters effectively demonstrate specific implicit barriers women face once becoming a pastor, most women did not recall experiencing *overt resistance* from their congregations like Laura experienced. However, some faced resistance from the local community. For instance, Anna, who graduated seminary in the middle of the Conservative Takeover and won the distinguished preaching award at her seminary, received her first full-time senior pastor position after searching for 25 years. Anna described the local community's response when she received the position of senior pastor:

> In my first year here, we had rocks thrown through the windows and all kinds of stuff on the front page of the paper every day for about a week.
> Interviewer: Really? Because the church hired a woman pastor?
> Yes. We had a couple that was at the international mission who were trying to be appointed as volunteer missionaries. Well, the trustee for the International Mission Board [of the Southern Baptist Convention] from the state of Alabama called the International Mission Board to say this couple has a female as their pastor and so their application was denied.

Despite finding a church that was open to hiring her as a senior pastor, Anna still faced aggressive opposition from community members who failed to believe women were worthy of the job. Additionally, congregants faced punitive consequences affecting their ability to become missionaries simply because they attended Anna's church. Here we see that the familiar dominant narrative of exclusion and marginalization followed Anna as well as her congregants even as she served in a church that openly supported her as senior pastor.

Many women did not face explicit resistance from their congregations or surrounding communities after becoming pastors, but they continued to experience opposition, silence, or lack of affirmation from their families and friends. Sophie, a senior pastor who graduated from seminary about 25 years after Anna and also received the distinguished preaching award at her seminary, reflected on the apprehension of her family:

> So back home I was always real quiet about [wanting to be a pastor] because I just didn't want to deal with people's reactions. . . . I mean my parents, they weren't really supportive, but my family sort of avoids anything controversial so it wasn't like we had direct conversation about it. Like when I was in college, my mom would tell people I was going to be a professor, even though I'd never said that. It was just easier for her, I guess, it just easier for her to get around it. They've definitely warmed up over time, particularly for my mom. I think when

she came for my ordination [and] that made a big difference for her. She didn't say that, but I think so.

While some women pastors' parents proved supportive, many parents never brought up the subject or were judgmental. Sophie shared that even after she decided she wanted to be a pastor, she was cautious about sharing her plans with people from her hometown because she didn't want to take the chance of hearing their reactions of disapproval or confusion. While not explicitly oppositional, the lack of reaction paired with her parents' silence or perceived positions of neutrality fails to disrupt the internalized messages and beliefs of exclusion that Sophie had received for most of her life and forces her to repress her professional goals about which she would otherwise be excited.

Male pastors noted that sometimes family members may disagree with their moderate-liberal theology, preferred that they choose a profession that made more money, or expected that they pursue lead pastor positions, but their maleness was never an issue of discussion with their families. Ben, an associate pastor, communicated that he had no desire to be a senior pastor in the future, and he and his partner, Ashley, commented on how congregants and family members typically respond to this notion:

BEN: I think people [congregants] are often confused by the fact that I don't ... that it's not an aspiration.

ASHLEY: Definitely, my family will ask when he will start looking for lead pastor positions and are surprised, maybe even worried, when I say he has no interest in doing that. I think they still think that women should, need to be taken care of by a man. Even though I have my own thing going on professionally, they need to be the breadwinners.

Such critiques or confusion around men's choices to not pursue being senior pastor suggest that they think men are not empowered when they are not making enough money or hold the most authority. In other words, because masculinity and power are conflated, men are expected to pursue goals associated with leadership, money, authority, and status, while women, even those with careers, should support their husbands in achieving this and have their husbands take care of them despite their abilities to take care of themselves. Although these expectations are unfair to men, they still assume men's dominance and, therefore, function as barriers to women pursuing positions of authority and leadership.

Having experienced different expectations than men, many women only considered pursuing a senior pastor position after serving in other ministerial positions and roles (often part-time) for several years. They typically credited their interactions and experiences with women senior pastors as partially responsible for their pursuit of lead pastor positions. For instance, when I asked Jane, an associate pastor, if she will ever pursue a senior pastor position, she responded:

> Yes. And I've only ever said that out loud to one other person, my husband, and it was just a few months ago. I'm in my forties and I'm just now thinking. Yeah, this is something I want and could do. I think it has been since working with Anna. I have learned a lot from her. And also, I'm starting to think more independently in terms of leadership. Just recently I noticed, she may handle something a certain way, and I think to myself, "Hmm. I might have handled that differently."

Despite her obvious giftedness and skill set, Jane—who felt called to be a pastor as a young girl and couldn't imagine it possible—had not even considered the possibility of becoming a senior pastor until working with Anna. Anna, both as an example and mentor, helped Jane realize that she was capable of being a senior pastor and further developed her ability to think independently and lead. Jane, being in a position to lead and further develop her management abilities, gave her the confidence to imagine herself as a senior pastor.

Finally, women pastors' past exclusion sometimes negatively influenced their ability to participate in activities alongside their male counterparts. For instance, Kristen, a co-lead pastor at a church not included in the study, reflected on a workshop activity at a denominational conference for pastors:

> I remember being at a denominational meeting. There was a room full of pastors and we were asked to call out the person in our lives who first affirmed our call to the ministry. So all of the men started calling out the names of people who affirmed their calling. I was sitting next to Karen, one of the only other women pastors in the room, co-pastor. We both remained silent during this process. As we got into the elevator to go back to our rooms, she asked why I didn't say anything. I said, "No one ever named that in me. I just always knew from within or I guess God." She said, "Me, too. And I thought it too presumptuous to say Isaiah!" [laughs]

Here, Kristen and her co-pastor were unable to fully participate in the workshop because gendered assumptions were built into the activity. Unlike the other male pastors in the room, who had been verbally affirmed by ministers or other people in their lives, "no one had named that" in Kristen or Karen. This activity further revealed disparate experiences of many women pastors and perpetuated their exclusion despite their status as pastors. This example also illustrates the utility and value of women pastors having relationships with other women pastors who share similar experiences. It is through Kristen's interaction with her colleague that this experience of exclusion was transformed into an exchange of mutual understanding and affirmation of their callings, a type of opportunity that is few and far between for women in Baptist life.

Steps Toward Change

In addition to becoming aware of the ways that normative Baptist gender structure remains influential in CBF congregations and particularly in the lives of women pastors, it is important to point out that CBF congregations are inextricably linked to the gender structure of dominant culture as well. In other words, women's underrepresentation in senior pastor positions in CBF congregations parallels dominant patterns in the gendered division of labor of other denominational entities and occupations on a national level. Women remain significantly underrepresented in the higher echelons of leadership in politics, business, medicine, law, and religion and underrepresented overall in fields like science, technology, and engineering. The likelihood of women having access to women role models in any leadership position, not just in the church but in society overall, remains comparatively low. Moreover, girls often receive implicit messages about "what they are good at" or "what they should do" early in life that perpetuate these outcomes. For instance, girls are often given dolls to care for, while their boy counterparts are given tools to build with or science experiments to exercise. Or girls are given nurse costumes when boys are given doctor costumes, and so on.

Therefore, in order for CBF congregations to effectively fulfill their mission of women's equal leadership and theological commitment to equality and justice for all human beings, they must work beyond officially stating that they support the leadership of women toward creating a gender counterstructure that stands in opposition to the unequal status quo of society. To do this, congregations must provide more opportunities for leadership and development specifically for young women and girls, invite more women as guest preachers in their congregations, and ultimately become more intentional about hiring women as pastors and seminary faculty.

At the end of one of my research visits with one congregation that had never hired a woman in any full-time pastoral position, one congregant asked about some of the themes that were surfacing in my study. I talked about some of the findings in this chapter, particularly about how women rarely receive affirmation about their ministerial callings. To this she asked, "Well, do you think it's just because women generally *need* more affirmation than men?" The data in this study do not point toward that hypothesis. These findings show that women pastors may need more encouragement and affirmation than do men pastors, not because they are *naturally* more insecure or socialized to have sensitive personalities, but because of internalized messages of discrimination and exclusion. Additionally, they receive consistent discouragement to pursue their callings from a young age and have a dearth of women role models demonstrating that being a Baptist pastor is possible, whereas men and boys constantly receive implicit encouragement and explicit affirmation. This study instead demonstrates women's resilience and ability to become pastors *despite* receiving little affirmation and experiencing judgment and exclusion along the way. My interaction with this congregant further demonstrates the pervasiveness of normative gender structure and, therefore, calls for further awareness of how our beliefs and assumptions remain significantly influenced by normative gender structure.

Discussion Questions

- Explain the influence of the dominant Baptist gender structure on women pursuing leadership positions in churches.
- In her theory of gendered organizations, Acker identified five gendered organizational processes (see Introduction). How many were at play in this chapter?
- Why was the presence of women role models important for other women in seminaries and churches?
- Think about the career of your dreams. Have you experienced encouragement or discouragement or silence in pursuing this field or position? Can you identify any same-sex role models in these positions? What about images in media or entertainment? Consider role models at the intersection of race, sexuality, and gender identity as well. What does the person who plays these professional roles in television or movies typically look like? Do you fit this dominant mold?

Supplemental Readings

Finlay, Barbara. 2003. *Facing the stained glass ceiling: Gender in a protestant seminary.* Lanham, MD: University Press of America.

Gansen, Heidi M. 2017. Reproducing (and disrupting) heteronormativity: Gendered sexual socialization in preschool classrooms. *Sociology of Education, 90*(3), 255–272.

Kane, Emily W. 2012. *The gender trap: Parents and the pitfalls of raising boys and girls.* New York: NYU Press.

Martin, Karin A. 1998. Becoming a gendered body: Practices of preschools. *American Sociological Review*, 63(4), 494–511.

Rosenthal, Lisa, Levy, Sheri R., London, Bonita, Lobel, Marci, and Bazile, Cartney. 2013. In pursuit of the MD: The impact of role models, identity compatibility, and belonging among undergraduate women. *Sex Roles*, 68(7–8), 464–473.

Sealy, Ruth, and Singh, Val. 2006. Role models, work identity and senior women's career progression-why are role models important? In *Academy of Management proceedings* (Vol. 2006, No. 1, pp. E1–E6). Briarcliff Manor, NY: Academy of Management.

3
Gender "Neutral" Hiring Processes

So really it was less a gender thing . . .

Gender is a foundational component of *organizational logic*, or the underlying assumptions and processes that shape work organizations.[1] Acker challenges the preconceived notion that organizational logic is gender neutral by arguing that there is a gendered substructure underlying the daily practical work activities that occur within organizations. [2] Organizational logic in its material forms refers to "work rules, labor contracts, managerial directives, and other documentary tools for running large organizations, including systems of job evaluation."[3] It also includes more abstract hiring protocols, job descriptions, hiring criteria, and the unofficial *ways of doing things* influenced by the conscious and unconscious assumptions, beliefs, and preferences of organizational actors.[4]

Like in many other workplaces, a committee of congregational actors is responsible for hiring and personnel processes in Baptist churches. Typically, the congregation selects a pastoral search committee comprised of five to seven congregational members. The committee conducts a pastoral search, visits pastors and observes their preaching, and typically chooses four or five candidates to interview. Once the hiring committee interviews all of the candidates, it usually votes and decides on a candidate to present to the whole congregation. This candidate is often invited to preach and engage in conversations with the congregants. After the candidate's official visit, the entire congregation votes on whether or not to hire. During this process, congregants' gendered opinions and attitudes are particularly influential to Baptist churches' organizational logic.

To varying degrees, all of the congregations in this study have established goals of inclusion and equality particularly pertaining to women and women's leadership. In fact, all of the pastoral hiring committees were represented equally by men and women members with the goal of eliminating gender biases throughout the hiring process. The following sections show how despite congregants' intentions of equality, gendered hiring criteria as well as congregants' conscious and unconscious gender biases perpetuate male pastors' advantage in hiring practices within these congregations.

Preacher Woman. Katie Lauve-Moon, Oxford University Press (2021). © Oxford University Press.
DOI: 10.1093/oso/9780197527542.003.0004

"Just Doesn't Feel Right"

I think there is some basic difference and I couldn't tell you exactly what I think that is. [laughs] The authority that a male can present. [pauses] Mainly because women have not been expected or allowed, not just in church but in our whole society. It seems that we have accepted it more in a political world than we have in church. I've wondered that about myself, trying to figure out, okay now what is it about this I don't like? [laughs] I don't know what it is. I can't tell you. But I do think there's a difference and I think it probably is those of us that are still around, and as time goes on that won't be as big of a deal. But you look at our church, you talk about the leadership and all the people who never experienced [a woman pastor]. And it's that we are open to the change, but still it just doesn't feel right. It's not that . . . it just doesn't feel right and we don't want to be mean about it or against it.

Similar to how many women in this study slowly evolved into realizing they were allowed to be pastors and could be pastors, it also took time for some congregants to "undo" their exclusionary biases related to women's leadership. This congregant, who had served on several pastoral search committees, struggled with an internal conflict that persisted between morally or intellectually supporting women's leadership in the church and it just not *feeling right*. Conscious and unconscious biases are often shaped by our social environments and driven by feelings of discomfort that influence our decisions.[5] Research shows that implicit or unconscious biases undergird institutional oppression and reinforce inequities in the labor force.[6] There is reason to believe that growing up in congregations where women almost exclusively served in support roles would influence how one *feels* when led by a woman. This congregant suggests this to be true in relation to his uneasy feelings associated with women's leadership in the church *despite* his openness to change.

The lack of women's leadership in this congregant's church simply serves as a microcosm of a larger societal gender structure by which women are underrepresented in positions of authority (e.g., CEOs) and overrepresented in support roles (e.g., administrative assistants). For instance, although he perceived women's leadership to be more widely accepted in politics, in the United States women still only represent about a quarter of US Congressional positions and about 13% of US Cabinet positions (2 women of 16 core Cabinet positions); currently, in 2020, there is only one more woman Cabinet member than there was in 1935 when the very first woman was confirmed as a US Cabinet core member over 80 years ago! The national political gender structure is mirrored on a global level as well, with only about 10% of countries led by female heads of state. Such an unbalanced gender structure suggests a standard for a normative mold of leaders and may further reinforce people's feelings of discomfort when they engage female leaders in the church who fail to fit the normative male pastoral mold.

Other congregants who supported women's leadership in the church noted similar feelings as well. For instance, while serving on a pastoral search committee, one congregant was unsure about hiring a woman as a senior pastor. Even still, he visited her church to observe her preaching and leading a service. After this experience, he stated, "Well, I see it entirely differently. This is a struggle for me, but I do see this differently." The pastoral search committee ended up hiring a man, but this congregant's observation of a woman actually "doing" the role of pastor caused him to intellectually and morally change his stance on women's leadership. While his being exposed to a woman pastor began to chip away at his bias, it did not fully eliminate his feelings of uneasiness with the idea of women pastors. It is impossible to know if this committee member's continued struggle with women in leadership directly resulted in hiring a male pastor for this position, but it is important to note that his feelings of uncertainty were inevitably present in the deliberation process.

Some congregants recalled feelings of discomfort when they first engaged a woman pastor but noted that this apprehension dissipated the more they experienced women pastors. One woman recalled, "Now I remember the first time I heard a woman actually preach and I have to admit that was a new feeling. I was unsure about it. I was unsure about it when we first hired Lynne [their first woman pastor], even though I knew it was right. But she was so wonderful, I didn't even think about it over time. I got used to it." Similarly, one pastor remembered the angst his spouse felt around the thought of experiencing a woman pastor for the first time: "She [his spouse] was very honest as we were preparing to get to church that intellectually she didn't have any problem, but she was really anxious about what it would actually feel like to have a woman pastor. We went that Sunday and we never visited anywhere else." These two examples further demonstrate how conscious and unconscious gender biases are not only experienced by men but women as well. Like men, if women primarily experience men in leadership roles and women in support roles, there is a good chance that experiencing a leader who does not fit into the normative leadership mold may illicit feelings of uneasiness that often come with experiencing something new or different for the first time. However, as noted earlier, in many cases these feelings can subside once a new normative mold is forged and expanded to include more types of people.

Studies show that unconscious gender biases influence hiring decisions in ways that most often negatively impact women's chances at being hired, particularly in leadership positions.[7] Gender structure is rarely situated in a way that intellectually, morally, or emotionally questions men's ability to lead on the basis of sex and so they don't encounter these same gendered barriers. Moreover, congregants' discomfort with women pastors is directly related to their familiarity and comfort with the normative leadership of men. Therefore, congregants' discomfort about women's leadership proves particularly advantageous to male pastors who are applying for the same jobs as women. The internal struggle that many congregants experienced in relation to women's leadership suggests that women pastors must be so exceptional that they not only convince congregants intellectually and morally that they are worthy and capable of effective leadership *but also* make them *feel* comfortable with their leadership. Furthermore, women's ability to become senior pastors and establish authority depends largely on congregants' willingness to be open to emotions associated with anxiety and feelings of discomfort related to women's leadership and develop a critical lens for identifying ways their personal unconscious biases may result in inequitable outcomes between, in this case, white heteronormative cisgender men and women.

Incongruence of Essentialist Assumptions and Intentions of Equality

Some congregants felt comfortable with women's equal leadership, but they argued that women and men are essentially different and, therefore, women should naturally function as different types of leaders than men. In interviews with pastors and congregants, I did not ask many questions that explicitly inquired about their attitudes or opinions pertaining to men and women because they were typically aware enough to respond with politically correct answers. However, for my closing question I sometimes would explicitly ask, "Do you believe that women and men are essentially different?" or "Do you think there is something essentially different between a woman doing the role of pastor and a man doing the role of pastor?"

Most congregants, especially women, in churches with a woman pastor often attributed differences between men and women pastors to individual personality traits rather than sex differences. These congregants, even women, would often reveal their gender biases unknowingly in more subtle ways. For example, one congregant evaluated his pastor, "She was the first woman lead pastor we had—but she was very assertive, did a good job." I pressed further and asked what he meant by *assertive*. He went on, "She was effective in leading services, preaching, you know—leadership." This congregant, who implicitly understands assertiveness to be a trait of good leaders, clarifies that *although* this pastor was a woman, she proved to lead assertively. This qualifying statement suggests that women must prove that they can be assertive and effective leaders *despite* being women.

Other congregants, almost exclusively in congregations that had never hired a woman senior pastor, explicitly stated that they understood women as essentially different than men but believed these differences should be valued equally. For example, senior pastor Brett, who had served on pastoral hiring committees at a church that had never hired a woman in any full-time pastoral position, responded:

> I think men lead aggressively, mechanistically sometimes. I think men are more focused on results and solving problems. Men are not as patient and able to sit in ambiguity as long . . . Women think—I don't know, I can't get any specifics, it's like a perceptual thing. I think women are typically better listeners in my experience. Women are typically more patient. I think women are typically more thoughtful. I think women tend to have a different kind of courage.

As illustrated in Chapter 1, the role of pastor is conflated with expectations of authority and leadership and, therefore, is intrinsically linked to masculinity. Although pastors are expected to engage in feminized skills such as being patient, being a good listener, and being compassionate, empathetic, and collaborative in order to establish their authority, the gendered significance of the role of pastor is situated in their ability to demonstrate strong leadership skills and embody authority effectively. Specifically, these expectations were referred to by congregants as pastors' ability to "stand their ground," "be tough," "be assertive," "be a senior pastor," and "not be pushed around," which are abilities and traits generally associated with masculinity.[8] Congregants also expected pastors to establish their authority through "good preaching" typically defined by pastors' ability to demonstrate a high level of intelligence, research and technical skills, and commanding attention in the pulpit, which are also qualities generally associated with masculinity.

Brett perceived that women typically embody traits of femininity like listening, patience, and thoughtfulness more often and effectively than men and observed men to have qualities that are most often associated with masculinity and, therefore, leadership. These observations are likely influenced by a gender structure most often characterized by the socialization of men into authoritative roles and women into caring roles. Although Brett placed equal value on the different qualities of men and women, he failed to see how these assumptions inherently reinforce a gendered hierarchy, with men being more suited for leadership and women more suited for support roles. As we continued our conversation, he pointed out examples of men and women who failed to fit these descriptions of essentialism, but Brett referred to these examples as exceptions and statistically atypical although he never actually cited specific statistics; countless studies actually show gender to be constructed and performative rather than natural fixed traits of men and women (see Introduction). Given Brett's understanding of differences between men and women, he will likely perceive men as more *naturally* able to embody pastoral positions of authority and leadership. As the exceptions to his notion of essentialism, which in and of itself contradict the argument of essentialism, women would have to prove that they have the qualities required to be strong leaders *despite* being women.

Brett's last statement distinguished between how men and women embody *different types of courage*. This further suggests that he assumes essential personality differences exist between men and women, so I asked him to clarify what he meant by this. He responded:

> Well, because women are part of a class in our society that has more experience being discriminated against, they're more likely to see things like that in the [biblical] text. When they preach, for example, they are able to further identify with people who are also discriminated against.

Here, we see that while Brett takes an essentialist position, he seems to have some understanding of how normative gender structure is constructed in ways that discriminate against women as well as influence the lens through which women pastors identify similar experiences in biblical texts and formulate sermons that speak to the marginalization of others. The significance of Brett's statement about women's courage lies in the word *different*. Brett's explanation suggests that he understands men's courage as *traditional* courage, a standard to measure all other types of courage against and women's courage as *a different kind of courage*. Therefore, Brett associates men's normative courage with traits such as strength, leadership, bravery, decisiveness, boldness, and risk-taking—traits usually characteristic of heroes in books and movies and typically descriptive of positions of authority. However, he understands women's courage as primarily related to their marginalized and subordinate status in society and their ability to empathize and speak out against discrimination.

Women *should* be considered courageous for preaching sermons on social justice issues that are considered controversial by church members, particularly given that congregants typically hold the power on whether or not pastors keep their jobs. I perceived any woman pastor who braved this masculinized profession as courageous for even trying in the first place. Moreover, I did not observe the courage women embody by risking their jobs in leading congregants to controversial and important places to differ from the kind of courage traditionally associated with masculinity, particularly in a modern world. While Brett's understanding of women's courage causes them to more freely be an advocate for the oppressed, a trait valued by only a handful of social justice-oriented congregations, his conception of men's courage better qualifies them for positions of leadership in general (e.g., being a problem-solver). Here we see that Brett's distinction between men's and women's courage is not simply one of difference but inherently one of value and status.

A different congregant who had served on pastoral search committees at a church that currently had a female senior pastor attributed essential differences between men and women to fixed differences in male and female brains. He stated:

> Male brains and female brains are not the same; male bodies and female bodies are not the same. You can do whatever you want, but women still bear children in our species and that's not going to change. I was thinking about the whole issue of female sexuality that is connected to stuff like [hormones]. Which I'll let you read on your own time, but it orients us in different ways. I think there was a need for the feminist critique of leveling the playing field and talking about ways that males and females are alike. That point needed to be made but it needs—also there is just, some leveling with the fact that men and women don't do things exactly the same way and probably never had and probably never will and that's that—can we be okay with that or do we need to be just really anxious about that? There's a lot of anxiety in our society about this issue.

While this congregant acknowledges the value of a feminist critique, he ultimately asserts that men's and women's personalities are essentially different due to their different bodies, brains, hormones, and relationships to procreation, and this will never change. In other words, despite more recent research that demonstrates how gender is a social construct, literature that critiques brain organization theory and biological sex difference research, and emerging work that suggests that any perceived differences between men and women cannot conclusively be attributed to differences in the brain,[9] this congregant understands gender to be something *we are* rather than something *we do*. To take it a step further, he also connects men's and women's biological differences to what he perceives to be *naturally* different approaches to leadership despite recent studies demonstrating a lack of connection between the two. He concludes by arguing that we need to accept the reality that men and women are different, but he does not think this reality should be a source of anxiety, particularly if we learn to value men's and women's behaviors equally. Similar to previous examples, this congregant fails to see that masculinity and femininity are not only constructed as different but exist in a hierarchical relationship with each other, with masculinity as dominant.[10] In other words, it is for good reason that society, particularly women, are "anxious" about the dominant notion that men and women as essentially different because it inherently leads to men's ascendance to leadership positions.

To be sure, despite his unconsciously sexist assertion that men and women are essentially different, this congregant felt strongly about the need for ministry to be reimagined in a way that could better value women's *natural* leadership styles. He explained:

> I'll use business as an example. I think it's easy for women to get pulled into trying to act like men and use that aggression and not listening. I'm not sure that anybody benefits from that. Yes, I mostly find that and I think that it would be easy for a lot of women to feel like they have to do ministry the same way that men do. I think probably we are at a time in our society, where there's enough creative thinking going on where there might be ways for a woman in ministry to not have to do it, just do it in a new job fashion. I hope so.

Despite his binary conceptualization of gender in the previous quote, here he suggests that women *can* engage in masculine approaches to leadership, their biology does not prevent them from leading in this way; it is just not perceived favorably when women do so. Or, more specifically, he would prefer that they not do so. Unlike in the previous quote, he does not state that men and women are different, but rather argues that men and women have different behavioral expectations and they should behave within these social norms. So he does not suggest that women are unable to embody forms of masculinity, but rather questions whether or not it is beneficial to anyone for women to act aggressively or *not listen*, thus rendering masculine qualities essential to leadership as the exclusive traits of men and reinforcing white, straight, cisgender men's more swift ascendance into positions of authority.

Similarly, another congregant, who had served on a pastoral hiring committee at a church with a woman associate pastor but had never hired a woman as a senior pastor, explicitly stated that he supported the equal leadership of women. However, he thought it was unfair that women were sometimes expected to fit into the masculinized mold of pastor and *lead like men*. Moreover, he felt that women should have the *freedom* to lead like a woman and that women sometimes try to *overcompensate* by acting like men. While this congregant supports women in leadership, he understands men and women as essentially different. He believes that women should be able to naturally lead *like a woman*, defined by feminine traits such as listening to others, being caring, and being relational. In other words, he thinks that masculinity is the natural quality of men while femininity is the natural quality of women. Consequently, he views women leaders who embody qualities of masculinity as unnatural or *overcompensating*, thereby restricting and judging women's embodiment of masculinity. He fails to understand that by definition it is impossible to lead without embodying qualities of masculinity at least some of the time. Here, women are expected to retain a certain level of femininity as they engage a role that requires masculine skills and traits; this is an impossible task. Moreover, I never heard congregants critique men for engaging more feminine qualities typically associated with ideal pastors (e.g., listening, caring), thereby suggesting a double standard.

This understanding of gender as something *we are* rather than something *we do* is problematic because qualities of masculinity are conflated with those of leadership and authority and, therefore, those of pastors. While the feminine qualities these congregants understand as natural to women are expected of all pastors (see Chapter 1), men *and* women, congregants also expect pastors to assertively lead and effectively establish authority, qualities understood as masculine. Therefore, women's exclusion from masculine qualities or judgment for embodying masculine qualities ultimately reinforces men's dominance in effectively "doing" the role of pastor. These types of assumptions likely reinforce a gendered division of labor by which men maintain most senior pastor positions and women occupy subordinate, support roles or at most, pastoral positions with fewer leadership expectations than senior pastors.

Moreover, while it is unjust that femininity is often undervalued in positions of leadership or considered less important than masculine qualities, it is equally unjust for women who embody forms of masculinity as leaders to be perceived as unnatural, inauthentic, or overcompensating. Gender equality is not achieved through women's freedom "to lead like a woman"; this only ensures men's exclusive access to masculinity and, therefore, their dominance and power. Rather, gender equality is achieved through women (and men and every gender in between) having the freedom to lead in ways that are authentic to who they are as individuals and ways that are necessary to do their jobs effectively. Despite these congregants' intentions of gender equality, they remain blind to the inherent hierarchical relationship between masculinity and femininity, how the assumption of essentialism undergirds the glass ceiling, and how women *must* embody forms of masculinity in order to establish authority and lead others. Since the role of pastor is ultimately masculinized, if congregants assume essential differences between men (i.e., masculine) and women (i.e., feminine), then men will be more likely to receive pastoral positions because they will be perceived (consciously or unconsciously) as better fits for these jobs. Additionally, women have the additional burden of presenting as *exceptions to their sex* and capable of establishing their authority *despite* being a woman.

"Gender-Neutral" Hiring Criteria

In every congregation, search committee members explicitly stated there were no differences between how they reviewed the résumés of men and women applicants. Instead, they believed they were looking for the *most qualified candidate* regardless of sex. However, most committee members failed to consider how women's unequal gendered experiences *prior* to the job market (as discussed in the previous chapter) intersect to reinforce men's advantage on the job market. For instance, most search committee members stated that they usually looked for someone who was younger (twenties, thirties, or forties).

> My husband was on the search committee for Kyle. I knew a lot about it. We
> knew he was young; we knew we wanted somebody young. All our churches do
> now. They want someone young. . . . Because we got older members now and
> our kids aren't going to church. We wanted someone young. We were a dying
> church with mainly older people so we thought having a young, vibrant pastor
> and a young family would bring more people.

While explicitly ageist, congregants' preference for hiring someone younger does not seem to intentionally advantage men over women applicants. However, this preference inevitably decreases the likelihood of women receiving senior pastor positions. As seen in Chapter 2, by the time many women find it possible and are prepared to pursue senior pastor positions (for various reasons), they have aged out of the preferred age range. Congregants consider this hiring criteria gender-neutral because it does not explicitly discriminate against women, but they fail to see how the gendered barriers women face prior to the hiring process negatively influence the likelihood that women applicants will be within the preferred age range. Consequently, criteria that privilege younger pastors not only exclude older applicants but disproportionately purge many women from the hiring pool, thereby rendering outcomes of this hiring norm gendered, not neutral.

Similar to the hiring criteria at most workplaces, pastoral search committees also considered applicants' work experience as a key qualification and, therefore, directly compared the pastoral experience of men and women applicants. Co-senior pastor Laura explained why this practice was problematic for women on the job market:

> By the time we graduated seminary, he [Michael, co-senior pastor] had almost
> 10 years of experience on me. And it's not just that he had more experience than
> me on paper, but he had opportunities to practice things like preaching. And
> so [motions hand toward Michael], who do you think they're going to choose?
> I feel like I have to go get my doctorate just to catch up.

Exclusionary beliefs and policies in Baptist life presented barriers to women receiving opportunities to develop pastoral skills like preaching. While Laura was being denied opportunities for pastoral experience in high school, college, and seminary, Michael was being offered these opportunities, thus making him more competitive and marketable on the job market. Similarly, Ashley, a congregant and ordained minister, described how women's experiences differed from men's in seminary.

> I know that while I was—and a lot of my girlfriends—were just trying to figure out what we were going to do in seminary. Like—"Yes! We got to come! Now what?" A lot of my guy friends were already preaching and senior pastors [while they were in seminary]. You know, they were part-time because the churches were rural and small, but they were still getting that experience. . . . I remember many of my guy friends talking about how they couldn't preach the [more moderate-liberal] sermons they wanted to preach at their churches because they would be pushing it too far. . . . I don't know of any women seminary students who were part-time [senior] pastors or preached at one of these smaller churches on Sundays—you know, because they [these churches] were too conservative. A lot of us also worked at [Southern Baptist summer camps]. Both males and females were allowed to be counselors and teach Bible studies. I remember having a woman director. And some of my guy friends were camp pastors, but I don't remember ever seeing a woman camp pastor. So that was another place they could get experience and we couldn't.

Ashley echoed Laura's point that she and many of her women colleagues spent much of their time in seminary developing their newly discovered pastoral identities. Meanwhile, her male classmates were serving as ministers and pastors or, sometimes, even part-time senior pastors in congregations. As a result, Ashley had significantly less experience than her male colleagues when she graduated from seminary.

Ashley also explained that her moderate-liberal male classmates received pastoral and preaching experience at more conservative congregations. In order to maintain job security, they often withheld beliefs that conflicted with conservative congregational theology and preached sermons that didn't "push it too far." By doing this, men were able to pass as more conservative despite being more theologically moderate or progressive. Women were less likely to pass as conservative because many conservative congregations and denominational entities consider the very notion of women pastors as theologically liberal. Through their complicity, men were benefitting from these churches' exclusionary gender beliefs while women were barred from experience. *Complicit masculinities* refers to when men do not necessarily support or fit into dominant exclusionary systems of gender and sexism but fail to challenge them or reinforce them by participating in them, thereby receiving some of the exclusionary benefits of these systems and reinforcing their dominance.[11] Men's ability to gain pastoral experience in *all* Baptist churches and affiliated entities, including conservative ones, results in their advantage on the job market. Consequently, when hiring committees directly compare the pastoral experience of men and women applicants, they reinforce hiring practices that produce sexist outcomes, not gender-neutral ones.

Some churches not only valued the amount of applicants' pastoral experience but also specifically required or preferred *senior pastor* experience. I observed the process that led to the hiring of one congregation's senior pastor, Olivia, the church's first woman pastor. The search committee narrowed down the search to five applicants, two women and three men. Although Olivia was one of the top five candidates, the search committee initially selected one of the male candidates, Sam, to be invited to preach, interview with the congregation, and be voted upon. Olivia and Sam were both in their thirties, the age range often sought after by search committees. In fact, the male candidate was actually younger than Olivia but already had several years of senior pastor experience while Olivia only had associate pastor experience. When the hiring committee announced that Sam would be coming to preach for the job, some women in the congregation disagreed with the decision because they thought it was time to hire a woman pastor, particularly one that was qualified enough to be one of the top five candidates for the job. After some controversy, these women's challenge to this male candidate partially led to the hiring of Olivia as the church's first woman senior pastor. One search committee member explained why Sam was first chosen instead of Olivia:

> [We had] a wide age variation, a very wide age range. Well, not that wide, maybe thirties . . . I don't think that the fact that she was a woman made any difference negative or positive. I think it was entirely neutral thing. Maybe to some, it did. But to me, she was a unifier and she knew how to respond to the congregation. She was a solid, well-trained pastor that fit in our mold. She was highly recommended by people we respected. . . . But to me personally, there is no stronger proponent of women in ministry than I am, but I really was looking at the person. To be honest with you, Olivia did not have senior pastor experience. That was what some of us were looking for. . . . But I'm telling you that what Sam did have, which certain people did think was important, he had senior pastor experience for a long time. I don't know for how many years, maybe five.

This female congregant explicitly supported women's equal leadership and described the hiring process as entirely neutral. However, because the committee preferred candidates who had previous senior pastor experience *and* were in a certain age range, the odds of women being perceived as qualified for the position significantly decreased. Although she thought Olivia was a strong candidate, ultimately Olivia had never been a senior pastor and, therefore, was not initially offered the job. Despite the committee's intentions of gender neutrality in the hiring process, preferring candidates to have senior pastor experience fails to consider the additional hurdles women face prior to the job market, reinforces a gendered division of labor, and, therefore, proves to not be neutral. The committee member went on to explain why many of the women candidates were not considered seriously for the job.

> I'm trying to think how many women versus men applied for the job. I would say, and this may not be accurate, 25% were women who were actually in the top contenders because there were women who didn't have pastoral experience at all, or women who had like taken strange twists and turns who may have been in our mold [what they were looking for]. One woman, she had taken on social justice issues and she was actually working with the homeless. That's an example. She was an ordained minister, but her full-time job was in working with say the homeless or working with prostitutes.

Here, we see that in addition to senior pastor experience, this pastoral search committee member prefers more direct professional paths to senior pastor positions. However, what she describes as "strange twists and turns" are actually the effects of the theological, interpersonal, cultural, and organizational barriers that many women professionals and, in this case, Baptist women pastors encounter prior to the job market. These types of gendered hurdles often result in a lack of opportunities and influence women's pursuit of alternative professional paths or forms of ministry. It seems the hiring committee interpreted these professional "twists and turns" as shortcomings rather than signs of their resilience and adaptability. Despite her support of women pastors, this congregant proved unaware of the influence of gendered barriers on women pastors' career paths and, therefore, understood these hiring criteria as gender neutral rather than as benefitting men.

Similarly, a woman search committee member at a church that had never hired a woman as senior pastor required similar criteria in the selection process of their last senior pastor and communicated that she later regretted this approach to the hiring process:

> I don't know how many women we had apply, but there was definitely one woman who—I would say that there was one woman, who for me anyway, would have been in maybe the top 15 that we were looking at. . . . I remember this particular woman and I've always, to tell you the truth, regretted that I did not push more for us to [consider her further]—I wish she'd been one of our top 10, and I wish we had listened to her preach, and I wish we had talked to her as a group and we didn't. We only talked to men, and I have regretted that, that I didn't do that, one of my regrets. . . . She had not been a [senior] pastor, I think

she had been an associate pastor, we eliminated anyone who had not been a
senior pastor, so really it was less a gender thing. But looking back on it, how are
you going to have women who have been a senior pastor if you don't let them be
a senior pastor?

Here, this congregant expected men *and* women candidates to have senior
pastor experience and, therefore, considered this criterion to be gender neutral
rather than masculinized. Like the previous example, this finding suggests that
this committee member was also not fully aware of the barriers women face prior
to the job market and how this hiring expectation actually *is* a "gender thing"
because it resulted in gendered outcomes despite the good intentions of the committee. She clearly regretted not considering one woman candidate more seriously; this revealed her emerging realization that congregations need to be more
intentional about hiring women in order to disrupt normative gender structure
and break the cycle of women not receiving senior pastor positions.

While it seemed that a few congregants valued or began to value being intentional about hiring women as senior pastors, some congregants were explicitly
opposed to this approach because they did not perceive it to be gender neutral.
For example, one congregant explained, "No, we did not set out to hire a woman.
We looked at men and women equally. We didn't want to be 'affirmative action-
y.' " Another congregant responded to the notion of intentionally hiring women
by stating, "No. I'd probably leave if we did something like that. It just seems unfair to not hire the best candidate and just hire a woman because she's a woman."
These congregants intend to create fair and equitable hiring practices, but they
fail to see how men's and women's paths to being considered for a pastoral position are already unequal.

The purpose of affirmative action policy is actually to produce outcomes that
equalize a unequal playing field and create a workforce that is an accurate reflection of the demographics of the qualified workers in the related job market;
essentially it is to break the cycle of inequality. Different from most of the hiring
committees' approach to equality, the affirmative action approach takes into account the gendered structural barriers women face over the course of their lives
and achieves equality by factoring these barriers into the hiring process and considering other less traditional, yet relevant, hiring criteria as well. Conversely,
some congregants considered an affirmative action approach in conflict with the
search committee's efforts to create an equitable hiring process because, from
their perspectives, it fails to consider the résumés of men and women equally.

In one congregation that had never hired a woman in any full-time pastoral
position, an "affirmative action-y" approach was attempted during a pastoral
hiring process but was ultimately unsuccessful. Brett, the senior pastor, served
on a pastoral search committee that was hiring candidates for two full-time

pastoral positions. These positions were not lead pastor positions, but this church maintained a flat leadership structure at the time, so they were full-time positions with theoretically as much authority, autonomy, and leadership as senior pastor positions. According to Brett, the top six candidates consisted of two women and four men. The search committee then narrowed down the pool to four candidates, three men and one woman. One of the positions was given to one of the male candidates pretty early in the deliberation process. For the second pastoral position, all three of the other candidates were seriously considered for the position. The committee debated over the two male candidates as essentially the same candidate because they offered *similar qualities*; both male candidates had been part of the congregation as members previously. The deliberation pertaining to the candidates was essentially about whether or not to hire the woman candidate or one of the two male candidates. Brett explained how this conversation occurred:

> When we met to discuss, I said, "Everybody, well I really think, it would be beneficial with two positions that we hire one male and one female. Because we have a lot of women in the congregation and it would great to have somebody that could minister to them." And [other committee members] were like, "I don't think that at all." And [one committee member] said, "That's offensive. That's offensive to me as a woman that you would say that."
>
> Interviewer: Did she you go on? Did you ask why that was offensive to her?
>
> Nope, she didn't. I go "Okay." I started to back off there and was like well we'll just see where the discussion goes; if she [woman candidate] can get there on her own merit, then I win anyways. I did want Meredith [woman candidate] because she was really talented, really talented and because she was female.

Here, we see Brett take more of an affirmative action approach to hiring a woman pastor than his fellow committee member. Since the church had an all-male pastoral staff, he valued the presence of a woman pastoral leader as a role model for girls and women in the congregation. One of the female committee members took offense to the idea of hiring Meredith *just* because she was a woman. In other words, she objected to the potential of a *token hire*, which is when workplaces hire a small number of people from underrepresented groups to give the appearance of diversity and equality, but the hire is typically perfunctory and holds only symbolic significance.[12] It did not appear that Meredith was a token hire though. Meredith was essentially a top-three candidate and clearly qualified for the job. Also, there were only three full-time pastors on staff, so hiring Meredith wouldn't have represented only a symbolic image of equality; she would have effectively made up one-third of the full-time pastoral staff. Brett's effort to hire a woman pastor in this instance should not be understood synonymously with the concept of a token hire but instead as an effort to disrupt the normative Baptist division of labor and provide the congregation with a woman pastoral role model.

Once the opposing committee member expressed that she was offended, Brett stopped advocating for Meredith. Another search committee member who was present for this conversation further explained that once she voiced her opposition, the conversation ceased because many perceived her as having the expert opinion on what was offensive in terms of gender because she was herself a woman. This assumption suggests that the committee generally understood women as a homogenous group with the same perspectives and failed to recognize how men *and* women often reinforce dominant gender structure. Additionally, although the hiring process was designed as a democratic one, Brett explained that search committee members viewed this particular committee member as holding a lot of unofficial authority and influence within the church, which also contributed to no one challenging her about the idea of hiring a woman. In the end, two men were hired for the two pastoral positions forming an all-male pastoral staff.

The majority of the committee members remained unaware of the effects of gender structure and how the lack of women pastors as role models reinforces images of men in leadership and contributes to girls' self-perceived capabilities of occupying positions of leadership. Women's representation in pastoral positions would have been particularly important at this church because it is located in a college town that also has a seminary. Hiring a woman would have provided a rare woman role model to college students considering the vocational ministry or any leadership roles. Not only would hiring Meredith have provided a qualified pastor to all congregants, men and women, it would have also provided a unique mentor to women seminary students and congregants as they maneuvered through gender barriers characteristic of Baptist life as well as sexist barriers persistent in society overall.

Despite search committees' good intentions of gender neutrality in pastoral hiring processes, most hiring criteria failed to recognize that many of these *preferences* advantage men. When hiring committees consider the résumés of men and women candidates in *completely the same ways*, this only reinforces a gendered division of labor skewed toward men in positions of authority. In order for Cooperative Baptist Fellowship (CBF) congregations and other workplaces to pursue their goals of gender equality most effectively, they must undo established gendered hiring processes and reimagine new hiring criteria. In the case of CBF congregations, in addition to attributes related to education, experience, and preaching, search committees could consider qualities that many women cultivate as they push against barriers on their paths to actually becoming a pastor such as intelligence, resourcefulness, strength, courage, an acute sense of self, determination, deep spirituality, inclusiveness, collaboration, creativity, discernment, adaptability, commitment, and patience—most of which are attributes that congregants identified as important pastoral qualities anyway but were not as often considered in the hiring processes (see Chapter 1).

Congregations could also be more intentional about considering, interviewing, and selecting women pastors. As previously mentioned, the majority of Baptist congregants are women and the number of women graduates in CBF-affiliated seminaries is almost completely even with the number of male graduates. Despite these numbers, women still only make up 5% of solo senior pastor positions. Therefore, an affirmative action approach would actually disrupt this pattern and enhance congregations' intended outcomes of gender equity rather than undermine this stated goal.

Successfully Hiring Women Pastors

As I identified the ways congregational hiring processes implicitly advantage men, I became curious about the specific cases in which women *were* hired as senior pastors. How were they able to clear these barriers? How were they able to convince congregants of their leadership skills? Were they *perceived* as having qualities other women candidates were not perceived as having?

In addition to all women in this study being exceptional candidates, I observed that when most churches hired their first woman pastor, the prospect of a woman leading the church did indeed cause at least some conflict between congregants. In more progressive churches, this conflict usually amounted to a handful of congregants who usually left or eventually got used to having a woman pastor. In conservative-moderate churches, the relatively open-minded committee members usually faced resistance from other congregants. Consequently, search committees often employed strategies or educational efforts to gradually help other church members who were resistant. For instance, when Laura and Michael applied for a senior pastor position as co-pastors, the church reached out to Michael first, who negotiated the possibility of co-pastoring with Laura and hiring her as well. When the committee agreed to this idea, they initially faced resistance from other congregants but were intentional about implementing strategies to alleviate concerns. When I asked about the congregation's response to hiring both Laura and Michael, one hiring committee member responded:

> It was a mix. It was tough. I mean, we had just come off of bringing a different female and we had a lot of pushback then. . . . They [congregants] weren't saying a lot, but we were getting indirect word about it. Even after we brought Michael and Laura, it was a painful process. You know, with the conservative people we

had, we didn't want to bring anybody in, if we didn't have 99% agreement. So we
had to do a lot of educating. We don't make those kind of rash changes without
process. Even down to the day that we voted we had two or three people who
weren't [on board.]

The search committee knew that hiring a woman pastor would potentially cause
members to leave the church and result in broken relationships and financial insecurity. In anticipation of this outcome, the search committee members put in
extra time to educate and prepare other congregants and were ultimately successful
in passing the vote for hiring both Laura and Michael. Although even after Laura
and Michael were hired, "it was a painful process" for the congregation; the search
committee's commitment to hiring a woman and educating the congregation ultimately disrupted the normative gender structure in Baptist life and granted Laura
the opportunity to serve as a senior co-pastor.

As previously mentioned, the pastoral search committee in the church where
Olivia serves as senior pastor actually decided to hire one of the male candidates
before hiring Olivia. However, when the decision was announced to the rest of the
congregation, a group of women organized and pressured the search committee
to reconsider hiring Olivia, who would have been the first woman hired as senior
pastor in this church's 100-year history. One of these congregants explained why she
felt this was necessary:

> I felt like that this was the time in history that we had—even [when we were] a
> Southern Baptist Church we have done so much to support women and their
> various roles. We stood behind them breaking away from—not so much the old
> ideology of the Southern Baptists but the more recent one. Why would we not
> want to continue in that vein? We just had a grand opportunity and we had this
> woman in our top five—I just thought it was time.

This congregant thought it was important that her congregation disrupt the status
quo of dominant gender structure. As a professional woman herself, she had experienced and observed the unequal effects of dominant gender structure faced by
professional women, and therefore, she understood the significance of being intentional about hiring a woman, particularly one who was as qualified as Olivia.
Carolyn along with a team of women pushed for Olivia's hiring and was ultimately
successful. Olivia received a unanimous vote from the congregation, and search
committee members have since stated that "she was the right choice." The decision
to hire Olivia was a result of these women advocating and pushing toward a new,
more inclusive image of pastors in Baptist life.

In other congregations, particularly those hiring a woman senior pastor for the
first time, women who had a previous relationship with the congregation received

the role of senior pastor. For example, one congregant described how their temporary interim senior pastor, Anna (who had been searching for a senior pastor position for 25 years), was hired as their permanent senior pastor:

> Two things—[the congregation] had progressed so far by then and they knew
> her. Just what she did was just come in and love the people like they were. She
> had no ambition to be our pastor when she came in. . . . In fact, at the time it was
> agreed that the interim could not be considered for pastor. . . . But they fell in
> love with her.

Given that Anna's position was temporary, the congregation was able to bypass any
controversial conversations about hiring their first woman pastor while simultaneously experiencing Anna as a pastor. As a result, Anna was given an opportunity to
prove herself, and the congregation eventually hired her as their first woman senior
pastor.

When another church considered their first woman lead pastor, there was not
only the issue of hiring a woman for the first time but also the issue of having an
exclusively female pastoral staff. At the time they had a woman associate pastor and
although this congregation was open to hiring a woman as senior pastor, the idea of
having *too many* women on staff was an issue for some. This finding is interesting
because having an all-male pastoral staff rarely surfaced as problematic in other
congregations unless related to issues of social justice. Like in other masculinized
professions, this finding illustrates the invisibility (or congruence) of men's sex with
the masculinized role of pastor and the centrality (or incongruence) of women's
sex with the masculinized role of pastor. Despite these anxieties, this congregation
narrowed down the search to a man and woman, and they ultimately hired their
first woman senior pastor:

> Amber [pastoral candidate] grew up in [our town], so we knew her parents.
> A lot of members of the church knew Amber. That was a more natural fit; it was
> somebody they were familiar with because it was like when I was ordained back
> in the dark ages, one of the comments was, "Well, I don't believe in women in
> ministry, but it's okay that you're being ordained."

The existing relationship between Amber and the congregation assuaged their
unconscious gender biases that initially caused them anxiety and ultimately led
to hiring their first woman senior pastor. Like Anna, Amber had the opportunity
and time to demonstrate her ministerial skills and capacities for leadership prior to
being considered for the job, thus ultimately rendering issues related to her status as
a woman inconsequential in the deliberation process. Other members of this congregation further explained that when they later hired their second woman senior

pastor, there was no conflict related to her sex. In fact, their top-three candidates in this subsequent job search were all women, which suggests a positive shift in conscious or unconscious gender biases after having a woman as pastor.

For every instance that a woman was hired as senior pastor, she either had a pre-existing relationship with the congregation, had a group of congregants strongly advocate for her hiring, or was the second woman senior pastor to be hired with the one prior having had a previous relationship with the congregation. These findings suggest that, despite unconscious gender biases, conscious strategies for overcoming those biases can open the door, and once in, women as lead pastors, specifically in the cases of women *solo* senior pastors, can diminish or even overcome those biases. Secondly, these findings show that women's chances of being hired as a senior pastor are closely linked with congregants' commitment to advocating on behalf of women candidates to other congregants who may be resistant or have more explicit gender biases. For this reason, it is particularly important for congregations to be intentional and active about hiring women throughout the entire hiring process. In this way, congregations can more effectively change the current masculinized division of labor in CBF congregations and more effectively work toward their goals of equity.

Steps Toward Change

- Create a congregational committee tasked with creating guidelines for hiring processes that work toward equity.
- Provide trainings for church members in how to establish best practices around equitable hiring processes.
- Critically examine job descriptions and evaluation methods to determine if they are implicitly gendered.
- Consider the conversation an ongoing one as different iterations of implicit sexism in hiring processes emerge.
- Host unconscious gender bias trainings in your congregation.
- Hire a church social worker who is qualified to lead and facilitate the above initiatives.

Discussion Questions

- How do you feel when you are led by a woman? Consider and compare various contexts, for example, home, church, classroom, politics, workplace. To what do you attribute your feelings?

- Is it possible to work toward gender equity in leadership while simultaneously assuming essential personality differences between men and women along a rigid biological gender binary? Why or why not?
- Should a well-intentioned individual who engages in seemingly gender-neutral processes that result in sexist outcomes be considered a sexist? Why or why not?
- Consider a different context than the ones presented here, for example, your personal congregation, workplace, social organization. What types of organizational processes seem gender neutral but actually result in sexist outcomes? What types of organizational processes actually result in equitable outcomes? How are these patterns similar or different than the ones presented in this chapter? Identify a research study or scholarly article that presents gendered organizational logic in workplaces.
- How may organizational logic discriminate against other marginalized and oppressed groups? What have you experienced or observed? Identify a research study or scholarly article that presents ways organizational logic is discriminatory at the intersection of gender and race, ethnicity, class, sexuality, able-bodiedness, or gender identity.
- Is having a discriminatory *unconscious* bias necessarily a moral issue? Why or why not?

Supplemental Readings

Banaji, Mahzarin R., and Greenwald, Anthony G. 2016. *Blindspot: Hidden biases of good people*. London: Bantam.

Bertrand, Marianne, and Mullainathan, Sendhi. 2004. Are Emily and Greg more employable than Lakisha and Jamal? A field experiment on labor market discrimination. *American Economic Review*, 94(4), 991–1013.

Britton, Dana M. 1997. Gendered organizational logic: Policy and practice in men's and women's prisons. *Gender & Society*, 11(6), 796–818.

Easterly, Debra M., and Ricard, Cynthia S. 2011. Conscious efforts to end unconscious bias: Why women leave academic research. *Journal of Research Administration*, 42(1), 61–73.

Eberhardt, J. L. 2020. *Biased: Uncovering the hidden prejudice that shapes what we see, think, and do*. New York: Penguin Books.

Fobes, Catherine. 2001. Searching for a priest . . . or a man? Using gender as a cultural resource in an Episcopal campus chapel. *Journal for the Scientific Study of Religion*, 40(1), 87–98.

Girod, Sabine, Fassiotto, Magali, Grewal, Daisy, Ku, Manwai Candy, Sriram, Natarajan, Nosek, Brian A., and Valantine, Hannah. 2016. Reducing implicit gender leadership bias in academic medicine with an educational intervention. *Academic Medicine*, 91(8), 1143–1150.

Kamphoff, Cindra S., Armentrout, Suzannah M., and Driska, Andrew. 2010. The token female: Women's experiences as Division I collegiate head coaches of men's teams. *Journal of Intercollegiate Sport*, 3(2), 297–315.

Miller, Susan L., Forest, Kay. B., and Jurik, Nancy C. 2003. Diversity in blue: Lesbian and gay police officers in a masculine occupation. *Men and Masculinities*, 5(4), 355–385.

Prokos, Anastasia, and Padavic, Irene. 2002. "There oughtta be a law against bitches": Masculinity lessons in police academy training. *Gender, Work & Organization*, 9(4), 439–459.

Sayce, Susan, and Acker, Joan. 2012. *Equality, Diversity and Inclusion: An International Journal*, 31(33), 214–224.

Yoder, Janice D. 1991. Rethinking tokenism: Looking beyond numbers. *Gender & Society*, 5(2), 178–192.

4
The Body

I feel like the main thing that happens for me is I feel like I get—
I've made up a phrase, I get grand-daughtered a lot. Part of me
understands it because a lot of times my congregants are old enough
to be my grandparents but they're just sort of like, "You're such a
cute, little pastor." I get a lot of that, I mean maybe not that exact
phrasing but just sort of like even when they're complimenting my
sermon or something you feel more like, "I'm so proud of your bal-
lerina recital." . . . I think I get a lot of pushback, not pushback but
just strange reactions based on my age and based on the fact that
I tend to look younger and sound younger than I am and I'm petite.
I don't always know how to separate when it's gender and when it's
age. I notice age reactions much more than gender, but I often feel
like the whole age thing—if I were a man and I had a deep voice,
I wouldn't be getting the same sort of like hesitancy or disbelief or
lack of respect or "Oh, you're so cute."

—Sophie, senior pastor

Despite the fact that senior pastor Sophie held more authority than anyone in
the congregation, even after she preached a sermon, the pastoral activity that
presents the most authority, congregants often approached her as if she were
a cute little girl rather than their pastor. Here, we see that despite her abilities,
skills, and position of authority, Sophie's embodied femininity proved more visible than her embodied authority. Sophie acknowledged that her age played a
role in these interactions as well, but ultimately believed that if she were a man,
had a deep voice, and fit better into the male-bodied mold of pastor, these
interactions would be structured in a way that respected her position of authority instead of a way that called her authority into question. In other words,
if congregants were engaging a male pastor of a similar age, his sex would be
rendered invisible because masculinity and authority are intertwined. Therefore,
despite some congregants' good intentions of complimenting Sophie, these types
of interactions infantilize her as she engages the masculinized role of pastor and
ultimately undermine her pastoral authority and professional credibility.

Preacher Woman. Katie Lauve-Moon, Oxford University Press (2021). © Oxford University Press.
DOI: 10.1093/oso/9780197527542.003.0005

Research shows that the female body and expectations of femininity under-gird women's uncertain relationship with what Acker defines as the *ideal worker*, which is reflected in the image of the male body with no emotions, no sexuality, and no relationship with procreation and whose life revolves around his full-time job while a wife (or someone who fills a traditional wife role) takes care of his children and personal needs.[1] In other words, the ideal worker is best under-stood through the *idealized quality content* of *hegemonic masculinity* defined by the male body and qualities such as being strong, decisive, rational, assertive, authoritative, confident, and the breadwinner.[2] This means that the female body and the *idealized quality content* of *hegemonic femininity* (e.g., supportive, nur-turing, passive, weak, emotional, passive, dependent) are incongruent with the ideal worker mold.[3] In fact, Acker argues, "Women's bodies cannot be adapted to hegemonic masculinity; to function at the top of male hierarchies requires that women render irrelevant everything that makes them women."[4] The notion that women's bodies can never fully be perceived as embodying hegemonic mascu-linity proves problematic for women professionals in leadership positions be-cause they will unlikely be perceived as fitting squarely into these positions in ways equal to men, particularly white, straight, cisgender, able-bodied men.

Other studies suggest that the assumed managerial body is inherently mascu-line, and perceptions of individual competence are closely related to the sex of the body with the normative female body often being perceived as weak or incompe-tent.[5] In fact, research shows that height has a positive relationship with salaries as well as perceptions of competence, cognitive ability, charisma, and ability to command attention, embody authority, and display strong leadership.[6] For ex-ample, in his book *Blink*, Malcolm Gladwell reports that only 14.5% of American men are six feet and over in height, while 58% of Fortune 500 Company CEO's are six feet and over. Furthermore, 3.9% of adult American men are six feet and two inches or taller while 30% of CEOs are this height or taller![7] Additionally, re-search shows that US presidential outcomes are partially predicted by the height of the winning candidate.[8] Given that *intelligence, charisma,* and *strong leader-ship* were all qualities congregants in this study valued in their lead pastors, the correlation between perceptions of these qualities and height prove relevant to those applying for pastoral positions, particularly women whose average height in the United States is five feet four inches.[9]

Such notions were further corroborated in the way many congregants described how pastors were able to effectively secure the attention of congregants and establish authority. Most congregants assessed pastors' ability to lead in rela-tion to how they presented themselves while preaching. Specifically, congregants perceived pastors as credible and commanding attention when they had "good material," usually characterized by thought-provoking, well-researched, well-written, and insightful sermons. In addition to being competent in the pulpit, congregants expected pastors to present a strong delivery, which was often characterized by body stature, voice, charisma, and the ability to retain congregants' attention. Some congregants characterized effective pastors with phrases like "booming voice," "took up a room," and "towered over everyone." In fact, when asked to describe characteristics of the most effective pastors they had ever experienced, some congregants described their charisma, intellect, voices, and statures as if they were all related.

> They were thought-producing sermons. Nothing flashy or showy about them. He occasionally employed a little bit of humor, but he was just not built for humor that much. But it was that week after week after week just solid good material and a solid delivery. He was tall and had a fairly resonant voice and good content. He commanded attention.

> Now he was someone who could get your attention. He was charismatic. He was smart, funny. He had a really broad frame and you paid attention when he spoke.

As illustrated here and in Sophie's quote earlier, in addition to describing effective pastors as being tall or having a broad frame, congregants also characterized some of their best pastors as having strong voices. In fact, some congregants considered women pastors' feminine voices problematic.

> She's not afraid to be a senior staff person from what I'd perceive. I think she knew when she came in that given her age, and her appearance, and her voice that she needed to be pretty assertive. My perception is she is . . . because as anybody who knows Sophie knows that there are times in which her voice is problematic because you talk to her on the phone you might think she's 12.

Here, this congregant described Sophie's voice as childlike, thereby disassociating high-pitched voices from authority and revealing her perceived mismatch of small statures and high voices with effectively establishing pastoral authority. Similarly, another congregant judged co-pastor Laura's preaching by applying her voice as an evaluation standard.

> I think they both have good preaching, but I need to hear it. Everybody can hear Michael. Laura has problems with that because her voice is—well it's different. It's soft.

This congregant judged both Laura and Michael as being good preachers. However, Michael was perceived as slightly more effective because he did not have a soft voice. Knowing that this was a common way of evaluating preaching, senior pastor Olivia always took an extra effort to make sure her preaching voice was one that carried well in the sanctuary and commanded attention. However, she noticed that sometimes congregants did not perceive the strength of her voice and power of her delivery as positively as congregants had perceived men's strong deliveries.

> I know that there was a guy who was coming for a while. And one of the sermons on race—he didn't say it to me, he said it to Ben [associate pastor], "I really don't come to church to be yelled at." He just felt like I was yelling. Ben tried to encourage him to come and talk to me, but the guy was clear just like, "I'm out." I wonder, if a man had said with passion some of the same things that I said, would he have been bold and brave? Would he have really been speaking out for truth and justice? Was it because I was a woman that it was perceived that I was yelling at him? I do wonder—I have gotten feedback from some of our more conservative, and conservative in the sense of cautious. We really just want to come to church to hear that God loves us and everything is going to be okay. They like when I'm very soft, and gentle, and affirming. That's when I do feel like they want me to be the mama that tells them it's going to be okay. Sometimes I'm okay doing that . . . but it's not my job to always do that.

This example proves different from the previous ones where male pastors established authority through their booming voices. I actually observed Olivia deliver this sermon. It was a contextually controversial sermon about race and she was bold, resolute, passionate, and strong in her delivery, but I did not perceive her as yelling. In fact, I never witnessed her yell during a sermon in the year of Sundays that I observed her preaching. This man's dissatisfaction with Olivia's tone suggests that he expected Olivia to be soft-spoken, more passive in her delivery, and affirming in her message. He expected her to act within the bounds of hegemonic femininity while engaging a traditionally masculinized task.

Olivia thought further about how this example related to feedback she received from other congregants and described the conflicting *dual expectations* of being both a woman and a pastor. She explained that some congregants would rather she embody qualities of hegemonic femininity like being maternal, caring, soft, gentle, or being a "mama" as she engages in her pastoral tasks. However, pastors are equally expected to establish their authority, be bold, assertive, and lead. Therefore, if Olivia meets their expectations of femininity all the time, then she is unable to effectively do these more masculine aspects of her job. Congregants' expectations requiring Olivia to act or speak in feminine ways conflict with their expectations of her effectively fulfilling her role of authority as a pastor; such conflicting expectations puts Olivia in what is referred to as a *double bind*. By contrast, when congregants expect men pastors to both *act like a man* and be a pastor, this results in a singular congruent expectation because masculinity and authority are conflated.

Congregants' dual expectations of femininity and masculinity prove to be an almost impossible standard for women pastors to reach. Consequently, they are constantly negotiating their embodied femininity and masculinity in an effort to successfully walk the very fine line between *hegemonic femininity* and *pariah femininities*, which is when women embody masculine qualities in ways that cause them to face negative social and/or professional consequences.[10] They must be feminine enough to not be negatively evaluated for not being womanly enough, and they must embody masculinity just enough to establish their authority and lead effectively. Some women pastors employed tactics for addressing this gendered predicament. Sophie explained her strategies for addressing negative perceptions around her size.

> I wear high heels on Sunday and never during the week. I like dressing up a little extra for Sunday and, to be honest, I like being a little taller—again, I feel like people take me more seriously, but heels are way too uncomfortable to wear with any regularity. . . . I am very petite so I wear a robe. It helps so much to wear something that automatically tells people I am the minister, and I [less often] have to deal with all the awkward conversation with visitors who think I am someone's daughter or granddaughter or who feel shocked or embarrassed when they find out they're talking to the pastor. I feel like it provides me with this sort of credibility in people's eyes.

Given that congregants associate large stature with leadership and authority, Sophie wears high heels to be taller and a robe to be broader and provide symbolic authority. In one respect, Sophie wearing heels and a robe is a positive, effective approach because this helps her establish authority *despite* how her small stature is perceived by congregants. However, wearing a robe and high heels also reinforces images of what leaders and authority figures, specifically pastors, *should* look like in order to be taken seriously. Being tall may have been a necessity in leaders hundreds of years ago in a world where physical strength was very much related to protection and survival, but not in a twenty-first-century society. Not to mention, heels are uncomfortable for many women. Although Sophie created a way to be taller and, therefore, a way to be perceived as having more pastoral authority, she does so at the cost of her own personal comfort. And, more importantly, rather than expecting the congregation to evolve and reformulate their ideas around what leaders look like, Sophie takes on the responsibility of manipulating her body so that it fits more squarely in a masculinized mold. These strategic steps not only add more to Sophie's already full job description, but these strategies of resistance simultaneously function as forms of accommodation and conformity and, ultimately, reinforce dominant ideals of the masculine mold of pastor.

It is important to note that in the case of Sophie's congregation, church members also organized efforts to prepare other congregants for Sophie's appearance and voice so that she could be as successful as possible.

> I think the search committee did a really nice job of doing that [preparing us] in terms of introducing her and her background, buying her book and providing it to the congregation. I appreciate the way the church took the time to really work on the microphone and the sound system in terms of her sounding the best. I like the way they prepared us for that [Sophie's voice] because I remember seeing her the first time she talked and I thought, "Oh, yes. This is what they were talking about." But I don't even think about it anymore and I don't think I thought about it after the first two minutes. I think they prepared me for having that moment. From there on, I was totally focused on what she says.

This example is significant for three reasons. First, the church perceived Sophie's voice as problematic so they went to extra lengths to build Sophie's credibility to the church and provide a sound system so that she could more effectively establish her authority as a preacher. This helped Sophie bypass the perceived barrier of her feminine voice and demonstrates the congregation's commitment to her success. However, again, such efforts reinforce the dominant idea of what leaders are *supposed* to sound like. The fact that the congregation thought it was important to prepare the congregation for Sophie's voice shows that normative and expected qualities of women, such as having a high voice, are considered undesirable or ineffective attributes of pastors.

Finally, after hearing Sophie preach, the congregant no longer perceived Sophie's voice as an issue, which shows that the congregant's visual and audible perceptions of authority in relation to the normative male body size and voice began to shift after spending time with a pastor whose voice and stature did not fit into this masculinized pastoral mold. This suggests that such biases may decrease as people experience different types of leaders who are able to showcase their skills effectively and successfully even while not fitting in the normative mold. With that said, it is also important to note that Sophie was an above-average preacher. She had won the distinguished preaching award at her seminary and published a book of her sermons shortly after graduating from seminary. Additionally, some of her congregants described her as prophetic, brilliant, and the "next Barbara Brown Taylor," who was a prolific, noteworthy woman preacher and trailblazer of her time. Therefore, Sophie's exceptional preaching skills and sermon writing were undeniable and contributed to her ability to overcome the hurdle of her voice and stature in ways that many other women may not have been able to do as effectively.

Expectations of Femininity

Women additionally faced congregational expectations of maintaining a feminine and attractive appearance as they engaged their roles of pastor. Dominant notions of feminine attractiveness are generally guided by the idealized quality content of hegemonic femininity.[11] The idealized quality content of hegemonic femininity is patterned throughout society. Ideal portrayals of women's bodies are dictated through advertising and media outlets, suggesting to women that they should be physically fit yet still feminine and thin. The fashion industry and celebrities offer idealized conceptions of beauty by showing women what clothes to wear and how to wear them as well as presenting expectations of long, flowing shiny hair and made-up faces. Although the idealized quality content of femininity may vary by context, these types of images generally serve as a measuring stick by which women often judge themselves and are evaluated by men and other women in dominant culture; they define how women *should* look and act.

These messages are so pervasive and dominant in the Western world that such expectations are often taken for granted as *just the way things naturally are and should be*. So much so, that women often face social consequences when they fail to fit into this particular mold; herein lies the hegemonic significance of gender. In dominant culture, it is only through women's effective embodiment and practice of hegemonic femininity that they receive full approval and acceptance. Likewise, women's failure to do so, or embodiment of masculinity often perceived as *pariah femininities*,[12] typically results in their discrimination and judgment by others.

The dominant conception of women as objects that exist for the pleasure, benefit, and judgment of others further exacerbates their visibility as women when they engage masculinized professional roles. Therefore, women leaders and authority figures are often experienced first as the feminine other and *then* as a professional, if at all.[13] In contrast, the male body, typically perceived as an autonomous individual rather than an object of desire, is conflated with professionalism, authority, and leadership. For instance, a male pastor is typically referred to as a "pastor," and a woman pastor is almost always referred to as a "woman pastor." A woman with power is referred to as a "power woman" and the power of a girl is referred to as "girl power" because femininity is generally perceived as incongruent with power and authority. The terms "power man" and "boy power" don't generally exist because hegemonic masculinity and power are one in the same. While women leaders are usually viewed first as the feminine other and then as a leader, a white, cisgender, heteronormative man in a position of authority is viewed as a man and authority figure simultaneously because hegemonic masculinity and authority are intrinsically linked. Therefore, women typically are evaluated by their ability to simultaneously embody femininity while they engage a masculinized professional role, an additional (often impossible) expectation usually not placed on men.

The incongruence of the ideal qualities of hegemonic femininity and the ideal worker results in women professionals' constant negotiation of their physical appearance, dress, make-up, and hairstyles as they engage masculinized roles. For instance, conventionally attractive, thin people (as defined by hegemonic femininity and masculinity) maintain higher potential for occupational success than less attractive or fuller-figured people (as defined by hegemonic femininity).[14] However, when women are sexualized by their make-up and dress, it results in negative professional consequences.[15] Research also suggests that while high-status occupations perceive attractiveness as an advantage for women acquiring new job opportunities, attractiveness functions as a liability for women when collaborating with male colleagues (like, for instance, being at risk for sexual harassment) and for being taken seriously as professionals in the long term.[16]

Congregations displayed such expectations of women pastors with various expectations of feminine attractiveness. For instance, co-pastors Laura and Michael conveyed how congregants often assumed methods of control only over Laura's weight.

LAURA: And then in the serving line at Wednesday night dinner—they will fill up his plate.
MICHAEL: They really do the whole, "Oh, he's a growing boy," sort of thing.
LAURA: Like pile it on for him, right?
MICHAEL: And load up my plate. But when Laura goes through . . .
LAURA: It's "Oh, you don't want bread, do you?" You know things like that.
MICHAEL: And they know we're both on diets and exercising, but they just do it to her.

Here, congregants encourage Michael to eat more because, as illustrated in the previous section, being big and strong is associated with authority and power, qualities of masculinity. Conversely, when they serve Laura's plate, they ask questions that suggest they expect Laura to maintain a small figure, which would be more characteristic of hegemonic femininity. This expectation reinforces dominant expectations of what women *should* look like and demonstrates that women are expected to be small and feminine in their stature, which are traits not perceived in relation to leadership and authority. Moreover, not only is there differential treatment concerning the management of Michael and Laura's weight, there is an assumption that Laura's body, perceived as an object of attractiveness, is available for congregants to judge and control despite having no functional connection to her role as a pastor.

Olivia, a senior pastor, experienced similar interactions with congregants who assumed her weight and body was an open topic of discussion.

> There are two women in church who are really proud of me when I'm losing weight, and would comment on it, "Are you just not eating? That's probably what you are doing right now. Oh, I'm so proud of you." And one male church member, for the first year I was here, every time he saw me eating something unhealthy, he would say, "That's 10 more pounds."

Similar to the expectations placed on Laura, these interactions not only reinforce expectations related to how women are supposed to look; they position Olivia as the sexual object which should be attractive and pleasing to look at, as defined by hegemonic femininity. Consequently, Olivia is seen first as a woman rather than a pastor, ultimately undermining her authority. To follow up, I asked the male associate pastor at Olivia's church if he had experienced these comments from congregants. He responded that although he was dieting as well, congregants never interjected concerning his eating habits.

Expectations of hegemonic femininity related to women's bodies are so pervasive that many women come to have these expectations of their own bodies and judge other women by these standards as well. In my conversations with Olivia over the course of a year, she often referenced her weight. Sometimes she communicated that she gained weight or that she needed to lose weight. Sometimes she would refer to her outfit and say, "I probably shouldn't wear this now that I've gained weight." Like many other women who have had their bodies judged and evaluated even from a very young age, Olivia's perception of her own body fueled a deep insecurity in her as well as pressure to fit idealized images of women. One time she described an interaction with a congregant who suggested she was overweight while she was engaging her role as pastor at a Wednesday night church dinner:

> A man [a congregant] called me fat tonight. Well, he insinuated that I was unable to button my red International Women's Day jacket because I've put on weight. And it hurt. And I crumbled like a sixth-grade girl being "mean girl-ed."

Even though she embodied the role of pastor, a role that is typically revered and respected, this congregant interacted with her as a woman whose body, as the sexual object, was open to judgment. When this occurred, she began to experience old feelings of insecurity. But because this congregant made this statement about her "red International Women's Day jacket" *on* International Women's Day, something shifted in Olivia. Consequently, she became more aware of the dominant gender structure and the unequal expectations placed on women's bodies. Olivia described this shift in consciousness:

> I have been thinking about my reaction and how tender I am to that kind of comment. And then I thought of my daughter's boldness. And the ridiculous industry and injustice that surrounds gender. And the story I am telling her with my life. And I thought, "No more." This body grew babies and sustained them. This body embraces and blesses and visits and comforts every single day. This body is powerful, and I say no more to the shame that my culture throws at women. I am proud of the woman I am. And I will document my life without commentary or judgment. And I will eat real bread with real butter with real wine because I am crushing it and won't apologize for not buttoning my bottom button.

Olivia compared the sensitivity, tenderness, and hurt she feels in response to people commenting on her weight to her young daughter's boldness and was reminded that women are not born with these insecurities. Further, she realized that the "industry" of gender unjustly shames women about their bodies to the extent that they begin to believe it and judge themselves by these same standards.

Olivia's shift in consciousness is important. This realization disrupts her internalized gender norms and bolsters her impact as a role model and mentor to girls and women. However, like Sophie, Olivia's reframing of how she personally views her body and commitment to "not apologize for not buttoning her bottom button" results in her exclusively shouldering the responsibility of change. Therefore, this approach alone does not disrupt the gendered expectations of congregants and address issues of gender on the organizational level. In order for these gendered assumptions to be changed, they must be addressed on the congregational level, or normative gender structure will be reinforced and Olivia and other women pastors will continue to bear the responsibility of personal growth and adaptation. Moreover, the congregants, who function as the human resources committees for these churches, will continue to expect women pastors to adhere to the norms of femininity and evaluate women pastors with additional criteria than expected of men.

In addition to regulating women's weight, congregants often expected women pastors to present other forms of femininity as pastors and preachers. Olivia recalled one of the first times she ever preached:

> One of the very first times that I've preached in that service, a really nice man came up to me afterwards and he's like, "You did a really good job today, but it

would have been so much better if you just would've smiled." So I thought about that when Hillary (Clinton) got picked on for not smiling and how she talks about all the issues facing the first woman President of the United States. And even then, I knew that that was inappropriate. So afterwards my mentor asked, "How did it go? How did you feel? Do you want to discuss any of it?" because he really wanted to help me. But I said to him, the first thing that someone said as I came out of that chapel was, "You should smile next time." And I said, "They never would've said that to a man. It never would've happened." But he was like, "Well, maybe that's true, but look at it this way, he knows you're going to preach again [laughs]." But I know that if I had gone to his wife, she would've been nice and righteously angry about that on my behalf, and it would've confirmed my suspicion.

Women are often expected to be pleasant, smile, and generally make the people around them feel good through their appearance and body language. Here, this congregant expected Olivia to deliver her sermon effectively *and* do it while smiling. This evaluation of Olivia shows that he thought it was permissible for Olivia to preach—in fact, he affirmed her preaching skills—however, he would have preferred her remain attractive and pleasant while doing so, an additional expectation of women that most men don't encounter. Olivia went on to say that she tried to explain to her male mentor why such a comment was problematic, but he simply did not get it. Despite his good intentions, as a male pastor, he likely had never faced the same *dual expectations* when he preached. He failed to understand the wide-reaching effects of dominant gender structure, how men and women are unequally evaluated, and how such comments reinforce barriers for women pastors. And again, her mentor's suggestion that Olivia reframe this sexist comment to mean something positive puts the responsibility on her to adapt to a sexist organizational culture rather than on the congregant to change his biased gender beliefs and behaviors.

Congregants, particularly women congregants, also expected women to embody hegemonic femininity through their appearance (e.g., dress, make-up, and hair). For instance, one female congregant described associate pastor Meg's attire when she came for her interview.

With Meg, when she first came, I don't think—this is total perception but I am close to Meg. I don't think she's spends a lot time worried about what she looks like. She's got some pretty features; she's got some things I'm sure she works on. But when she came to interview for her weekend with the church, she was very plain. She wore black slacks and a white shirt. That sort of thing. Almost to the extreme of "I don't want you making an assumption on anything other than what I'm saying and doing." And I think that is still a part of her and still part of her that I think is authentic. She wants to be—that being said, she's got a style of her own. And now that she's comfortable with us, she shows it. She doesn't—I don't think she tries to dress for the congregation. And I think she is comfortable with that.

I then asked the congregant if she thought congregants were comfortable with Meg not "dressing for the congregation." She responded, "Some probably aren't. [No], some people aren't."

Here, this congregant describes Meg as someone who doesn't spend very much time thinking about what she looks like or dressing for the congregation. While she attributes this to Meg's authenticity, she also suggests that the congregation has a set of expectations or preferences related to how women *should* dress that Meg does not fit into squarely. She also pointed out that Meg has some pretty features as well as some things that she presumed she worked on, which reveals her implicit expectation of women working to be attractive.

Despite these gendered biases, this congregant was astute in acknowledging the potential of women professionals not being taken seriously when they dress too femininely. She perceived that Meg dresses plainly (here understood as the opposite of feminine) because she fears the consequences of having her appearance evaluated instead of her words and actions. Despite her effort, though, Meg's appearance was *still* judged for not being feminine enough despite the fact that Meg's clothes style holds no relation to her ability to be an effective pastor. Meg was ultimately hired, but it is important to note the additional evaluation of her attire in her interview. This evaluative standard is not typically placed on men because traditional professional dress and traditional men's attire (as defined by hegemonic masculinity) are typically one in the same.

In a separate conversation with Meg, I asked if she ever received critiques on the way she dressed. Meg explained that she received comments on her dress primarily from other women:

Older women are the worst [most often critiqued her dress]. So, for example, one Sunday morning I was coming out of the restroom. I had on a button-up shirt and some slacks and she says, "Oh wow, you really can wear whatever you want to under that robe." [laughs]

Even on a Sunday morning, the day that pastors' authority is displayed the most, a congregant still negatively evaluated Meg's attire. This congregant's comment is significant for two reasons. First, dominant understandings of women as sexual objects to be gazed upon and evaluated are so engrained in society that women's appearances have become a normative entry point for conversations with other women and a common criteria by which to judge other women. Therefore, Meg's attire was this congregant's first and only point of conversation with her that morning. Secondly, this congregant implicitly communicated to Meg that her attire, which was a button-up shirt and slacks, did not meet her expectations of femininity, thereby urging Meg to dress more femininely. As a result, Meg's status as a woman, who is expected to wear feminine clothes, superseded her status as an authority figure and leader.

Similarly, Jane, an associate pastor at a church with a woman senior pastor, indicated that she felt pressured to meet women congregants' expectations of dress and appearance as well.

> I think about what shoes I have on. I do. It's fine for me to have painted toenails, but they should not be nasty, whatever looking, that would not be okay. And that's not necessarily my standard, I just would worry about what they would think. . . If I'm meeting with women—I dress up more if I'm meeting with women than if I'm meeting with men. If I'm meeting with men, I'd hardly even worry about what I'm wearing. But if I know I'm going to a women's lunch or blah blah blah, then I know I've got to look a certain way.

Jane indicated that she paid more attention to her attire when she knew she would be interacting with other women because they had a particular set of expectations related to her appearance. In other words, women congregants determined a "certain way" that women are supposed to look and dress, including themselves, and they hold Jane to this standard. Jane clarified that these expectations aren't her personal standards, but she conforms to these expectations because she would worry about what the congregants would think, which is important given the congregational power structure in Baptist churches. This shows that despite her own less feminine preferences, Jane remains constrained by expectations of hegemonic femininity at work.

When I spoke with male pastors, I asked if they experienced similar expectations related to their attire by congregants. Most male pastors didn't recall these types of expectations. Some stated that congregants preferred that they were clean-shaven and dressed professionally. Women were also expected to dress professionally, but unlike men, they had to find ways to be professional and feminine simultaneously. This is a predicament men don't face because dressing professionally is conflated with masculinity. One male pastor said that congregants would comment on his handsome looks and attire, but he did not face such comments frequently. Another male pastor mentioned that one time he received feedback that his hair was too fluffy, but he was single and it was often assumed that he needed this advice from female congregants because he was not in a relationship with a woman. Relatedly, most of the time congregants implied that male pastors' attire was their wives' domain and responsibility, so even if they were critiqued on their attire, it would fall on the wife of the pastor. For example, one pastor wearing a green shirt was asked by a congregant to tell his wife that "green is not your color." The absence of expectations of femininity on evaluating heteronormative male pastors reinforces their advantage and frees their time and energy for pursuing other requirements of their jobs while women continue to negotiate their dual expectations of femininity and professionalism.

But Not Too Much Femininity

When women pastors *did* express their femininity through their clothes, accessories, or make-up, congregants often found it distracting from their roles as pastors; women faced an additional *double bind*. Senior pastor Olivia succinctly described how this occurs.

> But the [woman] who always wants me to wear red lipstick, said to me recently, we were in the trustees meeting the other night, and she said, "I just got so distracted looking at you and thinking how beautiful you are. And how wonderful it is to have such a beautiful pastor. And it must've been that you had red lipstick on that night."

This congregant both expected Olivia to wear red lipstick and was also distracted *because* she was wearing red lipstick. In fact, if Olivia does not wear red lipstick, this congregant expresses to her that she *should* because Olivia being a beautiful pastor is important to her. However, if Olivia *does* wear red lipstick, the congregant views Olivia first as a woman or an object to be admired rather than a leader. Although the congregant was intending to compliment Olivia, she also diminished Olivia's authority by focusing on her looks and beauty, particularly within the context of a trustees meeting. Male professionals, who are not *typically* approached as objects of beauty, were never expected to wear make-up or look beautiful. Therefore, this never became part of the criteria by which they were judged and evaluated as pastors.

Similarly, Ashley, a congregant who was also an ordained minister in Olivia's church, recalled the initial response of another woman congregant immediately after she preached a sermon.

> I preached a sermon one time. I worked really hard on it. Spent a lot of time researching and practicing my delivery. Then when I finished, the first thing a woman said to me was, "I'm sure you preached a wonderful sermon, but I couldn't listen because I was so distracted by your cute shoes."

Despite the considerable amount of time researching, preparing, and practicing her sermon, the first feedback Ashley received was not about the sermon itself, but about her stylish shoes. Since cute shoes (or femininity) fail to fit the traditional pastoral mold, the congregant was too distracted to listen to Ashley's sermon, thus rendering her sermon and role as a preacher secondary.

It is obvious this congregant meant to compliment Ashley. Because most women have been treated as sexual objects over the course of their lives and are typically expected to dress up, wear make-up, and accessorize, these types of compliments often serve as a way for women to bond and affirm each other. These types of interactions are not necessarily malicious or entirely negative. However, it is important to acknowledge that there are many other topics that women value and can talk about with each other that extend beyond these subjects. Moreover, there are many other ways to affirm women. In this case, it would have been most relevant for the congregant to compliment Ashley's sermon; this way her hard work, credibility, and authority as the preacher would not have been undermined and reduced to her shoes.

Allie, an associate pastor, had a similar experience with a congregant in relation to her hair.

> One time when I finished preaching, one woman touched my hair and told me that I had split ends. She was a hairdresser and offered to cut my hair for me. [laughs]

Allie, unlike most women pastors in the study, had long hair and did not always pin it up when she preached. Consequently, just after Allie preached a sermon, a congregant's attention went directly to one of her feminine qualities. This interaction, directly after Allie preached, not only shows that the congregant viewed Allie's status as a woman as more definitive than her status as a pastor but also communicates to Allie that having healthy hair is an expectation of being a pastor.

Women pastors often deployed strategies for walking the fine line between femininity and professionalism (masculinity) so that they could *attempt* to meet these dual expectations. For instance, associate pastor Meg and senior pastor Olivia explained:

MEG: When I preach I almost always pull my hair back and wear no earrings because I don't want distractions. [Because] I had a friend who when she preached, she had some long earrings on one time and somebody told her that they couldn't hear anything she said because they were watching her earrings and not to wear them.

OLIVIA: I really like gray nail polish, and I have one that's a dark gray purple. And I'll put it on, like Thursday through Saturday. But almost always, I'll take it off before Sunday. Because I feel it becomes too distracting. If I'm using my hands, then you can really see that.

Congregants are accustomed to a particular image of a pastor that does not include accessories or nail polish. So much so that pastors are asked to stop wearing accessories or make-up that is distracting. Such expectations reinforce the masculine image of pastor, require pastors to repress forms of feminine self-expression, and (again) shift the responsibility of change to the women pastors rather than the congregation itself. By necessity, Meg and Olivia impressively negotiate the mismatch of their feminine expressions with the masculinized role of pastor, but this strategy also reinforces what congregants think a pastor *should* look like and fails to create new, more inclusive images of pastors.

Some women congregants additionally thought it inappropriate for women to expose certain parts of their bodies. For instance, when I asked one congregant if she had any particular expectations of how Olivia dressed, she immediately said, "No, I don't think so." Then she thought further and said, "Well, I don't want her to come to church with a low-cut shirt and tight skirt or something. I expect her to be professional." She implicitly assumes that parts of the female body are incompatible with professionalism. For this reason, they should be covered and definitely not accentuated. So we find that Olivia has the dual expectations of displaying femininity but not too much femininity, thus narrowing the tight rope even more and again resulting in a *double bind*.

Similarly, one congregant at Meg's church recalled an instance when there was a church pool party and Meg wore a two-piece swimsuit.

This just came to mind. We had a spring fling with college students, with kids and little toddlers playing in the swimming pool. Meg had on a two-piece bathing suit and she was out there playing with them. I have three grandkids and daughters, son-in-laws and all, that age doesn't know what—that's not even important to them—so probably half of the people [younger half] didn't notice, then half went, "Hmmm." But I've never heard anybody say anything about Kyle [male senior pastor] in situations like those. That's the difference.

As associate pastor, part of Meg's job was to attend church events. In this case, the event was a swim party for college students. Meg wore a normative women's swimsuit, but the exposure of her body made some of the older congregants feel uncomfortable. Here, Meg's body was sexualized and understood as unprofessional to some congregants who preferred she wear something that covered more of her body. However, the congregant observed that no one ever said anything about Kyle wearing his normative male swimsuit and rightly pointed out the different (and unequal) expectations of Kyle and Meg as they both wore otherwise socially normative swimsuits at a church pool party. While men's bodies and normative swimwear typically remain congruent with professionalism, we see that although Meg is expected to embody forms of femininity through her dress and appearance, *too much* femininity is not encouraged and is negatively judged by some.

I also observed co-pastors Michael and Laura in a similar situation. At a church pool party for Vacation Bible School, Michael and Laura were swimming with other congregants, including children and adults. When I walked into the pool party, Laura came to greet me and said, "I know, right? What does a woman pastor wear to a church pool party?" as she pointed to the dress she was wearing over her swimsuit even when she swam in the pool. Then she said, "What else am I going to do?" When I later asked Laura why she felt like she needed to wear the dress, she said, "They don't make swimsuits that cover the parts I'm supposed to cover! Like what women's swimsuit is still professional?" Most women's swimsuits are designed in a way that accentuates and sexualizes the female body. Therefore, Laura created a strategy for reconciling the conflict between her female body and professionalism. In this way, her female body becomes less visible and her professionalism hopefully remains intact. However, similar to other women pastors' forms of resistance, this strategy may be necessary and effective in the short term, but it also reinforces the perceived mismatch between the female body and professionalism and accommodates congregants' unfair dual expectations.

Women pastors' bodies and expressions of femininity were also treated as the objects of male congregants' attraction. In contrast to women congregants who expected women pastors to not sexualize their bodies, men in the congregation did just the opposite. For instance, Olivia recalled being objectified by male congregants even right after she preached.

> One time before I wore a robe, I preached and afterwards one man told me, "You really have some va-va-voom curves." And another person—a man who is close enough to my age, said—it was very awkward and changed my relationship with him forever—said something about how hot I looked that day, and Jack [her husband] must love those heels. . . . And I can remember doing a wedding once. At the rehearsal, where I'm leading and directing and pulling people together, I can hear the groomsmen talking about me and one of them goes like, "Oh, you mean kind of like a little hot-for-teacher situation?"

Despite her particularly visible role as the pastoral authority, these male congregants reduced Olivia to her body. In the second example, Olivia explained that one male congregant told her that she "looked hot that day" and said, "Jack [her husband] must love those heels." Here, this congregant sexualized Olivia's body and insinuated that her husband would experience as much pleasure as he was experiencing while seeing her in high heels. In other words, this congregant's comment defines Olivia as a sexualized object purposed for bringing him and her husband pleasure. Instead of being valued as an independent authority figure and leader, she was primarily valued for the pleasure she offers men through her appearance. In the last scenario while Olivia was in the act of doing her job, she was belittled through men's whispers and comments that objectified her body. The authority that Olivia held as pastor in these contexts was superseded by men's myopic attention to her body, an occupational hazard that Olivia has learned to work around, but shouldn't have to work around.

Other women pastors encountered similar interactions with male congregants as well. In fact, some women pastors noted that sometimes these interactions progressed from sexualized comments to physical touch. For instance, associate pastor Meg explained the difference in how male congregants approach her, in comparison to senior pastor Kyle:

> So, for example, Kyle doesn't have a lot of old men hitting on him all the time or even those who aren't hitting on him constantly talking about how he looks or how much they love him in that way or rubbing on him or whatever that—people think it is okay because you're a woman.

Meg explained that Kyle, the male senior pastor, doesn't have to maneuver through comments that reduce him to his looks nor does he have to deal with congregants touching him and hitting on him because there seems to be more respect for a man in a position of authority; here dominant gender structure is situated in a way that deems it inappropriate and socially unacceptable for women to pursue men in the same way. The combination of Meg's female body and her single status resulted in male congregants perceiving her as up for grabs whether it be by touching her body or hitting on her. These interactions fit squarely in the hegemonic relationship between masculinity and femininity, with men as the sexual pursuers and women as the objects pursued. Here, men interacting with Meg as the sexual object divorces her body from her personal desires, not to mention her role as pastor, and positions it as something to be enjoyed and had by others. Clearly, these men view Meg as a woman before they view her as a pastor, thus simultaneously disrespecting and undercutting her authority and, ultimately, her ability to effectively do her job.

Meg also experienced a couple of men in the congregation who were interested in her romantically. She described her experience with one of these men:

He was like always asking me to meet him places or for coffee. I finally had to have a conversation with him to tell him like it's not going to happen and I'm his pastor. So then I got out of that and then he just persisted and persisted and he would try to get me alone and he would—and Kyle [male senior pastor] thankfully, I let him know what was going on and he didn't believe it at first. [laughter] He was like, "Really? Maybe you're thinking a little too much, he's probably just being flirty," but then he saw it. [laughter] So he took care of it. He had coffee with him and told him that he could not talk to me anymore.

Meg explained that once she realized that this congregant was pursuing her, she made a point to tell him that she was not interested in a relationship with him and reminded him that she was his pastor. Despite her direct and assertive communication with him, he continued to push. This congregant's behavior exemplifies the hegemonic relationship between masculinity and femininity by assuming his dominance and expecting Meg's compliance despite her position of authority. Meg eventually told Kyle about the situation, and the congregant stopped pursuing her once Kyle talked to him. In this case, Kyle's intervention was obviously necessary because this congregant persisted despite Meg's appeals and status as his pastor. However, the fact that Meg had to call on Kyle to handle this situation and the congregant did not stop pursuing Meg until another man stepped into stop it reinforces gender hegemony. In other words, the need for Kyle's interference is a result of the structural relationship between masculinity and femininity and ultimately undermines Meg's authority.

Robing: Resistance or Accommodation?

As mentioned throughout this chapter, women, their male counterparts, and congregants occasionally made efforts to maneuver around professional barriers related to women's bodies and appearances. In fact, in an attempt to minimize the objectification and sexualization of their bodies, all of the women senior pastors in this study wore robes and required their ministerial staff to robe as well. Only one male pastor in the entire study said that he often received comments about his attire and decided to wear a robe to bypass these comments. In most congregations in this study, congregants typically critiqued the idea of robing because they highly valued the democratic structure of Baptist congregations. Therefore, some congregants and male pastors initially opposed the idea of wearing robes because they thought it created a visible separation between the pastor and the congregants. For instance, when senior pastor Olivia decided that she as well as other ministerial staff would wear robes during religious services, associate pastor Ben initially resisted this idea.

I initially objected to the idea of robes. I think it creates a separation between pastors and congregants that maybe shouldn't be there, especially as Baptists. I'd rather be one with the people. But the truth is, people take you more seriously when you're wearing a uniform. I think for me, I'm young, so the robe helped congregants take me more seriously. And for Olivia, it's probably age and because she's a woman—I know people kept making comments about her clothes or how she looked. But I think the robe kind of takes gender out of it—it's sort of an equalizer.

Like Ben, most congregants who initially objected or felt uncomfortable with their pastors wearing robes eventually got used to it, and their perceptions of pastors having too much authority when they wore robes lessened or went away completely after time. However, it is important to note their initial critique because women, who decide to wear robes to establish their authority and increase their perceived credibility, run the risk of being viewed as embodying *too much* authority within the context of these Baptist congregations. It is also important to note that the choice to robe is not equal between men and women. Although Ben noted that he was taken more seriously once he began to robe because he was a young pastor, Olivia and other women pastors would equally face the obstacle of age *in addition* to the issues that come with having a female body.

Ben further stated, "I think the robe kind of takes gender out of it—it's sort of an equalizer." Based on feedback from women pastors, the robe to some extent does seem to function as an equalizer because it helps to establish their authority and decreases congregants' comments about their appearances. On the one hand, if the robe signifies authority, then it is intertwined with masculinity. That is, it further accentuates the authority men already carry through their male bodies. On the other hand, the robe helps establish the authority of women by hiding the curves and other often sexualized parts of their female bodies. That is, it minimizes their femininity as they engage the masculinized role of pastor. Therefore, since authority is conflated with masculinity, it does not take gender out of it; it only takes femininity out of it. And even then, past examples show that women's bodies were feminized even while wearing robes or just after taking their robes off. While the robes help, it only acts as an equalizer partially and temporarily.

When Olivia was offered the job as senior pastor, she made sure she was explicit about her and the rest of ministerial staff wearing a robe.

Well, I knew [I would wear a robe year around] once I was in a position that I can make the decision for myself. Because I was in a church where, they already had a tradition that for whatever reason, the pastors robed in Lent and Easter and Advent and Christmas, but not in between. In the interview process here, I said that I would, that's part of it. I don't want what I'm wearing that day to be the source—even if it's something nice. "Oh, you're so cute today, that's just such a great dress." I don't want that to be what anybody's thinking in that moment. Then, of course, now there's always somebody still finding something like, "Is she wearing red lipstick?" Whatever part of me they can see, they stalk.

For Olivia, the robe masks her feminine features so that congregants are less likely to feminize her and more likely to focus on how she effectively does her job. However, she also noted that even with the robe, congregants always find something to comment on related to her dress or appearance. Since female bodies and feminine forms of expression are not characteristic of the normative pastor mold, they prove particularly noticeable and visible. Therefore, even with the robe, congregants still judge whatever feminine parts of Olivia they can see, thereby reducing her to these parts and diminishing her pastoral authority.

The second significant point here is that Olivia was in a position of power to decide whether or not she would wear a robe. As senior pastor, Olivia had the authority to make the decision to wear the robe every Sunday and, therefore, better maneuver around the gendered barriers she encountered when she did not robe during services. However, this means that only exceptionally successful women pastors, specifically those who are senior pastors, maintain the absolute power to make this type of decision for themselves. Otherwise, their ability to wear a robe is dependent on the willingness of the typically male senior pastor.

The mismatch between embodied femininity and the position of pastor requires women pastors to constantly navigate congregants' conflicting expectations of gender through their bodies and appearance. They are required to achieve a perfect combination of masculinity and femininity in order to be respected as women and pastors. Furthermore, this perfect combination of masculinity and femininity is subject to change by setting, by people, or by moment. In some cases, this fine line appears impossible to achieve and certainly impossible to sustain. Senior pastor Sophie, who is small in stature, wore high heels to be taller and better establish her authority, but when Olivia wore heels as a pastor, she was sexualized. This shows that women pastors' strategies of resistance for bypassing the consequences of their femininity are not permanent, certain, or reliable solutions for effectively engaging the masculine role of pastor. Moreover, although a ministerial robe functions as a tool for women to cover their bodies, decrease congregants' distractions, and establish their authority, it also reinforces the notion that the female body is incompatible with the role of pastor and masculine images of pastors. Therefore, women utilizing strategies to disrupt gendered patterns that disrespect or diminish their positions as pastors may be effective temporarily, but they fail to create significant change on the organizational level. Moreover, as illustrated throughout this chapter, the responsibility remains theirs to change and adapt to the gendered expectations of the congregation rather than on the congregation to change their expectations in ways that produce more equitable outcomes for women pastors or any type of non-conforming pastors.

Although women pastors may learn how to more effectively clear these gendered hurdles, pastors and congregants must be intentional about broadening their notions around how women *should* dress, look, and sound *as well as* how the ideal pastor *should* dress, look, and sound. It is important to note that in some cases, I observed congregants' normative ideals of professionalism at least begin to loosen in relation to gender. For instance, Sophie expressed herself through dying her hair neon colors and Olivia began wearing large, dangly earrings even while robed. These acts of resistance and expressions of femininity began to restructure persistent, historical images of the masculine role of pastor in ways that broke old molds and created more space for diverse leaders. It is only through these types of efforts along with reciprocated acceptance and openness on the part of congregations that women pastors may be *fully pastor* and *fully woman*. Otherwise, gender equality may never be reached on organizational and structural levels and women pastors (and women leaders in general) will continue facing and having to maneuver around unequal gendered barriers related to their bodies and appearances.

Steps Toward Change

- As a congregation, begin approaching gender as something we do rather than something we are, particularly in relation to the body and appearance. Be intentional about broadening the scope of internalized images of *both* women and leaders, specifically pastors in the cases of congregations.
- How do you construct beauty? Where do these ideas of beauty come from?
- Create discussion groups focused on identifying implicit congregational gendered expectations related to the body and appearance. Discuss how the assumption of a rigid gender binary reinforces inequalities between men and women. If you are in a welcoming and affirming church, consider how the assumption of a rigid gender binary may result in heterosexist expectations of LGBTQ+ clergy and congregants related to appearance and attire.
- Create a committee tasked with identifying ways women pastors face dual expectations in relation to the body and appearance and design strategies of congregational change.
- Hire a social worker qualified in leading and facilitating these efforts.

Discussion Questions

- How is the *ideal worker* defined in relation to the body and attire? (See Acker, 1990)

- Define hegemonic femininity and pariah femininities. How do you see these concepts play out in your congregation? In your world? How do these gendered concepts play out in relation to race, class, and/or sexuality? (See Schippers, 2007)
- What are dual expectations in relation to the body and appearance? What is the double bind in relation to the body and appearance? What other professions or social contexts do these concepts play out in relation to gender?
- Do you perceive women dressing and acting in a feminine manner to be a moral or theological issue? Do you perceive men dressing and acting in a masculine manner to be a moral or theological issue? For instance, would it be morally or theologically permissible for a male pastor to wear fingernail polish or lipstick? Why or why not? Does your response reinforce or disrupt dominant gender structure?
- How does expecting women pastors to adhere to hegemonic femininity in how they dress, walk, talk, and so forth support or conflict with your commitment to the equal leadership of women in the church? Explain and then extend this question to women leaders in general.
- Does placing an emphasis on affirming women pastors' professional abilities mean that it is absolutely wrong or regressive to compliment their dress or looks? Why or why not?
- How may commentary around the gendered implications of robing differ in your congregation?
- Hegemonic femininity is conflated with whiteness and heteronormativity (see Schippers, 2007). How may the intersection of gender and race or gender and sexuality create additional professional hurdles of appearance and body for Black, Indigenous, Women of Color (BIWOC), LGBTQ+ women, or LGBTQ+ BIWOC within workplaces or organizations where expectations of hegemonic femininity are salient? Draw from personal experiences or observations and find an empirical study that may help you discuss this question.

Supplemental Readings

Banchefsky, Sarah, Westfall, Jacob, Park, Bernadette, and Judd, Charles M. 2016. "But you don't look like a scientist!": Women scientists with feminine appearance are deemed less likely to be scientists. *Sex Roles*, 75(3–4), 95–109.

Butler, Judith. 2011. *Gender trouble: Feminism and the subversion of identity*. New York: Routledge.

Connell, R. W. 2005. *Masculinities*. Cambridge: Polity.

Davies, Karen. 2003. The body and doing gender: The relations between doctors and nurses in hospital work. *Sociology of Health & Illness*, 25(7), 720–742.

De Casanova, Erynn Masi. 2004. "No ugly women": Concepts of race and beauty among adolescent women in Ecuador. *Gender & Society*, 18(3), 287–308.

Dellinger, Kirsten, and Williams, Christine L. 1997. Makeup at work: Negotiating appearance rules in the workplace. *Gender & Society*, 11(2), 151–177.

Gerding Speno, A., & Aubrey, J. S. 2018. Sexualization, youthification, and adultification: A content analysis of images of girls and women in popular magazines. *Journalism & Mass Communication Quarterly*, 95(3), 625–646.

Harris, Deborah A., and Giuffre, Patti. 2015. *Taking the heat: Women chefs and gender inequality in the professional kitchen*. New Brunswick, NJ: Rutgers University Press.

Lindqvist, Erik. 2012. Height and leadership. *Review of Economics and Statistics*, 94(4), 1191–1196.

Patton, Tracey Owens. 2006. "Hey girl, am I more than my hair?": African American women and their struggles with beauty, body image, and hair. *NWSA Journal*, 18(2): 24–51.

Ridgeway, Cecilia. L. 2009. Framed before we know it: How gender shapes social relations. *Gender & Society*, 23(2), 145–160.

Schilt, Kristen. 2006. Just one of the guys? How transmen make gender visible at work. *Gender & Society*, 20(4), 465–490.

Schippers, Mimi. 2007. Recovering the feminine other: Masculinity, femininity, and gender hegemony. *Theory and Society*, 36(1), 85–102.

Toliver, S. R. 2018. Alterity and innocence: The hunger games, Rue, and black girl adultification. *Journal of Children's Literature*, 44(2), 4–15.

Weitz, Rose. 2001. Women and their hair: Seeking power through resistance and accommodation. *Gender & Society*, 15(5), 667–686.

5
The Third Shift

How are you going to do this job without a wife?

I was at a Wednesday night church supper sitting at a table filled with congregants. It was obvious they had all been well informed about why I was there as they were buzzing with questions about my observations and sharing their own gendered experiences within the congregation. One woman turned to the senior pastor, David, and asked, "Remember when you were being interviewed and a woman on the hiring committee asked, 'How are you going to do this job without a wife?'" "Oh yeah, I forgot about that," David responded. David was a single man and, therefore, congregants were concerned whether or not he would be able to handle the full workload of a senior pastor position, given that pastors' wives have historically played an integral (unpaid) role in relation to the paid work of their pastor husbands. Upon hearing this story, I began to consider new questions: How have these expectations similarly or differently impacted single male pastors, single women pastors, married women pastors, and/or pastors' spouses? What about pastors in non-conforming relationships? Are women pastors expected to be *both* pastors and pastors' wives?

Thirty years ago, Arlie Hochschild published her groundbreaking work introducing the gendered concept of the "second shift." While the modern workforce consists of both men and women, the second shift refers to the domestic and childcare labor that happens inside the home following a paid workday outside the home, and the second shift disproportionately impacts women workers. At the time, this research demonstrated that working moms put in about 672 more hours of unpaid domestic and/or childcare labor compared to their husbands every year (about four weeks a year). Twenty-five years later at a time when the majority of the US workforce is comprised of dual-earning families,[1] studies suggest this gap has begun to close but still remains. More recent research shows that on *a weekly basis* full-time working moms in heteronormative relationships put in an average of 5–7 more hours of unpaid work at home compared to their husbands.[2] Other studies find that breadwinning women spend 30% more time with children than their male partners,[3] make the majority of decisions concerning childrearing,[4] and are still responsible for the majority of daily childcare.[5]

Many women pastors faced expectations of the second shift from congregants, their partners, and in some cases even themselves. One study revealed that

Preacher Woman. Katie Lauve-Moon, Oxford University Press (2021). © Oxford University Press.
DOI: 10.1093/oso/9780197527542.003.0006

Methodist women's most significant challenge as pastors was avoiding professional burnout and balancing tasks at home with their jobs. In fact, one Methodist
minister from the aforementioned study stated that her greatest challenge was
"being the wife of a husband who still expects so much from me as a 'home-
maker.' There's no wife for me!"[6] Senior pastor Olivia recalled that while having a
family was often considered to be advantageous for male pastors, it proved to be
an additional hurdle she faced on the job market.

> I have heard some members of the search committee [say] that one person on
> the search committee just really felt that a woman with children wouldn't say
> "Yes" to the job. Because she needs to be with her children. I don't know if it was
> said that she *couldn't* do the job or just that she *wouldn't*, therefore, we shouldn't
> ask her to. I know it came down to a man with young children, younger than
> mine, or me. That we were the final two. They offered it to him [first but it fell
> through], which leaves me pretty much as the solo candidate.

While Olivia being a woman with children was never officially named by committee members as the reason she was not initially offered the job, here it is
important to acknowledge that the search committee member seemed only concerned with the woman candidate having kids, not the male candidate, who was
married to a woman, having kids. This finding suggests that the search committee
member carried an assumption that Olivia (understood as the wife in her marriage) would primarily be responsible for taking care of her and her husband's
kids while the male candidate's wife would be primarily responsible for taking
care of she and her husband's kids. Whether this assumption was realized in the
context of this decision or not, it certainly did not help Olivia's chances in receiving the job. One former congregant and one current congregant at Olivia's
church shared similar thoughts about Olivia being a pastor, a wife, and a mom.

BEVERLY: Well, I mean she's a pastor. Has a full-time job and she is a wife and a
  mom of two young children. That's just a lot to balance.
ERIN: But she's been doing it. Somehow she makes it all work.

Beverly seemed concerned about Olivia's stamina in being a full-time pastor as
well as a *full-time* wife and mother with the assumption that Olivia was the primary caregiver to her husband and children. These types of assumptions reinforce the notion that unlike men, women are created to be more naturally good
at cleaning, cooking, and caring for others and, therefore, should do most of this
work. However, when men participate in this type of unpaid labor to any degree,
it can be considered an anomaly and over and beyond what is expected of them.
This dual expectation of women creates a situation in which only the women (if

any) who can somehow figure out a way to balance a full-time pastoral position and their *womanly* duties can be successful as pastors. Notice, in Erin's response she does not suggest that Olivia's spouse helps out at home but rather that Olivia has somehow found a way to "do it all." The assumption that married women in the paid workforce are *having* to "do it all" perhaps contributes to married female clergy being paid less than single female clergy and all male clergy because they are presumed to not be as available as their counterparts.[7]

The congregational assumptions that women should be or are better at serving, caring, supporting, cooking, cleaning, and generally being hospitable were often patterned throughout congregations. For instance, many of the congregations had some version of a "hospitality committee" comprised of church members who were nominated by church members. Of all the congregations combined, only two men served on this type of committee, thereby giving the vast majority of men a free pass from showing up to church early to prepare and serve coffee, cook and serve food at banquets and dinners while everyone else sits and eats, and clean up after events. Also, most of the children's ministries or programs were largely dependent on congregant volunteers. Collectively, there were roughly 100 congregants who volunteered to care for children in the nursery during Sunday morning church services. Despite having close to the same number of fathers and mothers in the congregation, men made up less than 10% of children's ministry volunteers, thereby granting most men the opportunity to attend the service every Sunday while most women volunteers were on a rotation and attending the service every other Sunday or every few Sundays. Traditional notions of women pastors being tied to their husbands even in professional settings surfaced in some of the printed materials of a congregation. One congregation published a book reporting the history of the congregation, including when they ordained the first woman in the congregation, hired the first woman minister, and hired the first woman senior pastor. In all of these reports, the women ministers who were noted as *firsts* were referred to by the first and last name of their husbands, for example, Mrs. [husband's first name] [husband's last name]. In other words, despite these female ministers' accomplishments, they were not acknowledged by name, thereby primarily being presented as wives connected to their husband's names and identities rather than an as professionals who were individually responsible for these accomplishments.

I followed up with Olivia, the only woman senior pastor with young kids in the study, to understand how congregants engaged her as a pastor, a wife, and a mother. She explained:

> You know what I get a lot of? They [congregants] are constantly asking me "Are you okay?" You know, "How are you holding up? You feeling okay?" You know like "Tell us if this starts to get more than you can handle." At first I was really

touched by how much everybody cared, but then I thought, "If I were a man, you wouldn't be asking me this." Even if I were a man with eight children, they wouldn't be asking me that.

Although nearly all of the pastors in the study seemed overworked, none of the male pastors with children conveyed that congregants consistently worried about whether or not they will be able to continue in their jobs as a result of their responsibilities at home. While it is likely that the congregants asking Olivia about her well-being have good intentions, the assumption that underlies these questions actually suggests that they see Olivia first as a woman, then as a pastor, and they ultimately doubt Olivia's stamina to continue doing her job effectively given her presumed responsibilities at home; this is an example of *benevolent sexism*.[8] Olivia argues that if she were a man, congregants would not hold similar concerns about his ability to be a husband, father, and pastor. Moreover, Olivia perceives that even if it were a man with eight children, congregants would not worry as much about him because congregants would assume that his wife would be doing the lion's share of the work at home. This assumption holds merit because the expectations of a *traditional* father and husband prove compatible with the expectations associated with Acker's conceptualization of an *ideal worker*, who has little to no relationship to domestic or childcare responsibilities and has a spouse, typically a wife, tending to any responsibilities that may enhance his performance at work.[9] Conversely, the *traditional* expectations of a wife and mother prove incongruent with those of an ideal worker. In fact, no male pastors who were fathers conveyed they received these types of comments from congregants—actually any fatherly involvement at all was often noted and praised.

Internalized antiquated conceptions of fatherhood and motherhood often surfaced as "mommy guilt" for many women pastors.[10] Mommy guilt can be best understood as the residual effect of an old constructed narrative about women's ultimate purpose in life—birthing and caring for children. Despite twenty-first-century research that suggests that daughters of working moms are more likely to excel in education, achieve leadership positions, and be paid more as adults and sons of working moms are more likely to spend more time with their children and help out around the house as adults, 41% of Americans say that an increase in working moms is detrimental to society while only 22% think it is positive for society.[11] Today research studies demonstrating the benefits of children having a parent (and usually a mom) at home has dominated the narrative and has failed to communicate the ways in which having a mom that works benefits children as well.[12] Consequently, many women who were told all of their lives that it is their calling to be moms and to do otherwise would be harmful to their children are likely to face a fair amount of guilt when they prioritize their own dreams, hopes, and ambitions. Conversely, men are not generally expected to carry this guilt; their expected fatherly duties (e.g., breadwinner, provider) typically prove congruent with pursuing their goals outside of the home.

Children's pastor Jessica explained that she got married shortly after graduating from college in psychology. Not long after that she and her husband were expecting their first child. Jessica communicated that before finding out she was pregnant, she had plans to go to graduate school after her husband had completed law school. She recalled it being difficult at first when she found out she was pregnant: "At the time it was hard, it was hard because I kind of felt things that I thought were my dreams slipping away." Jessica explained further that once her son was born, her perspective changed: "Then, as soon as he was born, it was like, 'Never mind, I don't need that. I have him and that's all I want and that's all I need right now.'" Jessica further conveyed that she was quite satisfied as a stay-at-home wife and mom; now as a mother of three children, Jessica felt inspired by her work as a part-time children's pastor and valued having this part of her life. Jessica first put off pursuing graduate school so her husband could enroll and graduate from law school, thereby putting his goals before her own. While Jessica was staying home, her husband, a lawyer, was able to focus primarily on his career and, therefore, eventually excelled and received higher status opportunities. Consequently, his success and salary justified their family continually putting his career first, thereby leaving Jessica to do most of the housework and childcare in addition to her part-time job. Despite the fact that she had continually put others before herself, she still experienced mommy guilt while working her part-time job.

> I'm the lone ranger at home oftentimes and I have guilt. I know all working moms deal with this guilt. But I feel like I'm letting them down, and I also feel like I'm not as energetic and creative as I want to be here [at work]. I'm not as game to take on new things here, right? Because I just feel I need to protect myself because it's worn me down over the last year and a half. I actually was up here speaking to leadership team last night about, I need help.

Like so many other women, Jessica, a children's pastor, worked in a feminized job, which are typically overworked and underpaid.[13] The combination of being the primary caregiver at home *and* the lack of support in her feminized job left her feeling like she was failing both at home and at work and, therefore, ultimately left her feeling guilty. Women pastors taking on the majority of tasks at home likely contributes to what some researchers have identified as the "motherhood penalty," which results in male professionals' ability to spend more time on work tasks than their female counterparts with potential for more favorable work evaluations.[14] Jessica never indicated one way or the other if she *would like* to be a full-time children's pastor. She only stated that it would be impossible, given her husband's work schedule. Similarly, senior pastor Olivia recalls that she initially valued staying home with her children but soon wanted to pursue the goal of becoming a senior pastor.

> I knew that I didn't want to be a stay-at-home mom indefinitely, but I wanted to be home and present when they were little. And some of that was a psychological drive and some of that is my mom and aunt and grandmother all stayed home and that's what they did. There was certainly an element of pressure to it. Yes, that was a hard time, and I started—that's an interesting thing, invisibility and visibility—so then I started to feel invisible and I didn't like it.

Olivia suggests that her wanting to stay at home was partially a psychological drive as well as the fact that the examples of mothers in her life stayed home with their children and she implicitly expected the same of herself. Despite feeling conflicted about being a working mom, she grew unsatisfied staying home full-time and began to feel *invisible*. This feeling of invisibility often accompanies undervalued feminized jobs, particularly unpaid ones. Not to mention she had previously experienced fulfillment in her various paid positions in the vocational ministry and, therefore, knew the feeling of being seen and appreciated in relation to her talents, skills, and labor. This feeling ultimately urged her to pursue a part-time ministerial position as an associate pastor.

> While I was an associate pastor, I started to realize, "Oh, I have instincts for this" [being a senior pastor]. And I started at some point in those years, of having little kids, wanting to be a senior pastor, but I kept thinking I'm going to wait until my kids are older. So if I get a senior pastor position when I'm 50, they're in college and I still have 20 years that I can do this. So it's not that I was closed to the idea [of being a senior pastor] anymore. I just felt like it was something that will come in a different season of my life that I had more time, when it was more doable. But I started realizing, these instincts are big and people who are four years older than I am are coming to me, wanting my advice, and my counsel, and my input because they really trust me. I took it more as, these are just signs that your time is coming a lot sooner.

After becoming a part-time associate pastor, Olivia continued to feel that she should prioritize being more available for her kids and then once her children went to college, she would pursue her goal of becoming a senior pastor. Once she noticed that she was particularly skilled at being a pastor, her previous notions of how she *should* go about her career as a mother of small children began to loosen and she eventually pursued a senior pastor position (although having small kids actually played against her in the interview process—see earlier). Olivia evolved to a place where she believed that caring for herself, her calling, her talents, and her professional goals could result in positive benefits for her children as well.

For some women, this sense of guilt not only applied to parenting, but to pursuing their own ambitions as well. When associate pastor Allie resolved to go to seminary, for years she had been working various part-time jobs and doing the majority of household and childcare work while her husband worked full-time as the breadwinner. Although she ultimately decided to pursue professional ministry and her husband was supportive of this decision, she still felt a sense of guilt for pursuing her goals.

> I felt like when I was in seminary, I think part of me I felt like I owed it to him [Derek, her husband] in some way to keep doing what I had been doing [household and childcare responsibilities]. First, here I was, we were spending all this money for me to do this thing. I think I felt that if everything else could stay the same, then I could [justify going].

Allie felt conflicted about how to both meet dominant expectations as a woman while pursuing her professional goals. In fact, despite having contributed to circumstances that allowed her husband to focus and pursue his career for the majority of their marriage, Allie *felt like she owed* Derek once he supported the pursuit of her professional goals. Therefore, even as family dynamics shifted with Allie commuting to seminary, she continued to tend to the vast majority of household and childcare duties. Allie further explained that the division of labor at home continued even after receiving her first full-time pastoral position.

> No, there really wasn't a shift. I remember people at church would say to me something about, "Guess Derek is fixing meals and stuff." And it's like, well if I'm not there, then, yes. If I'm in town, it was still up to me. I still made the doctor's appointments for our son. There were some small things (he did), but overall I really felt the burden of it. I think part of it—I felt like I needed to prove something. That I can keep doing this stuff and I can add this (a job) to it. If I were doing it over again, I would have been more vocal about saying, "Alright let's renegotiate this."

Allie conveys that even after she was working full-time, she continued to take care of things at home and felt she "needed to prove something." Given that the success of a woman is often understood and judged in terms of how well she performs in the roles of wife and mother, women typically feel pressure from both internal and external sources to make sure they are meeting these expectations of dominant gender structure. In addition to being a wife and mom,

Allie wanted to pursue her career. However, the dominant notions of gender are constructed in such a way that being a mom and wife are often perceived as incongruent with professional ambitions, particularly full-time work or those positions not included in the list of feminized jobs like nursing or teaching. Conversely, the dominant societal expectation placed on a husband and father to be the primary provider for the family proves congruent with pursuing his professional goals and succeeding in his job. As a result, women often spend a lot of time and energy fighting against this gendered internal conflict and navigating through external pressures to single-handedly perform successfully as both a woman and a professional. Allie concludes by noting that if she could do it all over again, she would have a conversation with her husband about renegotiating their division of labor at home so that they may both come closer to reaching a sustainable work-life balance.

In fact, the women full-time pastors who were married with kids all agreed it would be almost impossible to do their jobs without a partner at home equitably sharing the domestic and childcare responsibilities. Senior pastor Olivia expressed how necessary it was to divide the housework and childcare equally between she and her husband once she took on the full-time position of senior pastor.

> I said yes [to a full-time senior pastor position], and that became kind of a new thing for our family, that I took that on, and figuring out how do you juggle small children and all of that. . . . I have a fairly flexible schedule and I'm very present in my home life. . . . And Ryan (husband) is good with the kids. We are figuring out how to make it all work.

As Olivia pursued her professional goals, dynamics at home began to shift and the division of labor needed to be reallocated between both partners so that they each could be successful in their jobs and be present at home as well. Other pastors agreed that having not just a supportive but collaborative partner is crucial to meeting all of the expectations that come with being a pastor. Associate pastor Jane spoke about how she and her husband divided childcare responsibilities:

> About the time that I started here, he left [his previous job] and went into business with a friend of his, doing a nonprofit—they have their own nonprofit. If he had stayed at [his previous job], it would have been a lot harder because his schedule would not have been nearly as flexible. And even though this job that he's in now required travel in the first few years, a lot of travel. When he was home, he was extremely flexible and that's what we wanted. Being on at a church, there is quite a bit of flexibility compared to a corporate world, but still

I'm the one that has to keep office hours, has to be here—But it really works well and he's a great co-parent and partner. He parents as much as I do. Right now during the school year, I pick [the kids] up two days a week from school, he picks them up two days a week from school, and I'm off on Friday. So then, I get them on Friday.

Jane and her husband both made a conscious effort to create an equitable parenting partnership. The relative flexibility of both of their jobs proved key in their ability to share the second shift in a way that worked for each of them as parents and professionals. Similarly, senior pastor Anna found that having a partner who fully supports her career is also key to her success both at work and at home.

He owns his own firm. But no one's career has ever been considered lesser than the other's. He's great. That's the bottom line.

Anna's husband has his own career but supports Anna's career as much as he does his own, thereby disrupting a dominant gender structure that prioritizes men's careers. Moreover, Anna conveys that the measure of a "great man" is defined by how well he collaborates with and supports his partner in her career, rather than how well he "provides" for her through his own career; this represents a vital shift in gender structure and a loosening of gendered expectations.

It is likely no coincidence that the women who were actually able to secure full-time pastoral positions were the ones with more equitable marriages. These equal partnerships seemed to be a significant factor in the success of women pastors. With this said, it is important to remember that these marriages do not exist in a vacuum. Even if the dominant gender expectations have loosened enough for spouses or partners to negotiate housework and childcare in a balanced way, we all remain constrained by the flexibility and resources (or lack thereof) of our associated workplaces. In fact, in many of the aforementioned examples, the women pastors attributed their more equitable arrangements to the *flexibility* of theirs or their spouses' jobs. In other words, the family-friendly policies and resources that workplaces make available to working parents significantly influence the division of labor between parents at home and, ultimately, women's success in their careers.[15]

In the last 50 years, the rate of moms participating part-time or full-time in the US labor force has increased from 51% to 70%;[16] today about 60% of households are dual-earning with women comprising half of the US workforce.[17] Despite these trends, the United States continues to be the only country among 41 developed countries to *not* mandate paid family leave (including paternity and maternity leave),[18] which proves consistent with Acker's argument that dominant notions of the *ideal* worker have no relationship to domestic or childcare responsibilities.[19] In the other 40 countries, mothers receive *at least* 12 weeks of paid maternity leave at childbirth and in some countries women receive up to 9 months. Moreover, fathers receive an average of 18 weeks of paternity leave among the same sample. These types of gender structures allow women to heal from childbirth, bond with their children, and return to work with all of the necessary resources; moreover, this type of system provides opportunities for men to contribute equitably to the childrearing process from the beginning, thereby creating a more equitable gender structure at home as well.

In a 2013 UNESCO global report comparing the well-being of children, the United States ranked 26th of 29 developed countries.[20] Children's overall well-being was measured by their material well-being, health and safety, education, behaviors and risks, housing and environment, and children's own subjective perceptions of overall happiness; the United States ranked between 23rd and 27th for every category. Some have attributed these low scores to the significant increase of working moms in the last 30 years, arguing that children's overall well-being improves when mothers are at home to care for them. At least, this has been the dominant argument in relation to white moms.[21] However, Hochcschild critiques this position by pointing out that, for example, Norway holds some of the highest rates of female employment in the world *and* ranks seventh in child well-being in the world.[22] Federally mandated family-friendly workplace policies and resources are arguably the difference between Norway and the United States' circumstances related to child well-being and women's employment. While the United States has no federally mandated paid family leave, Norway offers more than a year of paid family leave, thereby providing mothers and fathers resources to care for their children and avoid burnout in their jobs.

Of a sample of 74 ministers who graduated from Baptist seminaries, findings showed that only 64% of full-time or part-time women ministers receive paid maternity leave and only 21% of male pastors receive paid paternity leave. These results suggest that the majority of these ministers' congregations are more family-friendly than those US workplaces providing only the federally mandated 12 weeks of *unpaid leave*. However, these findings *also* reveal that a little over a third of female ministers are penalized for having children. Moreover, the lack of paid paternity leave for male ministers constricts fathers' ability to be involved in the care of their children and ultimately reinforces a gender structure by which women carry a heavier load at home. This pattern particularly impacted co-pastors Michael and Laura who were married and also planned to split parenting responsibilities evenly. The church at which they worked was conflicted about giving paid maternity leave *as well as* paternity leave. One congregant stated: "Why would Michael need maternity leave? I just can't understand that." This congregant could not seem to imagine a parenting arrangement by which fathers were just as involved as mothers even when there are more ways to feed babies than breastfeeding and more to caring for children than feeding them. Laura further explained that she and Michael were hired as part-time pastors to fill one position; therefore, giving both she and Michael parental leave would be the same as giving it to one pastor. She also indicated that they had other congregants advocating on their behalf regarding this topic, but the issue had yet to be resolved by the end of the study. This finding is important because whatever decision the church makes will ultimately influence how Laura and Michael can negotiate parenting responsibilities despite their intentions to share the load equally. In other words, their ability to actually have an equitable marriage in relation to parenting is constrained by the decisions and policies of their workplace.

After several months after our initial interview, I asked senior pastor Olivia if she and her husband, Ryan, were still successfully balancing the second shift together. Since our first conversation, Ryan had started working in a new job, and I wanted to note any changes. Olivia responded:

> I am feeling right now that this job is too hard for a woman with kids to do without a tremendous amount of support [at home and at church]. We have fallen into very traditional gender roles for parenting and are clawing our way out. The church is not getting my best anymore.

Like so many other working parents who carry the lion's share of the second shift, Olivia was experiencing an increased amount of burnout. Despite Olivia and Ryan's earlier intentions of co-parenting in an equitable arrangement, Ryan's new job required a more rigid schedule and demanded more of his time, and so they fell back into a parenting arrangement that more reflects traditional gender roles. Olivia taking on the vast majority of the second shift reinforces Ryan's chances for success in his job and compromises her ability to perform at the same level she had been in her job while in a more equitable relationship at home.

The Third Shift

In Baptist culture the historical role of "pastor's wife" is widely understood as the complementary other to that of a pastor, and to varying degrees this expectation holds true in many congregations today.[23] As the presumably male heteronormative married pastor engages in preaching, teaching, leading, managing, and guiding, his wife typically supports, helps, and assists him in these endeavors. In addition to the tasks that many pastors' wives are primarily responsible for such as childcare and household responsibilities and perhaps their own jobs, they may also be expected to play the piano at church services, organize potlucks, edit sermons, pack their husband's suitcase for pastoral conferences, host events at home, and anything else that occurs behind the scenes in service to the pastor and the overall well-being of the congregation. In fact, a more conservative Southern Baptist seminary, Southwestern Baptist Theological Seminary, even offers a Seminary Studies for Student Wives certificate. Given that in Southern Baptist entities, only men are allowed to be pastors, the wives of these male students are encouraged to take classes toward this certificate, which will only officially qualify them as pastors' wives rather than vocational ministers. The courses offered include Partners In Ministry, which provides "a survey of issues related to the role of minister's wife," and Ministry in the Home, which offers a "study of the theological foundation, skills, and attitudes for a ministry of hospitality and service through the home."[24]

Although the congregations in the study were not Southern Baptist, some churches intentionally or unintentionally retained symbolic and functional remnants of this notion of a pastor's wife. Like many feminized roles, the position of pastor's wife typically has no job description or associated salaries and, therefore, is unrecognized in terms of economic status in larger society. Recall the congregant's question to a single male pastor at the beginning of the chapter: "How are you going to do this job without a wife?" This example suggests that these congregants' understanding of the relationship between a pastor and (his) spouse was largely complementary in relation to gender. In other words, congregants understand the feminized role of pastor's wife as a supporter and helper to complement the masculine role of pastor as a leader and authority figure. Similarly, one ordained minister, Samantha, who identified as a lesbian, recalled that during her interview for a pastoral position, one congregant asked if her wife knew how to play the piano. This example not only suggests an assumption of complementarity between the positions of pastor and pastor's wife but also reveals the assumption of a heteronormative relationship between two women, one of which is understood to be the masculine person in the relationship (the pastor) and one of which is understood to be the feminine person in the relationship (the pastor's wife). In one case, these types of expectations even extended to the husbands of female pastors who were occupying the role of "pastor's wife." Associate pastor Allie illustrated how congregants understand the role of her husband:

> He's very extroverted, they call him "Big Mama" here. [laughter] The preacher's wife, they just own it right up front. He teaches Sunday school, but he doesn't play the piano.
>
> I've tried to be really sensitive to that and not to let him be my fallback if I need to get something done, like "Oh, I'll just get him do it." Because he's pretty laid back, I do think there are some expectations of him. That he's going

to be present. He's got to be willing to do whatever. I try to when I can carve out space where he doesn't have to be engaged. When I can just flat out say, "I don't expect you to do this. Don't come. Please don't."

This example suggests that while the position of "pastor's wife" proves to be inherently feminine both symbolically and functionally, in some contexts it may be occupied by someone who identifies as a man rather than a woman. However, it is important to note that instead of being called a "pastor's husband," congregants referred to Allie's husband as a "preacher's wife" and "Big Mama." This finding reveals the perceived incongruence of the term *husband* with this supportive or subordinate role.

All of these examples imply that the position of pastor is inextricably linked to that of a pastor's wife and, in some cases, there is a set of unofficial and uncompensated responsibilities (typically expected of a pastor's wife) tied to the official job description of a pastor. While Allie's husband did face some expectations of a pastor's wife that she worked to minimize by setting boundaries, most husbands of female pastors were not expected by congregants to fill this role. In fact, in one case, a children's pastor received feedback in her annual job evaluation from the congregation's Human Resources Committee that she depended on her husband's support *too much* in doing her job. Congregational expectations around the role of pastor's wife ultimately presented organizational barriers to single male pastors and female pastors. In the case of the one male single pastor, David, it seemed that other women congregants, administrative assistants, or the female associate pastor on staff also stepped in to fill in the gaps left by not having a pastor's wife unofficially on staff. For example, Allie, the associate pastor to David, shared that congregants often made comments like "He doesn't have a wife to tell him these things. You can tell him. . . . You're his church wife." Conversely, women senior pastors were often asked (or felt pressure) to take on additional responsibilities often reserved for the pastors' wives such as being more involved in children's ministries or helping with the hospitality side of events. In fact, while observing pastors preach from the pulpit, I never observed a male pastor pause his sermon to correct the behaviors of his children in the pews who were usually sitting with their mom, thereby allowing his pastoral authority to remain uninterrupted while in the pulpit. However, I did observe a woman pastor stop the service to parent her kids.

Given that the position of a pastor has so often been intertwined with that of a pastor's wife, associate pastor Ben initially felt nervous that his spouse, Ashley, decided to not fill the traditional role of pastor's wife. The congregants' reactions caused him to feel pressure to encourage Ashley to be more involved. However, as time went on and the traditional structure of gender began to loosen, their reactions became less severe. Ben explained:

At first, it was difficult because most churches' expectation is that your wife will be involved in the life of the church. People didn't know what to do at first because Ashley's choice not to be involved went against the status quo. I felt pressure for her to be involved and I'm sure she felt even more pressure. After a while, people adjusted though. I would still get the stray comment of "Where's Ashley?," not "How's Ashley?" but "Where?" I think folks eventually began to separate her involvement from my position in the church. As they should. If I were a doctor, patients wouldn't be like "Why doesn't your wife come with you to work and help out for no pay." Why should it be any different in the pastoral profession?

Ben explains that at first congregants were concerned less with *how* Ashley was doing and more with *where* she was when she was not at church, thereby suggesting there were at least *some* underlying expectations of a pastor's wife in this congregation, but as time went on these gendered expectations diminished. Ashley further described some of the congregational pressures she faced in their congregation:

I work about 60 hours a week. I have my own gig, which they [congregants] absolutely support and encourage. But then, [they] want me to also be supportive. I mean what other job is a spouse expected to be involved in their partner's workplace and help out for free? The other thing I get, is when I go out of town, congregants will ask, well what is Ben [spouse and pastor] going to do without you? And then they will like offer advice about buying frozen meals.

The pressure is definitely there. Sometimes they will say things to Ben (husband, associate pastor). Like, for example, one time I went out celebrating my birthday with some of my friends on a Saturday, and I didn't go to church the next day. One of the ladies asked Ben where I was and when he said I was at home resting or maybe working, she said, "So she can go out with her friends, but she can't come to church?" You know, little things like that. And I'm not sure she represents the majority, but it's still there. You know, it's kind of like you are always under a microscope.

Even though Ashely retained a full-time job, sometimes "wifely" responsibilities were placed on her such as making sure her husband was fed when she goes out of town. In other words, Ben was not expected to be responsible for such domestic duties. While these expectations rarely surfaced in explicit ways, Ashley explained that implicit expectations of being a wife and, more specifically, being a *pastor's wife* often surfaced. Similarly, Meg, an associate pastor at a different church, explained that congregants expected senior pastor Kyle's wife to be involved in the church for both symbolic and practical reasons.

It has gotten a lot better now because she [Kyle's spouse] has recently begun to do some real work around here with the children and stepped into a Wednesday night role. But until that, and I think people are very nice to both of them (Kimberly and Kyle, the pastor) and don't say anything to either of them, but they say a lot behind their backs. I don't know how much now, but I know I still hear chatter because for one thing she stopped, a couple of years ago, she stopped sitting with him (Kyle) up front and now sits in the back (of the church during Sunday services). And I think she did that because of her daughter, and she was worried about her acting out during the service. And there was talk about that. People didn't like that.

She's helped out with Bible school during the summers, and we're very grateful for that. She'll say, "I'm not the traditional pastor's wife," and that's fine. But I think as a church member in a church where so many of the members really work hard, you can't quite say that. You don't have to lead choir and everything. You don't have to be head of everything. But . . . [you should be involved]

Meg presents an interesting point. She and other congregants convey that they are less concerned with Kimberly filling the traditional role of a pastor's wife and instead emphasize the idea that in a congregation largely run by volunteers, every member should do their part. Here, we see that perhaps the congregation's expectations of having a traditional pastor's wife have loosened over time and their expectations of Kimberly are more motivated by utilitarian reasons. However, Meg also communicates that some of the congregants took issue with the fact that Kimberly no longer sat in the front pew with her husband during church services, which has more to do with appearance than to do with Kimberly actually contributing equally to the well-being of the church. This type of critique suggests that if only on a symbolic level, there is some expectation in this congregation that a pastor's wife should support her husband as he engages in pastoral responsibilities.

Different from most of the congregations, associate pastor Jim explained that his church did not maintain traditional expectations regarding the involvement of his spouse, Alice.

There were expectations of me at the beginning. The person in my position formerly, his wife worked at the church as well as the office manager. And there were expectations that I would do something (at the church) four to five nights a week when I first started. I quickly said no to that and said my wife—I did not work with my wife. And so, therefore, I value—she works full-time—I value my time at home with her. I will give you two, maybe three nights, but that is all.

Those expectations were put on me. There were never expectations put on Alice, and that's one of the reasons she's okay with being married to a pastor.

Because she does not have the typical expectations that pastor wives have, like playing the piano or attending or hosting church functions and things like that—weren't put on her. I do think though there's an automatic assumption that she wants to care and invest in our students. These assumptions are sometimes made, but no expectations are given.

Jim described the initial congregational expectations regarding him and his spouse as linked to the precedent the previous pastor had set before him. The previous pastor's spouse had worked as the office manager at the church and, therefore, they were both involved in church activities several nights a week. He further explained that congregants primarily placed these expectations on him rather than his partner, Alice, and he was clear from the beginning about how much time he was willing to give the church every week. In setting these boundaries for himself, he also created a standard by which his spouse would not occupy the traditional role of a pastor's wife. Jim conveyed that while congregants do not place the more traditional expectations of a pastor's wife on Alice, congregants sometimes made assumptions that she would want to care and invest in the students of the congregation in the same way he was expected to do as a pastor to students.

Stella, a pastor's wife at the same church, agreed that expectations in this congregation were considerably lower than they were at other churches, but she still sometimes felt pressure to attend church events.

I never thought I'd be in this situation [a pastor's wife]. This was never something that I thought about. It was never—whenever Liam came on there was never like "Oh it's Liam and Stella" blah, blah, blah. And I was very thankful for that because I hate doing stuff like that. And this is Liam's job, this is not my job. And that's kinda how I feel about it. I'm not getting paid for this, and Liam's not getting paid *much* for this. You know what I mean? (laughing) But I do feel a perceived—I mean there are expectations for me to be at things. If Alice was not there with me—I would probably assume that people want me to [behave in a certain way]. I feel like people have paved the way—Alice has paved the way for that to not be a thing and I am very grateful for that.

Stella expressed that despite congregants having fewer expectations than other churches, she still internalized gender expectations from her previous observations of pastors' wives. She further explained that the precedent that Alice had set before her as a nontraditional pastor's wife helped mitigate any additional pressure that she may have faced. Here, we see how a disruption in traditional gender structure lessens the effects of these expectations on those who come after the disruption, thereby representing an example of *undoing gender*.[25]

Given that most women still take on the vast majority of the second shift at home, I refer to the role of pastor's wife as the "third shift"—whether it be for the pastor's wife who is expected to do uncompensated church work alongside her husband while working the second shift at home and a job in the paid workforce or the female pastor who takes on responsibilities of the pastor's wife in addition to the second shift at home. Like the second shift, the third shift acknowledges feminized work that often goes unseen, unrecognized, and uncompensated as well as the additional gendered barrier that women pastors and working wives of pastors often face.

Steps Toward Change

Since the United States fails to require workplaces to ensure that working parents, particularly expecting moms, are adequately resourced, it is even more important that congregations prioritize developing paid family leave policies not only for the parent giving birth to the child but to the support parent(s) as well. The extent to which churches provide family-friendly policies to *all* of their employees determines the extent to which parents can *actually* negotiate equitable parenting arrangements. Moreover, it is even more imperative that single parents have access to adequate resources as well. While this study suggests that congregations are generally flexible in terms of when and where pastors can work, it is important that congregations continue to think about new ways that they can create more flexible workplaces for parents. And, especially in churches that already have an in-house nursery or preschool, perhaps provide free childcare to all church employees. Finally, as married folks renegotiate how to equitably split the work of the second shift, it is important that men request paternity leave from their workplaces. Historically, the powers that be are more likely to listen when the more privileged add their voices to the chorus and call for change.

Additionally, congregants and pastors must begin to unlearn old gendered narratives that position women as called to be the primary caregivers to their children and husbands on natural or moral grounds. Such reflection requires accepting a position of openness and self-critique. Those who may need to unlearn these old narratives the most may be working moms experiencing mommy guilt. The guilt and judgment that accompany the gendered notion that working moms are harming their children ultimately create gendered barriers for women professionals and, specifically in this case, women pastors as they pursue their professional goals and ambitions. However, it becomes easier to let go of personal guilt when those around you have stopped judging you. It is vital that congregations hold each other and broader society accountable in replacing oppressive gender narratives with more equitable ones and then re-creating partnerships or marriages in ways that better reflect these new narratives, particularly in families where both partners' dreams and goals extend beyond the household.

Finally, congregations must reimagine pastoral positions in ways that only include the work of one person rather than that of the spouse of a person as well. In other words, the position of pastor's wife often functions as a gendered barrier to women pastors and working pastors' wives in these types of congregations. Congregations must work toward redistributing or eliminating the tasks of the third shift in order to more effectively achieve gender equity in congregations as well as broader society.

- Work together to redefine motherhood and fatherhood in ways that result in more equitable outcomes between men and women.
- Reimagine and redesign pastoral positions to not include expectations associated with the tasks of a pastor's wife.
- Reflect on the ways mommy guilt is a constructed narrative that does not have to be accepted. Choose not to participate in it.
- Prioritize paid family leave. Make sure clear and formal paid family leave policies exist in your congregations and workplaces and that they are available to everyone with children. Be prepared.
- Reflect on ways your marriage or partnership could be more equitable in relation to household responsibilities. Renegotiate.
- Hire a social worker qualified to facilitate aforementioned conversations and workshops and design equitable paid family leave policies and processes.

Discussion Questions

- How does the concept of the "second shift" play out in your life? Growing up, who was primarily in charge of household and childcare responsibilities? Why? As an adult, who is primarily in charge of household and childcare responsibilities in your home? Why?
- Do you recall learning any theology or interpretations of biblical scripture that position women's role as primarily related to household work and childcare? What biblical texts contradict these interpretations? What theology supports the notion that the men should be the head of the household? How do these interpretations reconcile with Jesus's overarching messages of equity and inclusion? How do these interpretations play out in your life today?

- How does the concept of the "third shift" play out in your congregation? In your life? To what other occupations may it apply?
- How can the ways in which masculinity is constructed be harmful to men as well? Do dominant expectations of masculinity provide any incentives for men to engage in household responsibilities or take on the majority of childcare?
- Most of the women in this study were white, educated, and in heteronormative relationships. It is important to not assume that gender is constructed the same way everywhere. How do you think general expectations of being a stay-at-home wife and mom change at the intersection of race, class, sexuality/sexual orientation, gender identity, able-bodiedness, or various other contexts? Identify a research study that addresses some of these questions.
- This chapter demonstrates that in order to split the second shift more equitably, people must renegotiate the workload in their relationships at home *and* have access to family-friendly workplace policies. How are these two factors intrinsically linked?
- Unlike white women, black women have always been expected to work in the United States. How do such trends relate to Sojourner Truth's "Ain't I a Woman" speech?
- What are arguments for and against a federally mandated paid family leave policy? If you were to make theological argument for and against a paid family leave policy, what would it be?
- How does the concept of dual expectations and the double bind for women professionals play out in this chapter? How are Chapters 4 and 5 related?
- What is benevolent sexism? Can you identify an example of benevolent sexism in your own context?

Supplemental Readings

Barnes, Riché Jeneen Daniel. 2008. "Black women have always worked." In *The changing landscape of work and family in the American middle class: Reports from the field* (pp. 189–209). Lanham, MD: Lexington Books.

Barnes, Riché J. Daniel. 2015. *Raising the race: Black career women redefine marriage, motherhood, and community.* New Brunswick, NJ: Rutgers University Press.

Connell, R. W., and Messerschmidt, James W. 2005. Hegemonic masculinity: Rethinking the concept. *Gender & Society, 19*(6), 829–859.

Crittenden, Ann. 2002. *The price of motherhood: Why the most important job in the world is still the least valued.* New York: Macmillan.

Dow, Dawn Marie. 2019. *Mothering while black: Boundaries and burdens of middle-class parenthood.* Berkeley: University of California Press.

Frame, Marsha W., and Shehan, Constance L. 2004. Care for the caregiver: Clues for the pastoral care of clergywomen. *Pastoral Psychology, 52*(5), 369–380.

Guy, Mary. 2017. Mom work versus dad work in local government. *Administration & Society, 49*(1), 48–64.

Maume, David J. 2008. Gender differences in providing urgent childcare among dual-earner parents. *Social Forces, 87*(1), 273–297.

Milkie, Melissa A., Sara B. Raley, and Suzanne M. Bianchi. 2009. Taking on the second shift: Time allocations and time pressures of US parents with preschoolers. *Social Forces, 88*(2), 487–517.

Murphy-Geiss, Gail E. 2011. Married to the minister: The status of the clergy spouse as part of a two-person single career. *Journal of Family Issues, 32*(7), 932–955.

Porter, Nicole B., 2006. Re-defining superwoman: An essay on overcoming the maternal wall in the legal workplace. *Duke Journal of Gender Law & Policy, 13*, 55.

Raley, Sara, Bianchi, Suzanne M., and Wang, Wendy. 2012. When do fathers care? Mothers' economic contribution and fathers' involvement in child care. *American Journal of Sociology, 117*(5), 1422–1459.

Settles, Isis H., Pratt-Hyatt, Jennifer S., and Buchanan, NiCole T. 2008. Through the lens of race: Black and White women's perceptions of womanhood. *Psychology of Women Quarterly, 32*(4), 454–468.

Taylor, Erin N., and Wallace, Lora E. 2012. For shame: Feminism, breastfeeding advocacy, and maternal guilt. *Hypatia, 27*(1), 76–98.

Truth, Sojourner. 1851. Ain't I a woman. *Anti-Slavery Bugle, 6*, 160.

6

Women's Work

Women's work, characterized by sex composition and/or feminized skills and qualities, presents a long-standing relationship with devaluation and subordination.[1] Today, many professions largely understood as feminine such as nursing, teaching, librarianships, and any other jobs related to children or domestic work have undergone shifts from masculinity to femininity and, therefore, concurrently a downward shift in power, status, and value. For example, the originally male-dominated occupation of clerical work, which was initially comprised of white-collar, capitalistic, autonomous positions and characterized by masculinized tasks, served as a rung in the professional ladder to more prestigious administrative roles within workplaces. Once women began entering these positions, the jobs themselves transformed into subordinate, working-class, terminal secretarial positions with few opportunities for advancement and, therefore, an overall devaluation in perceived social status and monetary worth. In other words, the shift from male bodies to female bodies in these positions resulted in a less direct relationship with power despite the fact that women were engaging in many of the same tasks and responsibilities as the men who previously held these jobs; the feminization of this profession primarily resulted in a change in power, wages, status, and opportunity rather than function.[2]

Patterns of feminization and devaluation often carry a direct relationship with actualized and perceived deskilling of jobs. For example, veterinary practice had historically been described as a physical, scientific, masculine profession only suitable for men. As women began entering the field, they were often described as good at their jobs for feminized reasons unrelated to science or medical practice, such as being an animal lover, being patient, or good with grieving pet owners, despite engaging in the same scientific and physical skills as their male counterparts, which are often perceived to hold more value and status.[3] It is through the concurrent processes of feminization and deskilling that the devaluation of feminized occupations and women's work in masculinized fields and positions occurs. Since feminized skills are not valued equally to masculinized ones, some feminized occupations like teaching, nursing, and social work, a female-initiated occupation, have gone to great lengths to *professionalize* or masculinize the profession by recruiting men, focusing on measurable outcomes, and requiring licenses or certifications.[4]

Preacher Woman. Katie Lauve-Moon, Oxford University Press (2021). © Oxford University Press.
DOI: 10.1093/oso/9780197527542.003.0007

Heather, an office manager at a church with an exclusively male full-time pastoral staff, explained that the devaluation of her position was associated with the historical conceptions of the roles of secretaries.

> I also make sure—no one is allowed to call me "secretary." Nobody. Because I'm like, "No, I'm not the secretary, I'm the office manager." Other people may not think it's important, but to me it is so important. I will not work here if my job title is "secretary". . . I actually have a hard time being—there is no way I could be the secretary here. The office manager would do the same job. I understand it's nothing but name, but there are a lot of days where that's hard. . . . I have a hard time explaining it, but in my mind, secretary brings up the 1950s woman who didn't have any education, didn't have any other skills other than typing, and didn't have anything to bring to the table while the men did all of the work. When I think of secretary, it's like, "I'm there to serve your needs while you guys do the important stuff." That's the picture I draw up, and you know what? The vast majority of churches have female administrative assistants and office managers.

Heather points to the importance of language and its associated meanings. She associates the role of secretary with one that requires few meaningful skills. Therefore, she *distances* herself from this historically feminized role as well as the devaluation of this role by declaring a more masculinized title for this position, the office manager.[5] While she perceives the role of a secretary as characterized by subordination and support tasks, she understands the title of office manager to communicate more clearly the professional (masculine) skills that many secretaries (now commonly referred to as administrative assistants) possess such as management skills. By distancing herself from the title of secretary (and, therefore, femininity), Heather simultaneously reinforces the devaluation of secretaries and elevates her position to one hopefully perceived as requiring more skills and carrying more status, thereby situating the position of office manager as *less* feminized and *more* masculinized than the position of secretary.

To determine how the roles of church secretary[6] and office manager/administrator were conceived within Cooperative Baptist Fellowship (CBF) congregations, congregants were asked to provide two to three qualities associated with each job. Congregant responses illustrated slightly different understandings of each of these titles. The highest reported quality for church secretaries was related to *friendliness* (e.g., pleasant, warm, personable, welcoming, friendly face, positive), which proves consistent with how feminized jobs are rarely associated with what professional workplaces consider *technical skills*, and therefore, are devalued. The second highest category was connected to being *organized* (e.g., detail-oriented), which suggests some level of skill

although none that are connected to a particular area of study. The third hig_
category was related to being *knowledgeable*. However, 8 of the 11 respor..._
within the *knowledgeable* category explicitly referred to knowledge of the church
building, congregants, and/or church staff rather than a particular academic or
professional knowledge. See Table 6.1 for further details.

These data also suggest that congregants mostly associated qualities of femininity with the role of secretary, with *caring, supportive* (e.g., helpful, helpmate), and *happy* representing many of remaining responses. Congregants did
place some value on what was commonly referred to as "secretarial skills," which
were characterized by a good speaking tone, time management skills, typing,
and phone and computer skills. The *Other* category represented about 17% of
responses. Most of these responses were associated with femininity, including
qualities such as *respect for pastor's time and congregants, cooperative, a person
who can take directions and follow them, female, pastor's wife, calm, listener, patient, unselfish,* and *works behind the scenes*. Other descriptors in this category
included *self-starter, does not get sidetracked, professional, good communicator/
liaison, hard worker,* and *gets things done*. With the exception of responses related to *integrity*, there were no descriptors related to qualities typically associated with leadership. And, to Heather's point, no responses pointed toward the
role of church secretary being associated with *intelligence*.

Table 6.1 Qualities Associated with Church Secretaries

Category	Count	%
Friendly	37	27.0
Organized	23	16.8
Knowledgeable	11	8.0
Caring	9	6.5
Integrity	9	6.5
Supportive	8	5.9
"Secretarial skills"	8	5.9
Thorough	3	2.2
Happy	3	2.2
Flexible	3	2.2
Other*	23	16.8
Total	**137**	**100**

*Categories that included only 1–2 responses.

Congregants' notions of the role of office manager or administrator, which is functionally similar in many ways to that of the church secretary, brought forth a noteworthy difference in congregational perceptions with a greater emphasis on technical skills and lesser emphasis on femininity. The highest reported category was linked to being *organized* and *efficient* (e.g., clear and concise, multitasker, prompt, detail-oriented), which demonstrates some level of skill. The second highest reported category referred to being *trustworthy* (e.g., discrete, loyal, honest). Similar to the role of church secretary, congregants identified being *friendly* as an ideal quality associated with office managers as well. However, this trait only represented about 10% of responses in relation to office managers. The fourth highest category, *business-minded*, was distinct from that of a church secretary and directly related to a particular skill set, including other descriptors such as *financial acumen* and *familiarity with accounting principles*. Other valued qualities included being a *hard worker* (e.g., tireless), *diligent* (e.g., conscientious), and *dependable* (e.g., responsible, good liaison). The category related to being *thoughtful* is an important one because it included descriptors such as *analytical*, *decisive*, and *problem-solver*, which are masculinized qualities often associated with leadership and other more valued positions. The position of office manager was associated with fewer feminized qualities with *friendly* and *patient* comprising only about 12% of total responses. The *Other* category represented a large portion of responses. Of these, feminized responses included *a friendly face for the office*, *listener*, *servant*, *helpful*, *compassionate*, *female*, and *kind*. However, unlike the position of secretary, the *Other* category also included more valued qualities such as *intelligent*, *wise*, *confident*, and *purposeful*. See Table 6.2 for more details.

While this shift in language may alter some people's perceptions of these roles, the positions of church secretary and office manager both remain closely related to qualities generally associated with feminized jobs and, therefore, closely related to each other. Heather explained further that despite her insistence of being called an *office manager*, she still often felt devalued and disrespected in relation to her position.

One of the things that really brings it up the most is what other people assume about me, like when people call or come in and [it seems like] they're like "You're the dumb office manager" or "the office mom"—and they say, "Can I speak to an actual pastor, or somebody who can actually help me?"... Just like that I'm here and answer the phone and twiddle my thumbs and I have no actual skills kind of thing, which is why part of me wants to put a nameplate on my desk, that has my degrees listed on it ... I'm just like "You don't know anything about me." I get very frustrated at that kind of thing. I'm the only ordained person on staff. I know I'm not actually a pastor, but. . . Yes, I can talk to you

Table 6.2 Qualities Associated with Church Office Managers/
Administrators

Category	Count	%
Organized/efficient	44	28.3
Trustworthy	19	12.3
Friendly	16	10.3
Business-minded	10	6.5
Hard worker	7	4.5
Diligent	7	4.5
Knowledgeable of church and congregants	7	4.5
Dependable	7	4.5
Thoughtful	5	3.2
Patient	4	1.9
Other*	30	19.5
Total	155	100

*Categories that included only 1–2 responses.

about your problems—yes, I am the dumb secretary, but I am also the only ordained person here and the most educated person here, and I actually want to help you with your problems, so you're getting me.

Heather was frustrated because she held two graduate degrees in religion and/ or ministry and had been ordained into the ministry, yet she was treated in a way that reflected the perceived knowledge and skills of her job title rather than her *actual* knowledge and skills. In other words, despite all of her education and ministerial experience, Heather remained constrained by her devalued position.

I had the most terrible wedding coordinator to deal with, who just treated me like dirt, and then wanted to talk to a pastor. It was basically, "Can I speak to your manager?" It was like that kind of thing. I was just very frustrated with the—I don't know, the position she saw me as, like how much power I actually had in this context. I think I did tell Brett [senior pastor] that she just made me feel like a dumb secretary. He was like "I'm sorry someone made you feel dumb," but I was like no, it's not that they made me feel dumb, it's like she made me feel like a dumb secretary. He was like "Well, don't worry, you're going to go on to do bigger and better things." I will go on to do bigger and better things, but right now I want to be doing important things as well. It's like [he was saying] that I can't do anything meaningful here right now. That was how it came across, which made me really mad because I'd [like to think] it doesn't matter what I'm doing, it will be meaningful and important.

Heather felt exclusively defined by her position, one of which historically and currently seemed to not hold very much value and significance. She tried to explain to senior pastor Brett why this reductionist perspective was problematic, but he failed to fully understand. It was not that this woman hurt Heather's feelings or that Heather even consciously believed that she was actually dumb; it was that this woman reduced her to a position commonly understood as lacking skills and knowledge, thereby reinforcing the dominant patterns of devaluing feminized positions. Furthermore, Brett revealed his implicit bias related to the position of office manager by stating that Heather will eventually move on to "bigger and better things." Consequently, Heather thought Brett's response suggested that he did not perceive her role as office manager to be meaningful · or important; whether this was Brett's intention or not, it is important to be aware of the gendered history and current trends of devaluation pertaining to women's work as well as the weight these types of comments may actually hold for women in typically devalued positions and how they reinforce a larger inequitable gender structure.

Similar patterns of devaluation persist for other feminized jobs such as those related to children and youth. For instance, in the early nineteenth century, men held the vast majority of American teaching positions. After the Civil War, women in southern and eastern states outnumbered men, and many men who survived the war moved west to pursue new employment opportunities.[7] White women were then encouraged to move into the then available teaching positions with very little bargaining power to negotiate salaries due to their limited employment opportunities. In fact, white men who remained in teaching positions were regularly paid higher salaries than even the highest paid women. Such trends point to the notion that the value of men's jobs during this period was most often measured by the worth and importance of the work. Conversely, the value of women's jobs was traditionally determined by the perceived needs of the worker, a woman who depends on others (e.g., husband, father) for primary support and has no dependents. The assumption of women's domesticity and dependency seemed to warrant lower wages, and women's lower wages engendered their continued economic dependency.[8]

Traditional ideologies related to women's *roles* in society were often used to justify both women's movement into the workforce *and* the devaluation of women's work. For example, in 1853, First Wave feminist and educator Catharine Beecher contended:

> To make education universal, it must be moderate in expense, and women can afford to teach for one half, or even less the salary which men would ask, because the female teacher has only to sustain herself; she does not look forward to the duty of supporting a family, should she marry; nor has she the ambition to amass a fortune.[9]

Here, we see that Beecher devalues the worth of women's work in order to promote women's entrance into the workforce. Beecher further advocated for women to move into teaching positions by illustrating a clear connection between teaching and what she perceived as women's *natural* roles. She states:

> Most happily, the education necessary to a woman to be a teacher is exactly the one that best fits her for that domestic relation she is primarily designed to fill.[10]

Florence Nightingale took a similar stance when she wrote, "Every woman is a nurse."[11] Of course, similar essentialist arguments have been made in opposition to women's entrance into particular positions of power. For instance, on the topic of library *administrative* positions, one author wrote in a 1904 issue of *Library Journal*:

> It is quite generally conceded that in positions which do not involve the highest degree of executive or business ability but which require a certain "gracious hospitality," women as a class far surpass men.[12]

Here, the author presents a statement of *benevolent sexism* by calling attention to the perception of women's *superior* characteristics, such as humility, charity, and hospitality, which are actually inherently subordinate and devalued in the context of labor and comparatively undervalued in positions of leadership. The author writes further:

> Women are quite generally acknowledged to work under a handicap because of a more delicate physique. This shows itself in less ability to carry calmly the heavy burdens of administrative responsibility, to endure continued mental strain in technical work.

These types of arguments were commonly drawn upon to justify women's lack of opportunity in administrative roles and positions of power. Additionally, such ideologies undergirded the notion that it was unwise to invest in women in administrative roles because their presence in the workplace would only be temporary due to eventual marital, domestic, and childcare responsibilities for which they would leave their paid positions in the workforce. Moreover, some drew on these perspectives to suggest that women are *naturally* drawn to subordinate and low-paying positions:

> A woman's primary attachment is to the family role; women are therefore less intrinsically committed to work than men and less likely to maintain a high level of specialized knowledge. Because their work motives are more utilitarian and less intrinsically task-oriented than those of men, they may require more [bureaucratic] control.[13]

Such dominant discourses positioned women as intrinsically designed for subordination and serving and caring for others. Single women shouldered this responsibility either in professions related to children, caregiving, and domestic work or in jobs inherently subordinate to masculinized positions such as secretaries and assistants. Married white women often stopped working in the paid labor force after getting married or having children and fulfilled these caregiving roles at home or, in many cases, oversaw a woman of color taking care of these responsibilities at home. Whether or not they agreed with this ideology or even had an interest in children or the available feminized jobs, women's employment options were predominately regulated and controlled by the white men in positions of power. For instance, until the mid-1940s, over half of American school systems prohibited married women from occupying teaching positions. Given that women were commonly expected to be solely responsible for domestic and childcare duties, they were also understood to be intrinsically conflicted between their family and employment roles and, therefore, less committed and skilled than men in the workplace. In the context of vocational ministry, these types of assumptions are suggested in research demonstrating the devaluation of married female clergy's work, with married clergywomen making lower salaries than unmarried clergywomen as well as married and unmarried male clergy.[14] Conversely, married male workers often make *more* than single male workers, although further research would need to be conducted to determine this trend within vocational ministry specifically.[15] For a more extensive overview of the development and devaluation of women's work, refer to *Still A Man's World: Men Who Do Women's Work* by Dr. Christine Williams.

Researchers demonstrate that the overall value of women's work today remains determined and influenced by the aforementioned historical ideologies pertaining to women's roles and the perceived low value of women's work; little has changed or been done to reposition feminized work as equally valued to masculinized work today.[16] In a society culturally regulated by growing expectations of political correctness and emerging research illustrating the lack of difference between men's and women's brains,[17] there is a lower likelihood that individuals will explicitly express essentialist opinions of women's roles in the home and the labor force. As presented in previous chapters, study participants most often implicitly revealed traditional gender biases rather than explicitly. However, gendered outcomes and disparities in the American workforce present a story more closely aligned with essentialist ideologies reflected in the history of women's work. For example, to date 97.7% of preschool/kindergarten, 79.3% of elementary and middle school, 58.5% of secondary, 47.7% of postsecondary, and 85.6% of special education teachers are women, while women only occupy 67.7% of top administrative positions in the vastly female-dominant field of education, a phenomenon referred to as the glass-escalator.[18] It is important to note that as the students grow from children to adolescents to adults, the number of male teachers increase while the number of female teachers decrease. This trend is further demonstrated with women representing only 49% of postsecondary teaching positions, thereby suggesting that women's *perceived* relationship to children more strongly indicates their representation in teaching positions rather than an intrinsic professional skill set related to teaching.

Feminization of Pastoral Positions

Similar gendered trends emerge in the context of the CBF. Let's revisit the graph from Chapter 1 to examine the relationship between devaluation and feminized jobs within these congregations (see Figure 6.1).

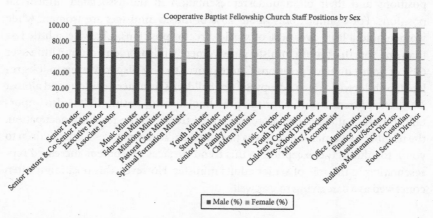

Figure 6.1 Sex composition of church positions on denominational level.

As illustrated in Chapter 1, here we see that generally as power, authority, and status decrease, the number of women increases; as power, authority, and status increase, the number of (white) men increases. The graph reveals a couple of exceptions in the bottom category of the professional hierarchy. These include the positions of building maintenance director, a job often associated with masculinity and manual labor, and custodian, which was often held by persons of color, who are typically relegated to the subordinate positions in society as demonstrated by the vast underrepresentation of people of color across most professional occupations and in pastoral and administrative positions in the CBF, specifically. By and large, in the CBF white women hold the vast majority of church jobs related to families, children, hospitality, and/or domestic work as well as nonministerial and/or support positions such as coordinators, directors, bookkeeping, secretaries/assistants, office administrators, and accompanists. Moreover, these findings show that the vast majority of ministry associates/ assistants are women.

The graph also reveals disparities between directors/coordinators and ministers. The terms "directors" and "coordinators" are often used to refer to women's positions in churches theologically opposed to women in church leadership. In these churches, women are theologically barred from holding the positions of "ministers" and "pastors," even though while serving as coordinators/directors they often engage the same tasks and responsibilities as ministers. These positions comparatively lack monetary worth, power, status, and authority and are typically subordinate to the ministerial and pastoral positions. Although CBF congregations theologically support women's leadership in the church, director and coordinator positions still persist as distinctly different from ministerial positions and are typically part-time and paid less than ministerial positions. Here, the graph reveals women's overrepresentation in director/coordinator positions and their often underrepresentation in the associated ministerial positions. For example, only about 25% of music ministers are women, while women hold a little over 60% of music director positions. Likewise, a little less than one-fourth of youth ministers are women, while women occupy a little over 60% of youth director positions. There proves to be a disparity even in jobs related to children; women occupy 80% of children's minister positions and almost 100% of children's coordinator and preschool director positions. It is also important to note that similar to aforementioned trends in the teaching occupation, the number of women decreases as the target audience matures from children to youth to adults. The exception to this trend surfaces in women's increased representation in the role of senior adults minister. However, this position is often conceived as a caregiving role as well.

The Children's and Youth Pastor

To gain a better understanding of the relationship between female-dominated positions and the processes of feminization, deskilling, and devaluation, I asked congregants to offer two to three attributes they most associate with children's pastors/ministers. The vast majority of ideal qualities associated with children's pastors were feminized and unrepresentative of any specific skills. Of 150 responses, almost 30% of associated attributes of children's pastors related to feminine qualities such as being nurturing, loving, patient, caring, and sweet. In fact, some responses directly denoted being a woman; these included "female," "mom," "matronly," "pastor's wife," and "Disney princess type." Moreover, about 10% of responses included being enthusiastic (e.g., upbeat, energetic, positive, fun), and another 10% related to being friendly (e.g., welcoming, relational, outgoing, personable). A little less than 10% of characteristics actually included any mention of particular skills or competencies (e.g., *professional, educated in relevant field, skilled at teaching the Bible to young minds, knowledgeable about children, can answer children's questions thoughtfully*). Only a couple of these responses specifically suggested that children's pastors should have some sort of training or degree related to ministry or theology, which is often a requirement of other pastoral positions. For a full list of attributes, see Table 6.3.

The attributes listed here are distinctly different from the qualities commonly associated with positions of leadership and authority in broader society. Even the role of senior pastor within CBF congregations, which includes more feminized qualities than other masculinized jobs and positions of power, carries more descriptors of leadership and power. For example, congregants reported "intelligence" as the second highest preferred quality of a senior pastor. Only one person in the entire sample indicated that intelligence was a quality associated with children's pastors. Moreover, only one person each listed "confidence" or "leadership ability" as important attributes of children's pastors. This collection of descriptors demonstrates that congregants largely associate feminized qualities with the position of children's pastor rather than qualities typically associated with leadership, thereby suggesting that the role of children's pastor holds less value than other pastoral roles despite its pastoral status and title. These findings support other research that illustrates the association of feminized qualities with professions related to childcare or children's education.[19] For example, even though teachers are consistently required to be assertive and directive in their classrooms as well as skilled and knowledgeable in their academic fields, their jobs are often described in relation to children and femininity (e.g., sweet, kind, nurturing, patient) rather than management, leadership, intelligence, expertise, skillfulness, or professionalism (masculinized qualities), thereby contributing to

Table 6.3 Qualities Associated with Children's Pastors ($N = 150$)

Categories	Count	Percent
Nurturing/caring	44	29.3
Enthusiastic	16	10.7
Personable	15	10.0
Competent	14	9.3
Likes kids	11	7.3
Able to work with parents/volunteers	11	7.3
Creative	9	6.0
Organized	7	4.7
Female	5	3.3
Integrity	4	2.7
Flexible	2	1.3
Intelligent	1	0.67
Confident	1	0.67
Leadership ability	1	0.67
Inspiring	1	0.67
Other	8	5.3

the devaluation of these positions (i.e., being overworked, underpaid, holding lower economic status).

The devaluation of the role of children's pastor may be further illustrated through examining the case study of Jessica, a children's pastor. Jessica was employed part-time, earned about half the salaries (or less) as other pastoral positions on staff without health benefits, and had by far the smallest office despite having significantly more supplies than any other pastor. Jessica was the only woman in a pastoral position at a church led by a male senior pastor. Jessica was employed for 20 hours a week despite the fact that the number of children in the church had increased exponentially over the last few years and children continued to be the church's fastest growing population. To gain a better understanding of the value of this position, I asked Jessica to give an overview of her tasks and responsibilities for a typical week and Sunday morning so that I could then compare these to the number of hours she was compensated for every week as well as the tasks and responsibilities of the full-time pastors on staff.

I need, of course, to secure volunteers for the week. But I have a rotation, so most of that is pretty set, but I might need to find some replacements from time to time in the summer—that becomes a big deal. But that becomes very time-consuming, making sure that I have everybody in place, because everybody's schedules are a little bit more up in the air. I have good numbers of volunteers, but making sure that I have the right number every week is hard. That process usually happens on Thursday. I do my writing [curricular writing for Bible lessons] on Tuesday or Wednesday for the week, I look at the lectionary passage, if I am writing for the lectionary that week. Get all of that, just sort of get a vision and direction for where the lesson is going to go. Then, I plan centers and activities for our different classes—we do hands-on when they first come in. Some of that is color sheets and worksheets, but I try really hard to incorporate like a game that they would encounter in life. . . . So I plan the game, write up the instructions for the game, and all that kind of stuff. Then, the Bible story happens. Then after that, is the crafts, which that takes a lot of time, because I have to buy all the supplies, if we don't already have them. I have to write up the instructions, pretty detailed instructions so the teachers can do that without me having to hover, because we have kids in so many different places [classrooms]. . . . The craft prep, I cut everything, I prepare as far as I can and sort as best I can. Depending on how many supplies, sometimes I sort them into individual bags so that the teachers can just hand children the bag of supplies. . . . As soon as I get the rooms settled and centers started, I make sure the teachers know what's going on. Then, I check on babies and if there's a crier, then I stay in there for a little while. If there's not, then I go to the toddler room and see if there is anybody that needs my assistance there.

Jessica was responsible for an entire event every week; she was essentially running her own church inside the larger church. In fact, Jessica refers to the children as her "congregants" for whom she assumes full responsibility. For the larger adult service, every other pastoral position was responsible for a particular part of the service. For instance, on a typical Sunday, the music pastor coordinated the band and songs to be sung and liturgy, a different full-time pastor prepared the announcements and coordinated volunteers, and a different full-time pastor prepared and delivered the sermons. It should be noted that one pastor was charged with coordinating adult Sunday school classes, but these functioned pretty autonomously once the teachers were assigned. Generally, each pastor was responsible for a particular piece of the Sunday (adult) service. Conversely, Jessica was in charge of the entire event happening behind the scenes in children's classrooms every Sunday. Of course, she utilized children's ministry volunteers, but she was responsible for making sure they were prepared. If the volunteers did not show up or did not follow instructions, this was ultimately understood as a reflection of her job performance, not theirs. In addition to the regular weekly tasks, Jessica was also responsible for coordinating and facilitating annual events and special occasions such as Mother's Day, Father's Day, baby dedications, and Promotion Sundays.

It quickly became apparent that Jessica's job required far more than being warm, nurturing, enthusiastic, and personable as indicated by the congregants' perceived qualities of children's pastors. In fact, Jessica functioned as the leader and manager of this weekly event and consistently engaged more highly valued qualities commonly associated with leadership like being a visionary, directive, assertive, confident, and intelligent than indicated by most CBF congregants in the study. Jessica was also required to effectively communicate with and meet the different needs of three distinct groups: children (infants–junior high), volunteers (almost all of which were women/moms), and parents. Additionally, like a senior pastor engaging in the congregationally valued skill of writing and delivering sermons, Jessica spent a lot of time writing Bible lessons and developing relevant activities for different age levels of children's Sunday school classes. This was an important and appreciated aspect of this particular children's ministry because this church valued a moderate theology that generally steered away from the more evangelical lessons typically found in Southern Baptist children's curriculum.

Since the lectionary occurs on a three-year cycle, Jessica noted that she could eventually stop writing every week and recycle the Bible lessons from the previous years. I asked whether she understood her position to be a 20 hour/week job without writing the Bible lesson every week.

> I feel like, yes, it's a lot for 20 hours a week, but what almost makes it too much is the fact that there are no breaks. Like a teacher even gets summer break, gets two months off in the summer. I know they're doing continuing education and things like that, they're still thinking and planning for the next year. . . . But they still have a planned time when they're not having to be at school every day and not entertain, educate kids, engage kids every day. But the way our church has it structured, there's really no opportunity. Because I'm a part-time employee, I don't get sabbatical. . . . I get vacation. I get, I think, six Sundays off, but preparing to [leave]—like this last week [when she was gone], I had to stay up late into the night to make sure the curriculum was done to a point where I can hand it off. I had to educate [a volunteer] where she needs to be when, and the processes. . . . I still have to have everything done. It's almost more work, because I'm not going to be on hand to answer any questions. . . . I have to be overprepared and to the point where I need to hand it off to someone who, a lot of times, they might volunteer in a classroom, but they don't know about what I do during the service. How I organize the classroom. The ins and outs of every

single classroom, and what to do if—It's difficult to be able to step away and even still I was on hand Sunday. I have my phone and my watch ready just in case. She [the volunteer] did have a few questions here and there that I needed to be able to respond to quickly.

Unlike the full-time pastors on staff, the part-time status of Jessica's position disqualified her from taking sabbaticals. Therefore, Jessica had no official opportunities for taking breaks and recharging. Moreover, Jessica was still ultimately responsible for organizing volunteers, developing lessons and activities, and providing the required supplies on the Sundays she was away. In fact, she felt like she needed to be on-call on the Sundays she missed. Other full-time pastors were not necessarily held to these same expectations. For instance, if the senior pastor missed a Sunday, he would typically ask one of the other pastors or an external preacher to fill in for him without having to write the sermon for the substitute preacher the week prior despite being employed full-time and receiving a full-time salary.

Later, Jessica described one instance when her daughter was in the hospital and had to unexpectedly miss a Sunday. She did not feel comfortable "dumping" her responsibilities on other staff members. In fact, in addition to asking volunteers from the congregation, Jessica asked her parents, who were not members of the church, to take on some of her responsibilities on that Sunday morning. Jessica also explained that she frequently asked her husband to fill in when she was short on volunteers or with any tasks that required an additional set of hands; however, in her last annual review meeting, the church's Human Resources committee noted that she leaned on her husband too much in the course of doing her job. It is important to note that this finding proves significantly different (opposite) to historical and even current expectations of the senior pastor's wife assisting him in his job responsibilities and ministry. One pastor also noted that he did not appreciate when she brought her kids to work despite the fact the church offered no childcare resources, her spouse worked full-time, and she would almost break even if she used her small salary to pay for childcare. For clarity, I asked Jessica why she felt like she could not turn to the rest of the church staff to fill in when she missed a Sunday, particularly if the expectations were that she not utilize the service of her spouse as much.

Like through this season I felt I needed more encouragement and that's not really always been there. I come to them [church staff] with a problem and sometimes—I'm a very creative person and up until this point in my career here, I've been the one that generates the ideas [related to the Children's Ministry]. I've been the one that has figured out how to solve the problem whatever it might be. At this point my energy is sort of drained and my creative juices not flowing as well as they typically do. I'll come to them and say, "I've got this problem. I need help" and they're like, "Well, what do you want to do about it?" I am like, "I don't want to have to decide what to do about it. I need your help. I need you to say, 'All right, we're gonna fix this problem,' " and that has not necessarily happened. I'm needing a little more help, leadership, guidance. . . . We are a team and we're all friends, there is no conflict between staff members. I think we're fairly autonomous in what we do, children's ministry especially. I just kind of do my own thing and I've always been responsible and taking care of whatever it is that is going to happen in my realm . . . it's kind of been a let-down. I consider these people my friends. I know they care for me, but I feel like I've needed more. In marriage, I would have said to [my husband], "I need more from you right now . . . this is what I need from you right now." But it's harder to do that when number one, when it's part-time. Number two, I'm not here every single day. I do feel a little bit disconnected from the goings-on.

Jessica communicates that she feels isolated in her position as children's pastor and, therefore, she has felt undersupported when she solicits the rest of staff's help in brainstorming problems related to the children's ministry. She notes that historically she has worked autonomously and proven to be resourceful and creative in meeting the needs of the children's ministry and the expectations of her position. However, given the demands of her job and at home, she has been feeling burned out and lacking the necessary resources for effectively doing her job. This finding is particularly interesting because some congregants and church staff described Jessica as well as the woman who held this position before her as *easily stressed* or *easily overwhelmed* with little to no speculation about the ways in which the actual job position may be overwhelming or stressful in comparison to the other church staff positions.

Jessica considers her fellow church staff to be friends who care for her, but she feels uncomfortable expressing her needs and advocating for herself be-cause of the part-time status of her job (and perhaps because of past notions of appearing *overwhelmed*). Here, we find that the subordinate status of her job not only creates a situation in which she is overworked and underpaid but also iso-lated and unsupported in a demanding feminized position. I later discovered that Jessica's feelings of isolation were likely reinforced by the design of the pas-toral staff retreat, which was open to all pastoral church staff. The pastoral staff retreat was held at the unoccupied apartment of a congregant and while Jessica was invited, she was the only woman and part-time pastor in attendance. She was also the only pastor to not spend the night because, as noted by one of the male pastors, it was "inappropriate for her to stay overnight," thereby suggesting that Jessica is not only constrained by the status and function of her job but by the status of her womanhood. In other words, this pastor conflated the presence of a professional with the presence of a woman's body and the notion of sexual (im)morality; he also implicitly assumed that none of the male pastors present would be attracted to each other, despite sexuality commonly being understood as a spectrum. Given Jessica's status as a woman and that she was perceived to be in the gender minority, she was excluded from the full experience of the professional retreat. In this case, the other male pastors designed a retreat that prioritized their full experiences rather than one that would include all of the pastors equally.

Jessica further described her annual review meeting with the church's Human Resources Committee. She noted that the committee asked that in addition to her current responsibilities, she also spend more time cleaning and restocking the classrooms, tasks typically expected of other feminized roles despite having nothing to do with her official job description.

> They would love for me to do more in the classrooms as far as like cleaning, organizing, just classroom management. Keeping them more up-to-date, going through toys and pulling out some puzzles or missing pieces, those sorts of things. Supply management, try to get all the supplies from the last week out and restocked back into our room, which still does not have shelves. It's just like tubs stacked on top of the tubs stacked on top of the tubs. That's like a labor-intensive process, I'm hoping that once the shelves come, [it] will be better. But at this point, it takes a while to do that. That would be like a work day for me, getting all that done.

In response to these additional expectations and lack of breaks, support, and resources, Jessica eventually proposed that the position of children's ministry *assistant* be *re-created*; it is important to note that the person who held the position of children's pastor before her had also previously requested and received an assistant.

> I need help so much and I'm not good at administrative stuff, and the idea in my [job] review, that was the main thing that they wanted me to improve on, was training volunteers and communication with volunteers, communication with family, all the administrative things. That's not my gifting. Right now at the place in life where I am and the energy level that I feel, the vigor that I feel that I have, I don't even think I want to take on growth. I'm just trying to keep my head above water. . . . The HR is wanting me to remain at 20 hours and then added a 10-hour position. I wanted to say, "But you were more than happy to ask me to do it all within 20 hours." When you were reviewing my job performance and said I needed to grow in these areas, you weren't going to add hours to my day or pay. You were perfectly happy to expect me to do it within 20

hours, yet when I say I need help, you're like "Yeah, well, we'll add a 10-hour position and you can keep doing everything else you're doing."

The Human Resources Committee ultimately approved Jessica's request for an
assistant, but the process seemed to reinforce some of the issues that contributed
to needing an assistant in the first place. In Jessica's annual review, HR added
new responsibilities such as tidying the rooms and keeping the supplies stocked
in an up-to-date, orderly fashion. They also identified that Jessica could grow to
become more effective in volunteer management and communication. Rather
than recognizing that this position was already well beyond 20 hours a week
and structured in a way that inevitably resulted in a pattern of extreme burnout
and ultimately requesting an assistant, Jessica was asked to do more and to grow
with very few resources and organizational support, with the exception of the
volunteers for whom she was responsible. This outcome put Jessica, a part-time
pastor with the least amount of power and pay, in a position of having to advocate for herself, which proves to be a precarious situation by which women are
often perceived as complaining or being ungrateful or incompetent or, in this
case, overwhelmed.

Consequently, Jessica requested that the position of children's ministry assistant be created but felt ambivalent when it was approved. With the approval of
the position, HR acknowledged there was a need for additional resources but
failed to recognize this in Jessica's annual review and, in fact, requested that she
perform more effectively and be responsible for additional tasks without changing her status to a full-time pastor. Only after she formally appealed to them
for help did the committee offer her the support she needed. However, this arrangement did not particularly alleviate her workload. The assistant mainly took
on many of the new responsibilities and helped with some of the administrative
tasks associated with coordinating volunteers for which Jessica claimed to lack
the giftedness. It is important to point out that administrative skills are typically
ones that come with experience, training, and mentoring, which, as illustrated
in Chapter 2, come far and few between for women ministers in Baptist life.
Furthermore, the status of Jessica's job did not allow for a mentoring structure or
equitable opportunities for attending conferences and trainings that were given
to the other pastors on staff. Finally, the structure of Jessica's job did not allow for
the time and energy to focus on growing in leadership and administrative skills,
as it was a revolving door with no actual breaks.

As Jessica continued to speak about this situation, she revealed that another
reason she felt strained was because her husband had recently received a new job
that caused him to work longer hours and be out of town more. In many logistical ways, she was operating as a single parent with three kids, which intensified
the lack of support she was experiencing at work. For whatever reason, Jessica

included the details of her personal situation in her appeal for an assistant and, subsequently, some of HR's conversation around granting the assistant took the form of *benevolent sexism*.[20] In other words, some of HR's rationale for creating the position was out of sensitivity to Jessica's situation at home rather than ex-clusively an acknowledgment that her position was overworked, underpaid, and undersupported regardless of what was happening at home, thereby framing the issue as one specific to Jessica rather than the church or the job itself. I later asked Jessica if she would accept the position if instead of offering an assistant, the Human Resources Committee extended her job to 30 hours a week or full-time. She indicated that it would be impossible because the demands of her husband's job would not allow for her to be full-time and she would feel guilty for being away from her kids so much. This response illustrates how gender structure re-mains at play even outside of the workplace. Given that Jessica's husband was in a masculinized job that paid significantly more money and carried more status than her feminized part-time job (and he had time to invest in his career while Jessica took care of his needs at home and in childcare), it did not make sense to prioritize her job over his for the sake of their family. Additionally, different from Jessica, her husband was likely not socialized in a way that resulted in his feeling guilty for not being responsible for most of the childcare and domestic responsi-bilities. Therefore, the prevailing gender structure proves more constraining for Jessica than her husband.

Grace, a children's pastor with aspirations of becoming a senior pastor, who was employed at a CBF church with a woman senior pastor, presented a slightly dif-ferent experience. While her role was part-time with a lower salary, she explained she had considerably more status, support, and resources as the children's pastor of her church. For instance, the church formed a Youth Education Committee, which was created to support the children's pastor in developing the vision of the children's ministry and strategies for educating the children and youth in the congregation. Some congregants conveyed that Sophie, the senior pastor, even attended these meetings in support of the children's ministry and children's pastor. This congregation also hired children's workers to be in classrooms on Sundays rather than solely depending on volunteers; this decreased Grace's time spent coordinating volunteers and improved the consistency of labor in the classrooms. However, Grace, who was in the process of hiring a new children's worker, indicated that some congregants were debating the *need* for employing children's workers against simply utilizing the service of volunteers.

Youth pastors are similar to children's pastors in that they are often part-time positions, paid less, and carry less status and power than senior pastors (although the position of youth pastor is typically a stepping-stone on the ladder to the senior pastor position while the children's pastor position is not). These trends may be related to the increased representation of women in these positions and this role's involvement with children and youth. While this position proves more feminized than senior pastor positions, congregants often attributed ideal qualities like *charisma* and *good role models* to youth pastors; these qualities are often associated with positions of leadership.[21] Matt, who served as a youth pastor at the same church as Grace, expressed that senior pastor Sophie was supportive of his ideas related to the youth ministry.

> Sophie has been very supportive, working through ideas and helping make them practical and also saying, "You might want to talk to x y and z," and then half the time she'll get involved and we'll both make it happen.

Sophie seemed intentional about creating an environment in which she supported and worked alongside Grace and Matt in their ministerial work. Different from Jessica's experiences of isolation, this type of environment allowed the children's and youth pastors more collaboration, support, and inclusion in their roles than Jessica. Yet, despite Sophie's collaborative leadership style, Grace and Matt's respective ministries often functioned separate from the goings-on of the larger congregation. Matt indicated that he was "trying to integrate youth and adult congregants more, so more adults will be involved and more adults will care," which suggests that there remains some level of marginalization as it relates to the more feminized youth and children's ministries despite some efforts of inclusion and support by leadership.

Associate Pastors

The case study of associate pastor Allie suggests that more masculinized pastoral positions may be conceived as *more* feminized once occupied by a woman. Congregants often understand the position of associate pastor as second in command to the senior pastor. It is typically the second highest in priority when it comes to congregants making this position full-time and providing benefits and resources. It is also typically the second highest in authority; an associate pastor will to some extent share preaching responsibilities with the senior pastor, a skill that is conflated with authority and leadership, and is usually charged with ministering to a subset of the congregation or leading a particular ministry like religious education, missions, or spiritual formation. Additionally, congregants generally understand the position of associate pastor to be a prerequisite to being hired as a senior pastor. To better understand the ways in which CBF congregants conceived of this position, I asked that they offer two to three qualities associated with associate pastors (see Table 6.4).

Table 6.4 Qualities Associated with Associate Pastors ($N = 205$)

Category	Count	Percent
Supportive/team player	31	15.1
Kind and compassionate	25	12.2
Willing to work hard and serve	20	9.8
Relational	17	8.3
"Jack of all trades"	16	7.8
Energetic	12	5.9
Creative	11	5.4
Organized	9	4.4
Leader/preacher	7	3.4
Thoughtful	7	3.4
Knowledgeable	6	2.9
Good listener	4	1.9
Missional	4	1.9
Integrity	3	1.5
Open-minded	3	1.5
Other*	31	15.1

*Categories that included only 1–2 responses.

The qualities associated with associate pastors proved to be quite nuanced and complex in their relationship to masculinity and femininity. The "willing to work hard and serve" and "jack of all trades" (a gendered phrase) categories suggested that associate pastors are expected to be "able to support and assist as needed"; congregants seemed to understand associate pastors to serve as the catch-all pastor. The "jack of all trades" category included phrases like "well-prepared in all areas," "takes on tasks that others do not want," "ability to adapt and quickly serve in other areas as needed," "works with all ages," "team member willing to do what is necessary for the church," and "attentive to all." In addition to other feminized qualities like being "kind and compassionate," a "good listener," and "relational," congregants most often linked associate pastors to being "supportive" and a "team player," particularly to the senior pastor. This category included phrases like "supportive of pastor," "assists in worship and leads as requested by senior pastor," "loyal and supportive of pastor," "back the lead pastor," "supportive of church and senior pastor direction," "works under direction of senior pastor," and "collaborates with ministerial staff." These qualities suggest that this role is inherently subordinate to the senior pastor and, therefore, more feminized than the role of senior pastor, which may explain women's increased representation in these positions compared to senior pastor positions. In fact, these themes of being supportive looked quite similar to those of a church secretary. The distinction between these two positions may be found in the more masculinized attributes related to associate pastors such as the expectation to being *knowledgeable* in relation to specific professional expertise (e.g., "excellent biblical knowledge," "very well educated"), being *thoughtful* (e.g., "good mind," "thinker," "intelligent," "wise"), and *leading* (e.g., "active in leading activities," "can work closely with senior pastor to lead church," "willing to take on leadership roles," expectation of "preaching"). While congregants understood associate pastors to be subordinate to senior pastors, these qualities also suggest that congregants expect that associate pastors are at least capable of engaging in the same functions as senior pastors with some congregants explicitly stating that associate pastors should hold the same qualities as the senior pastor and serve as an "excellent back-up for the senior pastor." Different from church secretaries, office managers, and children's pastors, associate pastors are expected to at least sometimes practice leadership *while* being subordinate to the senior pastor. In fact, one congregant summarized this theme concisely by stating that the associate pastor should be a "strong person, but willing to accept his/her role."

In addition to playing a support role to the senior pastor, congregants suggested that associate pastors should balance this role with phrases like "complements role of senior pastor and works well with that person" and "complements gifts and skills of senior pastor." This theme emerged in Chapter 2 as well with the relationship between senior and associate pastors being characterized as "yin" and "yang." Religious understandings of *complementarianism* are often utilized to justify traditional heteronormative relationships between men and women by which men are the leaders (i.e., masculine) and women are the supporters (i.e., feminine), thereby complementing each other in these ways. Allie found that congregants often conceptualized her role as a woman in the position of associate pastor under the leadership of a male senior pastor in this way as well.

The way people view my relationship with Paul [senior pastor]. That I'm his church wife. That I have this special role to fulfill—that I didn't sign up for. Some of it will be somebody coming up to me and saying something like—there was something about what he wore one day [congregants did not approve of]— saying, "He doesn't have a wife to tell him these things. You can tell him." I don't care what he does. Just other things like that. . . . Some of them [congregants] are people who adore him, adore me, who love this church, who would do anything for this church and anything for us personally. Yet they don't understand what it sounds like, when they're saying to me, "You're his church wife."

Congregants not only assume that Allie should complement the senior pastor professionally, but personally as well. In other words, her status as an associate pastor calls for a complementary and supportive relationship with the senior pastor while her perceived status as a woman calls for an *additional* complementary and supportive relationship with the senior pastor, one that is not included in her job description nor one to which she agreed, thereby creating an additional level of subordination in her role as associate pastor. Moreover, this additional job criteria simultaneously increases the amount of femininity associated with her position and decreases the value of her position because she is expected to take on the additional role of *wife* while not being paid additionally for the associated tasks.

Allie spoke more about the value of her position in relation to the tasks included in her job description. As an associate pastor, she was certainly responsible for a variety of different areas, including children, youth, families, missions, and preaching occasionally. When she was first hired as associate pastor, it was a 25 hours/week position that expanded to 30 hours/week after two years.

> It was just impossible. That was the constant source of frustration of "Here's my job description. There's no way. There is no way I can make that fit into 30 hours." ... I can't halfway do something. I'm going to do it, it's going to be done well, and it was such a relief when the church finally made me full-time, because for me it was not about the money at all, and it's never been about that. That's been a blessing for me to be at this stage of life, and for us to be financially secure as a family. I've watched other women coming out of seminary who are like "I've got to find something. I've got to take something because I got to have income." And it was a blessing for me not to have to worry about that, but the gift of time shouldn't be ignored. Even though when I went full-time the way it was validated—the way that they packaged it was, that's when I got the youth pastor.... I've really been wrestling with how to balance all the things that are in my job description. I have gotten a lot better at self-care, at knowing just when to draw the line. But I was describing my position to somebody recently and they were like "That's three positions."

Allie explained that while her position is now full-time, her job description expands well beyond that of one full-time job. Allie does not receive overtime pay, which decreases the actual value of one hour worked. Patterns of being overworked and underpaid prove consistent with those of working women and other feminized professions. Given the feminine attributes (e.g., listening, empathetic, loving, relational) of all ministerial positions, all professionals working in the vocational ministry, even senior pastors, are typically monetarily valued less than workers in other more masculinized fields such as science, business, medicine, and law. In fact, research shows that on average non-Catholic male clergy make about 34% less than those in the general working population. However, non-Catholic female clergy make about 48% less than the general working population.[22] Allie further explained that her status as a woman likely contributes to the further devaluation of her position.

> I don't think the church, I could be wrong about this—I don't think the church would have given a man the job description that I have. I really don't. You know the guy that was the youth minister before who, as I said, they had bumped up to associate pastor; they were going to give him a few additional duties. But it would not have looked anything like my job description. . . . They would not have expected him to be, you know, coordinating children's Sunday school and all these other things that are on my plate. And I know that some of the things I take on is because I see something that's not being done and I want to fill that gap. So that's part of my, you know, personal drive there. But no, I don't know another man anywhere who has a position that looks like mine does.

Allie's womanhood and perceived relationship to femininity seem to intensify the monetary devaluation of her position. This study did not collect the salaries of participating pastors, but even if Allie was given the same salary as the male associate pastor before her (she was not earning more), the monetary worth of her work would be less because she is responsible for additional duties.

Given that research shows that women are often perceived as less valuable or cost-worthy,[23] patterns of devaluing women's work may also be reflected in the gender pay gap between men and women clergy. In 2016, the U.S. Census Bureau reported that female clergy make 86.9% of the average salaries of male clergy, which suggests that the wage gap is actually lower than the national wage gap with women earning on average about 79% of men's earning across all professions (the gap broadens even more for women of color specifically). A different study actually found that the wage gap has decreased drastically from women clergy making an average of 63 cents to every male clergy's dollar in 1976 to an average of 93 cents to the dollar in 2016. However, researchers argue that this relative closing in the pastoral gender pay gap is largely attributed to the slow rates of income growth for male clergy over the same time period. Moreover, the slow growth rates in male clergy's salaries may be related to the overall decline in religious membership across denominations or be explained by the monetary devaluation of the overall profession as more women enter the field.[24] For instance, one study shows that when religious denominations hit a "tipping point" of 30% female clergy, then the gender pay gap becomes even more distinct, particularly in lower level positions.[25]

While much research suggests that the gender pay gap more broadly persists even after controlling for additional factors such as education or experience,[26] other research presents an adjusted gender pay gap that controls for both personal characteristics of employees and job characteristics. The adjusted pay gap suggests that even after controlling for additional individual and structural characteristics, American male workers still make an average of 4.9% more than women across all professions.[27] Many point to this significantly lower gap between men's and women's salaries as justification for the lack of attention to the issue. However, it is important to consider three important questions regarding gender pay gaps: (1) Why does a pay gap exist even after adjustments?; (2) What "personal" factors are actually structural? Meaning, should women's lack of experience compared to that of men's be considered as an individual trait or, as seen throughout the chapters in this book, are there actually gendered structural barriers that contribute to their abilities to gain experience? Additionally, why is it that women pastors are more likely than their male counterparts to receive jobs at smaller churches with smaller budgets?[28] Finally and relatedly, (3) Why may an unadjusted pay gap persist? The unadjusted wage gap suggests that, on average, women make an average of about 20% less than men in the United States while not controlling for job type, thereby suggesting that women are working lower paying jobs than men. With this being the case, why are the lowest paying jobs in society predominately occupied by women (and, while we're here, Black, Indigenous, People of Color [BIPOC] and the intersections of these)? In particular, why do clergywomen predominately occupy the lower ranks of church work? This chapter provides some insight into the relationship between feminization and devaluation in lower status positions within CBF congregations. Further research should be conducted to better understand this trend and ways in which the more masculinized position of senior pastor is perceived as being worth less when women hold this position.

Steps Toward Change

- Reevaluate the roles and job descriptions of the most feminized and devalued positions in the church. Is the value of these positions determined by antiquated gendered ideologies undergirding the current gender structure in Baptist life? Or is the value of these roles being determined by actual job tasks, responsibilities, and time spent? Given this, are there part-time feminized jobs that should actually be full-time?

- Examine ways children's pastors may be underresourced, excluded, and overworked and work toward change, if needed.
- Use more current terminology for "church secretaries" such as office managers or administrative assistants, as these terms impact the perceived value of the position.
- Reflect on the ways in which you may perceive femininized positions as less valuable in church, at home, at work, and society overall and work to change this thinking.
- Prioritize and account for feminized skills in job descriptions and compensate for these skills in ways equal to masculinized skills.
- Hire a social worker to guide you in these efforts.

Discussion Questions

- In what ways do you conceive of the value of feminized work? How may you reconceive feminized work in a way that adds value and equity?
- In what ways are masculinized skills often invisible when enacted by women? For instance, think of adjectives often used to describe kindergarten teachers. Are they more masculine or feminine? Now, think critically about what teachers actually do. How would you now describe their skill set?
- What types of trends establish a direct relationship between feminization and devaluation? Think about various contexts from the workplace to playground activities. For example, are girlish activities valued equally to boyish activities when boys and girls both engage these? Identify a research article that examines this relationship.
- Identify some of your unconscious or implicit biases when you consider the role of an administrative assistant, an office manager, and a children's pastor. What about other feminized professions (e.g., social workers, nurses, teachers, domestic workers)?
- How does *distancing* reinforce the devaluation of femininity (e.g., from secretary to office manager)? Why may *distancing* be necessary for success? Do you ever take strides to distance yourself from femininity? Why? See Rhoton (2011) below for more information on distancing.
- Is it possible to close the pay gap if the belief that there are "men's jobs" and "women's jobs" persists? Moreover, is it possible to close the pay gap if the belief that masculine skills are worth more than feminine skills persists?
- White women typically fill jobs that white men understand to be too undervalued or holding too low of status. Who do jobs go to when white women perceive certain jobs to be too undervalued or holding too low of

status for them? Reflect on types of patterns that emerge in your context and identify a research study that speaks to this. Who do the lowest status jobs go to in the context of the CBF? Reflect on the devaluation of jobs at the intersection of gender and race, class, age, and ability. How does this play out in your life?

- For social workers, how do you perceive the profession of social work's relationship with feminization and devaluation?

Supplemental Readings

Alfrey, Lauren, and Twine, France W. 2017. Gender-fluid geek girls: Negotiating inequality regimes in the tech industry. *Gender & Society*, 31(1), 28–50.

Davies, Margery. 2010. *Woman's place is at the typewriter*. Philadelphia: Temple University Press.

Duffy, Brooke E., and Schwartz, Becca. 2018. Digital "women's work?": Job recruitment ads and the feminization of social media employment. *New Media & Society*, 20(8), 2972–2989.

Duffy, Mignon. 2011. *Making care count: A century of gender, race, and paid care work*. New Brunswick, NJ: Rutgers University Press.

Irvine, Leslie, and Vermilya, Jenny R. 2010. Gender work in a feminized profession: The case of veterinary medicine. *Gender & Society*, 24(1), 56–82.

Levanon, Asaf, England, Paula, and Allison, Paul. 2009. Occupational feminization and pay: Assessing causal dynamics using 1950–2000 US census data. *Social Forces*, 88(2), 865–891.

Rhoton, Laura A. 2011. Distancing as a gendered barrier: Understanding women scientists' gender practices. *Gender & Society*, 25(6), 696–716.

Schleifer, Cyrus, and Miller, Amy D. 2017. Occupational gender inequality among American clergy, 1976–2016: Revisiting the stained-glass ceiling. *Sociology of Religion*, 78(4), 387–410.

Webber, Gretchen R., and Giuffre, Patti. 2019. Women's relationships with women at work: Barriers to solidarity. *Sociology Compass*, 13(6), e12698.

Williams, Christine L. 2013. The glass escalator, revisited: Gender inequality in neoliberal times, SWS feminist lecturer. *Gender & Society*, 27(5), 609–629.

Wingfield, Adia Harvey. 2009. Racializing the glass escalator: Reconsidering men's experiences with women's work. *Gender & Society*, 23(1), 5–26.

Supplemental Reading

7

Preacher Woman

As a kid, I was really shy, really soft-spoken, pretty passive. Partly, I was finding my voice through becoming a pastor. It's like the most rebellious thing I'd ever done. [laughter] Which is sadly true. I've always just been this rule-follower and not-rock-the-boat goody two shoes. It's like my MO; it's like keep everybody happy. I started to find my voice just because I had to sort of go against the grain to even become a pastor. . . . I think that's probably where I got a backbone. I got an extremely hateful response to something I had written from somebody I knew who severely misinterpreted what I was saying. It was really upsetting but at the end of it all, I decided this isn't going to stop me, I'm still going to keep writing. I just always felt like that was—that was just a defining moment where I realized it's more important to be authentic and to say what I think and what I feel and want to say even if people disagree or misunderstand what's happening. I think that was like the beginning of me deciding that I wasn't going to cower. It doesn't mean I always say everything I'm thinking. I still make decisions and discern, but there's a difference between choosing not to say something or how to say it versus just like—[not saying it] . . . you realize there are worse things than losing your job.

—Sophie, senior pastor

Standpoint theory argues that the perspectives of the oppressed and marginalized actually offer a more objective view of the world, particularly in relation to power and systems of oppression.[1] In other words, those who actually experience oppression are more equipped to identify, understand, and address systems of oppression than those who do not experience oppression. Paradoxically, those who are often listened to and making decisions about the lives of the marginalized are typically those who already have power; in Western culture this group most likely consists of white, cisgender, heteronormative Christian men. In the earlier quote, senior pastor Sophie had written an article speaking out against a social justice issue. As a woman who had faced several gendered barriers in her

Preacher Woman. Katie Lauve-Moon, Oxford University Press (2021). © Oxford University Press.
DOI: 10.1093/oso/9780197527542.003.0008

pursuit of becoming a senior pastor in the male-dominated field of Baptist ministry, Sophie was keenly aware of various forms of sexism and often spoke out
against these issues. While as a white woman, Sophie likely retained blind spots in
relation to racism, for instance, her personal and professional experiences of discrimination and oppression as a white woman ultimately caused her to be more
likely to learn about and speak out against other forms of oppression and discrimination such as those impacting Black Indigenous People of Color (BIPOC)
and LGBTQ+ people. Like many women, particularly women of color, who have
come before her, she is more equipped to identify and understand systems of
oppression that others in dominant society have failed to see or cared to understand. Consequently, Sophie sometimes faced resistance when she brought these
issues to light in her role as senior pastor. As illustrated in previous chapters, the
relationship between Baptist pastors and congregants proves similar to the one
between politicians and constituents; so when pastors speak out on what some
congregants may understand to be a controversial topic, they are taking a risk because congregants ultimately control whether or not they keep their jobs.

Sophie recalled receiving a "hateful response" to something she had written
in relation to a social justice issue. For some pastors, this type of response would
have perhaps resulted in more cautious and conservative stances. For Sophie,
this response solidified what she perceived as a need to speak out in the first place
and further demonstrated the lack of awareness (or acceptance) around the issue
at hand. She thought about backing off, but ultimately she realized that there
were "worse things than losing your job" like being silent about injustice and
failing to advocate on behalf of the marginalized and oppressed (and herself).

Sophie considered the practice of revealing unjust power structures and educating congregants as part of her calling as a Christ follower and, ultimately, her
role as a senior pastor. However, Sophie was not alone in this approach to her
job; many of the other women ministers also led in riskier ways. In fact, the congregational surveys requested that congregants list three words describing their
senior (lead) pastors. Responses indicated that only the women pastors in the
study were described with the following words: daring, courageous, open, truth
seeker, fearless, prophetic, and organizer. None of the male pastors in the study
were characterized in these ways. This is an important finding because the aforementioned descriptors are highly masculinized and, yet, in this context they are
most associated with women pastors. Congregants certainly described *both* men
and women pastors with other masculinized characteristics such as intelligent,
knowledgeable, wise, good preacher, skilled, thoughtful, and hard-working as
well as feminine traits such as loving, caring, kind, and personable. However,
congregants reserved these particular attributes for the women pastors (some
of who were solo household earners at the time of the study)—daring, courageous, open, truth seeker, fearless, prophetic, organizer—masculine qualities

commonly associated with critiquing and changing unjust systems and, there-fore, taking risks. This is an important finding because it counters other studies that suggest women are less likely to take risks than men.[2] Many of these studies attribute differences in men's and women's risk-taking behaviors to scientifi-cally antiquated *naturally* occurring physiological reasons (e.g., different brains) with little analysis of the sociopolitical factors that may produce such perceived differences between men and women and, therefore, prove completely inaccu-rate or, at least, limited in scope.[3]

At first I considered the possibility that congregants found these risk-taking qualities noteworthy in describing their pastors simply because their pastors were women and dominant narratives often position women as risk averse and tentative. Perhaps congregants noted that their (female) pastor was *courageous* because they did not expect her *as a woman* to be courageous. Whether or not unconscious gender biases influenced how congregants characterized their pastors, it seems that women pastors demonstrated in other ways that they *do* consistently take more risks than their male counterparts. On the whole, women pastors in the study more readily took on controversial topics in the pulpit, emphasized inclusion, and led social justice initiatives related to issues of sexism, homophobia, heterosexism, and racism. These trends reinforce findings of other studies demonstrating that women pastors are typically more political and social justice oriented.[4] Some studies suggest that women are more likely to be social justice minded because they *naturally* are more empathetic and their commit-ment to helping others is emotionally driven.[5] However, the data of this study reinforce other findings that suggest that women's commitment to social justice and helping others can be attributed to their own experiences of discrimination and oppression.[6] In other words, women pastors' capacity for empathy and com-mitment to addressing injustice primarily stems from their acute understanding of discrimination, marginalization, and oppression rather than their *natural dispositions*. It is important to note that one male senior pastor in particular was strongly committed to social justice issues and had taken the risk of affirming LGBTQ+ equal membership and leadership in the church; his church was sub-sequently kicked out of the congregation's state denominational entities and lost membership. However, he was the exception in relation to other male senior pastors in the study. He attributed his attention to social justice to the exclu-sionary experiences of his mother, who eventually became a pastor over 30 years after her calling.

Women pastors' commitment to raising the voices of the oppressed and working toward a more just world, even perhaps at the expense of their jobs, seemed particularly influenced by their interpretations of their roles as pastors. When asked how senior pastor Olivia approaches topics that may be difficult for church congregants to engage, she responded:

It's a sense that I have to say this thing. And to not say this thing is denying truth—whatever feels like is burning in me. So if it's a Black Lives Matter sermon, or if it's about marriage equality, any kind of justice issue, I feel like I'm compelled to go there on Sunday.

For Olivia, failing to speak out against injustice is *denying truth* and Olivia understands her role as a pastor in relation to bearing truth; to Olivia, truth and exposing social injustice are interrelated. From a standpoint perspective, Olivia's ability to see truth and her inclination to act on truth are enhanced by her awareness around her experiences as a woman in a male-dominated profession and a male-dominated world. Olivia continued to explain how her commitment to being *on the right side of history* and the right side of justice was more important to her in the end than her job security.

What are the stories that I want my kids to hear that I've told? And there needs to be actions that back this up and not just my words. The Black Lives Matter movement happened, and I hopefully spoke on the right side of justice and was on the right side of history. When marriage equality finally came to the United States, and I made space for it to come to the church, too. When other mothers have chosen their bad theology over their own sons and daughters, I hope that my kids have heard different in me. . . . So, initially that race sermon where people came and lined up and wanted to talk to me—it was four people. What I have to remind myself is that when I finished that sermon, there was applause and Amens, and I think somebody hooted. [laughs] But as most of us do, what I walked away with—what made the most impact on me that day were the four people who wanted to come talk about race with me. And so, at that point I did become more frightened because I felt, when we moved [to take this job]—like this has to be forever. And I have to be in this church for years, and our children will graduate high school here, and we'll grow old here, and this will be our forever home. And I feel much less anxious about that now. I now feel like I would rather live from truth and live from what my sense of right is, and have it be short, than end up in a job for a really long time and not be—I don't want to feel like [the church] owns me. I would rather be here for three years than be a puppet.

Olivia's commitment to justice and what she understood to be *right* proved more important than her commitment to her job if ever the two became mutually exclusive. These values explicitly influenced her willingness to take on what others may perceive as controversial topics and her overall riskier approach to leadership. Associate pastor Meg carried a similar approach in response to congregants leaving once her church became an LGBTQ+-affirming congregation:

I think we just knew that what we were doing was right, welcoming people into the church is right. Like that's what you do. If you have to go because you can't be around certain people then, as much as I love you, I'm not going to beg you to stay and tell them to go. So, I think just knowing that we were doing the right thing was enough.

Meg's understanding of what was *right* was informed by her experiences and observations of the invisibility of women in the church (as noted in previous chapters). Through her experiences and observations of exclusion in the Baptist gender structure, she was able to stand firm in her conviction of creating spaces of inclusion and equality—what she understood was right.

Similarly, associate pastor Allie drew on her experiences of gender exclusion to call attention to how being part of a more inclusive congregation may not adequately prepare people, particularly youth, for how unequal and exclusionary the rest of the world can be.

I was in seminary with too many women who were gifted and followed their call, and then got out. Some of them never found churches, or some of them found a church, but then didn't stay in it very long. Ministry is hard, you know that. I think that we have to work hard, and not just what we do in this church, but we need to be a part of a larger conversation. I try to be real intentional with the youth so that they—this is their norm. When they go off to college, and go to [wherever] I want them to be aware. Here are questions you need to be asking, here are things you need to be thinking about, you've taken this for granted, you take for granted that girls got to stand up and read scripture on a Sunday, or help with communion, or that I got to preach. That is not happening in the vast majority of churches that have Baptist in the name.

Allie understood that centralizing issues of sexism and gender inequality in her youth ministry was key to her role as associate pastor. Since women occupied leadership roles in her congregation, she wanted to educate her students on ways in which sexism plays out in different pockets of the world, particularly other Baptist churches, so that they may better understand the lived experiences of other girls and women and be prepared to respond with strategies of inclusion, equity, and resistance. For Allie, to be able to understand and address forms of oppression and discrimination was to be able to live out the Gospel and do her job well.

In addition to understanding issues of justice as part of their callings, women ministers often approached change with more of a sense of urgency than male pastors. Ordained minister Ashley explains why she understands this approach to change as important.

The "it just takes time" phrase is really interesting. And by interesting, I mean frustrating. (laughing) This phrase belongs to the privileged—it's usually said by white straight men. And, first of all, as a woman in a male-dominated field, believe me, I am very much aware of how slow change is or can be. The fact that you think you need to explain this to me is so ridiculous on so many levels. And secondly, why? Like, why does it have to take time? I mean I get that if you don't personally experience discrimination that the whole idea of social justice is just a political issue for you. Like a buzz word or something. But for some people it's their actual lives. It's my actual life. When we talk about taking things slow—we are really saying we don't want this to be uncomfortable for people it doesn't affect. Basically for people who are already comfortable, who have been comfortable. But for those it's been uncomfortable for, for a very long time— they can continue to wait. Like let's not talk too much about sexism because it makes people who aren't experiencing sexism uncomfortable. Seriously? So when weighing out what the bigger problem to avoid is—we are going to con- clude it is the comfort level of those not experiencing discrimination rather than those actually experiencing discrimination? I mean the first group is dealing with an uncomfortable idea and the second group is dealing with an uncomfortable life—to say the least. You know, the first group may be excluded because of a negative opinion they hold about other people; the second group is being excluded for being themselves. There's a difference. This is happening in churches across the country with gay membership. Pastors feel especially concerned for the church members who disagree with LGBTQ persons par- ticipating in the full life of the church and so keep putting off the decision to be LGBTQ affirming. Meanwhile those church members could go to literally any church they choose, and lesbian, gay, transgender people face bullying, have significantly higher suicide rates, and are dealing with being rejected and unac- cepted by their schools, families, and churches. Really, what's more important? Actually, what's more biblical?

For Ashley, *the political*, *the personal*, and *the moral* are all one in the same be- cause of her *social positionality* as a woman.[7] She suggests that those who do not face discrimination have the privilege of disconnecting the political from the personal. Moreover, she conveys that since the political and the personal are one in the same for her and many others, then what some understand as merely polit- ical must also be considered in relation to morality or, more specifically, biblical scripture. For these reasons, Ashley calls into question the concept of *incremental change* and pushes for *transformational change* instead by prioritizing the lived experiences of the marginalized. Ashley echoes others who critique incremental change by suggesting this approach largely prioritizes the experiences of the more privileged while she understands her calling as a Christian and minister to be centralizing the lives of the marginalized and oppressed.

While not all women pastors were as committed to a transformational change model as Ashley, they were overall more intentional about working toward a more equitable or inclusive outcome. Most of the male pastors in the study with the exception of one took on more incremental approaches to change, particularly around social justice issues. For example, one male pastor in the study hosted panels and discussions about LGBTQ+ membership and leadership in the church, but he did not feel like it was necessary to announce publically an open and affirming status. Another male pastor initiated congregational conversations about the full participation of LGBTQ+ people in the life of the church in order to build consensus but not necessarily with the purpose of moving the church to a decision that prioritized the marginalized. Women pastors appeared more clear and intentional about eventually landing in a more inclusive and equitable place, even if this plan included incremental steps to getting there such as panels, workshops, educational trainings, and one-on-one conversations.

Given that women often centralized values and initiatives of social justice, they were also the only pastors in the study to be described in the following terms: *biased, challenging, agenda-driven*. Male pastors were never described in this way in survey responses. These types of adjectives are commonly used to describe women acting on feminist values of liberation, inclusion, and equity in various fields, including religion and politics. In particular, the words *biased* and *agenda-driven* suggest that these pastors were pushing more than what others perceived to be the *neutral* mission of the church or the status quo. In other words, rather than using their platform and position for a *neutral or centrist* message, some congregants perceived women pastors as instead using their voices to push a more *leftist* feminist agenda. Those who hold this view fail to see and understand how society and, in this case, Baptist gender structure already skews toward masculinity and reinforces men's success, access to resources, and dominance in leadership as evident by the significantly low proportion of women in pastoral positions and the gendered processes identified in the chapters of this book. Therefore, maintaining the current *dominant* gender structure renders *neutrality* impossible. In other words, when a pastor or any leader for that matter seeks to maintain the status quo by not addressing issues of inequality, oppression, and marginalization, it is often understood as claiming the middle ground or remaining neutral. However, when the current status quo proves to be inherently oppressive, inequitable, or exclusionary toward a particular group of people (in other words, inherently privileges the dominant group), then *remaining neutral* is anything but neutral. Taking a feminist approach actually works more in the direction of neutrality than does maintaining the status quo of gender inequality.

While women pastors were less concerned with losing their jobs, some did seem uneasy with being associated with terms like *biased, agenda-driven,* and in some cases, *feminism.* I observed senior pastor Olivia greeting guests before a wedding ceremony. One of the attendees asked Olivia if she was the pastor's wife. She responded by saying that she was actually the pastor. When she recounted the story to me, in relation to her correcting the congregant, she said, "I just really didn't want to be perceived as an *angry feminist* or an *angry woman.*" Often the term *feminist* is accompanied with the word *angry* because feminism is inherently committed to addressing forms of sexism and working toward structural change; this means that feminists often critique and call attention to unjust systems. Sometimes women's critique of sexism is misconstrued as *complaining* or *angry* or *being ungrateful,* particularly given that women are often socialized to be passive and selfless and, therefore, are expected to act in these ways. Therefore, the branding of feminism as something angry and negative functions as an additional constraint to women's leadership, particularly those working toward gender equality. Here, Olivia's (likely rightful) concern with correcting the wedding guest reinforced a structure in which women should make sure everyone feels as comfortable as possible and constrained her from educating this person on the implications of such gendered assumptions.

Heather, an ordained minister, similarly conveyed that she used to feel insecure about bringing up issues of sexism or feminism.

> I also was kind of shy or weird about bringing it up. I didn't want people to see me as a feminist, like a crazy person. Or super-sensitive about—like "You can't say anything around me or I'll flip out." Now, I'm just like "No, you need to learn."

Heather feared that she would not be taken seriously as a result of speaking on matters of feminism and sexism. She once understood that being perceived as a feminist may also mean being perceived as crazy or super-sensitive. In a professional context, these types of assumptions would cause her to lose her credibility as a leader and teacher and ultimately not be listened to by others. Therefore, the meanings that others attach to various forms of feminism or even notions of raising awareness around sexism influenced the extent to which Heather felt she could speak out against gender issues or explain why gendered assumptions and behaviors may be problematic, thereby reinforcing the current gender structure. Eventually, Heather grew to understand that raising awareness and educating are more important than the opinions of those who do not fully agree with the ideals of feminism or understand the implications of dominant gender structure.

In only a couple of cases did congregants actually leave because women pastors in the study espoused feminist perspectives and ideals. This may be due to the fact that the most open-minded and socially conscious congregations in the study were the ones that actually hired women pastors. Senior pastor Sophie explained a response of one of the congregants after including some feminist commentary in her sermons:

> We've only lost one person that I know of and [we] talked. According to her, she didn't really leave because of the LGBT stuff but she did leave because she said that I'm a man-hater. I asked her [what she meant], she said, "Well you talked about abuse and rape in your sermon." I was like "Well, yes, I'm against abuse and rape, I'm not against men." She was like "I'm against it, too." It didn't really add up and I had one sermon where—this is just a joke I thought everybody thought was funny because they laughed—Easter Sunday I was talking about the women coming back to the tomb and the disciples not believing their story and I just talked about it being as a poignant example of mansplaining. I almost get the sense that she and I had very different definitions of what mansplaining is, because she kept saying "mansplaining" as if I had cussed.

Sophie's congregant labeled her a "man-hater" in response to her utilizing a feminist frame in a few sermons. The assumption that placing a feminist frame over a text results in man-hating suggests that this congregant retained little understanding of how gender structure works. A feminist hermeneutical frame does not necessarily replace a neutral frame; it likely replaces a masculinist hermeneutical frame. Yet I never observed or heard of any congregant accuse a male pastor of being a woman-hater for preaching a sermon in a way that, for example, reinforces the implicit silencing of women, minimizes the perspectives of women represented in the text, or misrepresents women's involvement in the ministry of Jesus. These traditional approaches to Scripture were established by way of a man's perspective; they are only considered traditional because men were given the power and privilege to record their interpretations first and, therefore, are not neutral. Sophie used her platform to raise awareness around a social issue related to the enactment of hypermasculinity on feminine bodies (whether it be men or women). She also joked about the established gendered trend of *mansplaining*, which ultimately further prioritizes the voices of men and silences women.[8] It is important to understand that such critiques are directed at a dominant gender structure that skews toward men and perhaps those that reinforce this structure rather than toward men in general; this congregant failed to understand this distinction. Moreover, it is important to understand that there are multiple forms of feminism even within the church; it is not a homogenous group or concept.[9]

It is important to remember that standpoint theory does not necessarily suggest that all women, for example, will be able to identify structural sexism when it happens or that they are completely exempt from reinforcing it. As illustrated throughout the chapters of this book, women are often socialized by the same dominant gender systems as men. Many women, particularly in the case of cis-normative, straight, educated, white women, more often engage feminized spaces and, therefore, perhaps have fewer opportunities to observe or personally experience the variety of ways in which sexism and other oppressions persist. Moreover, some sexist traditions and assumptions have become so engrained in the fabric of society, it sometimes proves difficult to see a different approach to life or ways in which the current approaches produce inequitable outcomes between men and women. For someone who has only known one particular way to "do gender," especially if those in power assert that this particular way is God ordained, it may feel unsettling or threatening to engage critiques of or calls for change in the current social order. For this congregant, this new and critical perspective of the world and Scripture was too much for her, and she ultimately left the congregation.

Women pastors were rarely completely silenced on issues of feminism. Most of the women pastors in the study consistently embodied values of feminism and utilized a feminist lens in writing their sermons. However, it is important to note that even in female-led congregations, pastors and congregants facilitated or hosted significantly fewer initiatives directed at understanding or addressing issues of sexism and gender inequality than those directed at other social issues such as racism, LGBTQ+ rights and inclusion, immigration, mass incarceration, or poverty. One congregation had recently become involved in issues of domestic and sexual violence, but no congregations explicitly addressed other gender issues such as the devaluation of women's work, unequal gender socialization, the wage gap, or the glass ceiling in broader society. Perhaps the notion that sexism had already been solved through the establishment of inclusive theology or hiring a woman senior pastor influenced the lack of focus on issues of sexism within these congregations. Whatever the case, congregations engaged issues of gender inequality far less often than other social issues.

Finding Allies

I really don't get why we consider sexism to be a "women's issue." Like we aren't responsible for creating sexism—maybe some women. Yet whenever there is an opportunity to learn about it or try to change it or whatever—only women show up. How does that help? Like we are well aware of how sexism works—we aren't the ones that need to learn. Yet when you show up for *Nevertheless, She Preached*—all women. I get that part of that is really good because women need a space where they are actually heard and listened to about this stuff and understood. And most of us aren't finding that in our churches. And it's space for women who haven't been given opportunities to

lead. That can be really healing. But women's exclusion from leadership in the church isn't just our problem—it's everybody's problem.
And if you aren't actively working against it, then you are complicit and a part of the problem. And we mostly see women actually doing the work to change things. . . . I think going to something
like [*Nevertheless, She Preached*] would be good for them [men].
Many of them seem to still have trouble imagining a different reality
(laughing). This would help them see what's possible.

Ashley, an ordained minister, calls attention to the issue of sexism as a structural
problem rather than simply a women's issue for which they are solely responsible for solving. She argues further that since everyone plays a part in creating
and reinforcing dominant gender structure, then everyone should be part of the
solution. Instead, she observes mostly women putting forth the time and energy
to work toward more equitable spaces in congregations. However, she acknowledges that giving women the opportunity to engage mostly women spaces such
as the *Nevertheless, She Preached* annual conference offers inclusive and equitable experiences they are not receiving in their own churches and other religious spaces (hence the need for the conference in the first place). Heather shared
similar feelings when she discovered that even while working as an ordained
minister and office manager in a congregation that theologically supports the
leadership of women in the church, she still faced unconscious gender biases
and a lack of understanding in relation to sexism and feminism by some of her
coworkers.

I know it's not mean-spirited, which is why I don't get too mad, but I do get
tired, if that makes sense. . . . I'll be honest, I do get tired, really tired. It's just like
"Here, too, [in] my safe space? Okay."

Heather recognizes that interactions with some of her male coworkers are not
intended to be mean or insulting, but her coworkers still fail to see some of
the more implicit ways they enact structural sexism and reinforce gender inequality. Heather assumed that when she took the job at a church that affirmed
the equal leadership of women in the church, she would be engaging a space
free of gendered assumptions and implicit sexism. Instead, she learned that
inclusive theology and good intentions do not effectively eradicate sexism in
churches. Although she was somewhat comforted by the good intentions of her
coworkers, she still ultimately faced outcomes of sexism and marginalization.
These gendered patterns tired her and, like many other women in the study, further increased her potential for burnout, which is commonly understood in relation to (1) diminished personal worth or accomplishment in the workplace;

(2) emotional exhaustion, and (3) depersonalization. It is important to note that the causes of burnout are often the effects of sexism and feminized work as well.[10]

Heather hoped that if her male coworkers did not explicitly identify as feminists, that they would at least function as allies willing to step out of their comfort zones and actively disrupt the dominant gender structure rather than reinforce or be complicit with it. The presence of allies offers the potential to create more energized and hopeful spaces rather than exhausting ones. Some describe allies as those who leverage their privilege for those who do not have the same privileges. Others understand allies to be those who are willing to die (or lose a job) for a cause that does not affect them. Martin Luther King Jr. once called for allies who prioritized justice over order. Most women working in these churches did not consistently find such committed allies in their male colleagues. In some cases, the absence of allies may be attributed to a lack of awareness of gender structure. For instance, when asked what his church does to address sexism, Jim, a male pastor at a church that had never hired a woman in any full-time pastoral position, stated:

> Gender is something we don't address a lot, because that's something that we would say we've dealt with and we want gender equality, especially in the church.

For Jim, gender equality had been achieved in his congregation since his church organizationally and theologically affirmed women's leadership. Jim lacked a sociological understanding of gender and inequality and, therefore, failed to see the many ways women, particularly staff members, often faced gendered hurdles in his own congregation. He also failed to understand how even if his congregation *was* far along in "undoing" gender inequality in the church,[11] his congregation was inextricably linked to broader society. In other words, over half of his congregation was comprised of women who likely engaged forms of sexism in their homes, schools, workplaces, or society overall, yet sexism was rarely addressed in this church. Moreover, Jim's logic for not addressing issues of gender in the church did not stand in relation to this congregation's efforts to raising awareness around issues of racism. This church never maintained exclusionary theology or discriminatory organizational values pertaining to Black Indigenous People of Color. Therefore, by Jim's logic, this church had already addressed issues of racism, yet the church staff remained intentional about educating the congregation on issues of racism and race inequality through education and other initiatives.

Brett, a different pastor of the same church, seemed to lack awareness around gender structure as well. One of his coworkers, office manager Heather, recalled how Brett wrote a letter to the congregation that focused on how much progress their church had made in terms of gender equality because it affirmed women's leadership in the pulpit and church overall. Heather explained:

> One of the examples he gave was when we were hiring [two new full-time] pastors, 100 people applied for the job, and we narrowed it down to 10, and four of them were women. Yes, we gave the job to two men but we had four of them who were women. It was things like that, those were all his examples of how we [have achieved gender equality]. I was like "You know the person who says, 'I'm not racist, I have a black friend,' or, 'I had a black friend once,' or, 'my neighbor's black.'" That kind of thing, and you're just like "That's not a good example, it doesn't really mean anything" and actually it kind of makes you sound maybe a little more suspicious." I was like "To be honest, that's how your [letter] came across." He was like, "Really?" I was like "Yes, that's like saying this church is diverse because we almost hired a black person once." Then it was the other thing, "And we have a female office manager on staff." I was like "It's like all of [office managers] and the entire denomination is female; that's not an accomplishment, that's the standard." And again, having a female children's pastor and then almost hiring—not even almost hiring, but you narrow down some women to possibly hire for a position, five years ago—those don't count. Those do not count as examples of how we're really good with women in this church. We had a long talk about that.

Heather calls attention to the continued invisibility around how sexism and gendered processes that play out in her congregation. First, the assertion that the congregation had made significant progress toward gender equality was from the perspective of a man who went straight from seminary graduation to the equivalent of a lead pastor position; this telling of events did not centralize the standpoint and experiences of women who had actually engaged this particular congregation. Yet, since he was the senior pastor of the church, he acted as the voice of authority on the issue. Secondly, the notions of women in the positions of office manager and children's pastor actually reinforced the current gender structure because these positions are typically understood as highly feminized and, therefore, most often held by women. To be sure, any progress in gender equality should be celebrated. *Some* of Brett's examples of progress seemed to be noteworthy. For instance, this congregation established the title of children's pastor rather than children's coordinator, which is often the title given to children's pastors at other congregations and is a title that diminishes the function of the position. They also consistently asked women guest preachers to fill in on Sunday. However, Brett's omission of the various other gendered issues that continue to persist in this congregation further silences the lived experiences of

women and renders invisible sexist patterns and outcomes within his congregation as well as broader society.

Associate pastor Allie recalled a similar example to describe the lack of understanding of gender structure by her male colleague, David, who was serving as
the senior pastor.

> One of the conversations that I have had with David which has been a point
> of friction, relates to Baptist women in ministry because every year, they pro-
> mote a month called the Martha Stearns Marshall month of preaching. They
> want churches to provide women with opportunities to preach. I preach here
> probably once every other month. I said something to David about "Can we
> officially promote this?" He just batted it down. His perspective is, that he is
> supportive of women in ministry and he doesn't see the value in pointing out,
> "Look a woman is preaching." His perspective is that it's somehow devaluing
> it. Which that doesn't make any sense to me, and we've gone back and forth
> with this.

Allie understands the barriers that women aspiring to be pastors face when
seeking out opportunities to preach. In Baptist life, there are far *fewer* churches
that affirm women in the pulpit than there are ones that prohibit women
preaching. Therefore, Allie and other pastors (men and women) in the study
argue it is important for those churches which affirm women's leadership to be
intentional about providing opportunities for women to preach so they have a
better chance of competing with men on the job market. Senior pastor David explicitly supports women's leadership in the church. In fact, in my conversations
with David, it was apparent he was integral in hiring Allie as an associate pastor.
However, in this case, Allie conveys that David's overarching values of gender
equality and the fact that he leads a church with gender-inclusive theology
should suffice. Furthermore, Allie stated that David does not "see the value in
pointing out, 'Look there's a woman preaching.'" David failed to see how providing preaching opportunities to women preachers disrupts a gender structure
in Baptist life by which women are vastly underrepresented and disadvantaged as
they pursue opportunities for professional development. Allie further explained
David's resistance to the idea:

> In his opinion, this [hearing a woman preach] is normative. But I'm like "Okay,
> it's normative here, but it's not out there. It's not." And last year I tried to have
> the conversation again, and said the purpose of this, it's not so much just to
> go to put a checkmark and say, "Oh, Allie preached in February, so there was
> a woman preaching. Check, we got that." It's supposed to be an opportunity
> to give women who don't have a place to preach a supportive environment in

which they can come in and preach maybe their first sermon, or certainly an early sermon in their career, where they can get affirmation, they can get experience. It's a way we contribute to the greater whole.

Allie suggested that David understood the occurrence of women preaching as "normative" in their congregation because Allie preached about every other month as the associate pastor. In other words, David had successfully demonstrated the value of gender equality in the church by hiring a woman as associate pastor who effectively acted as a visible and consistent leader in their congregation. In Allie's words, he was able to put a checkmark next to women preaching in their specific congregation. However, Allie was able to see the broader implications of Baptist gender structure and the ways that her congregation remained inextricably linked to inequitable gendered processes that persisted outside of the walls of their church. Moreover, she pushed David to see the ways in which their congregation could play a vital role in disrupting or resisting the barriers of Baptist gender structure that many women Baptist ministers were facing. Allie continued:

> And he was not having it, and his comment was something to the effect of—he just didn't want somebody who's not experienced to come in. But I'm thinking, "You had me come in here and preach a sermon before you hired me. You'd never heard me preach, and in fact I'd only preached once before at my church. And you let me come in here and do that. I was not experienced." So I don't know. That's something that he and I just don't see eye to eye. I have tried to talk through it with him and I just—and actually I said this to him recently, that I think some of his resistance to it is, he looks at his own experience, as being a single man, and that was a hindrance in him finding positions. I think part of him says, "Nobody was being an advocate for me." [laughs] I'm like "Well, okay, I'm sorry nobody was an advocate for you, but we . . ." I just know how hard it is.

Allie's description of David's perspective suggests that David wants to apply *equal* selection criteria to both men and women who are invited to come preach in their congregation. In other words, he would never ask an inexperienced man to preach in his church, so why would he ask an inexperienced woman? This notion proves similar to what some perceived as *gender-neutral* hiring processes in Chapter 3. David does not see how applying equal selection criteria actually maintains and reinforces an unequal gender structure, given that women have significantly fewer opportunities to gain experience, particularly in preaching. Allie points out that David invited her to come preach with very little experience, but it seems that was the anomaly.

Allie also suggested that David's resistance to intentionally provide a space for women to gain experience in the pulpit may be related to gendered barriers he faced as an unmarried male minister. Findings of this study (particularly those presented in Chapter 5) certainly suggest that congregants prefer pastors, particularly male pastors, to be married. While this gendered hurdle did not ultimately prevent David from occupying a couple of different senior pastor positions, it did present challenges for David as he pursued this position. Allie wondered whether or not David's unequal experiences influence his approach to providing additional preaching opportunities to women pastors. While I did not follow up with David to see if this was the case, it is not uncommon for those who have successfully overcome multiple barriers on their paths to success to understand it as unfair to make it easier on others who are on similar paths and, therefore, withhold resources. Conversely, Allie's experiences of having few opportunities to preach while on the job market and knowing "how hard it is" urged her toward creating a more equitable gender structure for other women on similar paths. Since Allie was the associate pastor rather than the senior pastor, the congregation ultimately took David's approach and did not promote Martha Stearns Marshall Month of Preaching in the way that Allie hoped.

Senior pastor Sophie also conveyed instances of colleagues failing to understand fully the effects of gender structure. For example, Sophie recalled a time when she attended a small pastoral retreat with other Cooperative Baptist Fellowship pastors and she was the only woman pastor in attendance. She indicated that the male leader of the retreat kept calling attention to her as a woman pastor and asking for her "perspective." The notion of asking a woman for her perspective is tricky. In some cases, women are asked for their perspectives because in a group of white, straight, cisgender men, they often carry unique experiences of marginalization, discrimination, and oppression that they can typically identify and address more effectively than others in the group. In other cases, women are asked to give a woman's perspective simply because they were born a female and it is assumed their perspectives will be categorically different from men's perspectives as a result of essential differences between men and women (e.g., different brains); in these instances, women are often understood as a homogenous category and asked to speak for *all women*. The latter centralizes the notions of essentialism and tokenism, which ultimately reinforce inequality. Sophie described a different time she was tokenized by a congregation without a woman pastor on staff.

Once I was invited to preach at First Baptist at [city], that was maybe my first or second year of seminary. It's one of the first few churches I preached at. I was honored that they asked me. I got there and they just—it was a Sunday night, and they just made a big deal throughout the whole service. "We're having a woman around. Look how progressive we are." I thought I was invited because [the church] saw potential in me and thought I was a good preacher and the whole thing made me feel like "I'm here because I'm a woman"—like the only qualification. That may not have been what they were thinking, [but] the way they played it up so much, it was uncomfortable. I've had several experiences that are something like that when people are—they're trying to be supportive and encouraging, but it ends up feeling more like patronizing.

In some ways, this scenario seems similar to the preaching opportunities Allie was pushing her congregation to provide to women seminarians and ministers. A congregation had invited Sophie, who was quite inexperienced at the time, to preach at their church. However, Sophie's interactions with church staff and congregants suggested that she was primarily being used as a symbolic token of gender equality in this congregation. In other words, the congregation providing Sophie with a rare opportunity for professional development in Baptist life seemed secondary to the congregation being able to wave the metaphoric flag of gender equality in their church through having a visiting woman preacher. What Sophie experienced as a form of tokenism, which tends to superficially mask rather than eradicate forms of sexism, felt more patronizing than empowering. Rather than explicitly valuing Sophie's particular voice, standpoint, and developing skill set, they seemed to position her as a checkmark in their pursuit of gender equality in the church. Conversely, Allie hoped to establish an organizational culture that sought gender equality through consistently providing a platform for women to use their voices and develop their preaching skills. The types of experiences covered in this section call for the elevation of women pastors' voices and standpoints, which can better speak to the various processes associated with dominant gender structure, as well as *listening* by those who have more difficulty seeing processes of gender inequality; this will mark the first step in developing effective allies in the church and working toward organizational change.

Keys to Creating Allies

All of the congregations in the study sought to cultivate cultures of openness and learning. Most often congregants' willingness to be open and challenged by new ideas proved apparent in their overall approaches to biblical Scripture. None of the congregations in the study approached Scripture as a literal or inerrant text overall; most congregants maintained that the Bible was a sacred text with historical, cultural, economic, and sociopolitical underpinnings and should be approached thematically rather than literally. This approach to biblical Scripture allowed for more opportunities to think critically and call into question dominant interpretations of the Bible that were exclusionary to particular groups. Moreover, this approach offered congregants opportunities to practice being uncomfortable with *not knowing* and lean into a process of reflecting and learning. To varying degrees, the common congregational values of openness, questioning, and learning resulted in a higher potential of openness about social justice issues as well. Associate pastor Meg describes how this culture of openness manifests in her congregation.

> Yes, but I think that part of it is—it's who this church is and they don't come to us and say, "We are unsure about this or we don't know about this, so you have to stop." We don't have that kind of relationship with our church, which is really wonderful. I think because we are surrounded by so many teachers and people who think further that they feel like they can challenge us and we feel like we can challenge them back, and that's part of our relationship together, which is really nice because there are some congregations where you couldn't keep pushing stuff. You would just have to stop or you would be fired. But this is not one of those.

Meg communicates that openness and challenging the status quo were key parts of the ethos of their congregation. Meg's experiences as a woman in Baptist culture played a part in propelling her toward addressing issues of social justice in and through her congregation. Additionally, Meg worked alongside senior pastor Kyle, who was also deeply committed to social justice initiatives. Kyle indicated that his mother felt called to be a Baptist pastor when she was in college, but at the time there were no pathways for women to become pastors in Baptist life. She put off her calling for 40 years and finally became a pastor in the Methodist denomination. Being an intimate observer of his mother's unequal experience in relation to her calling contributed greatly to his commitment to gender equality and social justice overall. Kyle and Meg alongside their congregants continued cultivating a culture of openness and taking the lead among other congregations in acting on important issues of inequality, injustice, and exclusion.

With the exception of Kyle and Meg's church, the most open congregations in the study proved to be those led by women senior pastors. In some cases, this culture of openness had been established by socially conscious male pastors during the civil rights movement as many of the then Southern Baptist churches split on the issue of racial segregation. The older churches in this study were those who supported racial integration and, therefore, had at least some history of being social justice oriented. A couple of the female-led congregations began ordaining women in the 1970s; one female-led congregation ordained a lesbian minister in the early 1980s. These types of congregational values were likely influential in these congregations being among the first in Baptist life to hire women senior pastors.

The extent to which congregations welcomed the discomfort of new ideas and tugs toward progress often manifested in conversations about gender-inclusive language when referring to God. No congregation in the study was organizationally opposed to referring to God with gender-neutral or feminine pronouns, but there seemed to be more pockets of resistance in male-led congregations. Some congregants perceived the practice of gender-inclusive language when referring to God as simply a perfunctory act of political correctness that seemed to not hold very much meaning in the big scheme of things. Others found having to think about how they referred to God to be *annoying* or *uncomfortable*. Some congregants stated that they just felt more comfortable with the language they were taught when they were younger because it was familiar. These perspectives failed to take into account those who consistently feel uncomfortable when they feel excluded by the language typically used to refer to God and, as such, reinforces a dominant gender structure. Through examples like these, I found that congregants' ability to be uncomfortable served as a fair measure of their ability to let go of their established privileges and serve as committed allies in social justice issues.

Female-led congregations overall seemed more open to discomfort and critiquing language typically used when referring to God. While not explicitly related to gender, one congregant at Sophie's church critiqued the notion of referring to God as "King" or "Lord," stating that these terms reinforce notions of antiquated monarchies or hierarchies. Another congregant argued that God encompasses both masculinity *and* femininity and, therefore, it seems more accurate to use both masculine and feminine pronouns when referring to God. A different congregant explained that referring to God as *she* or *mother* was liberating because she had had an abusive father. Some congregants took this notion a step forward by stating we should not use any gender-specific language when referring to God in order to be inclusive toward gender-nonconforming individuals. In one of my last conversations of this study, I asked Lily, a senior pastor who identified as a lesbian, if she understood the purpose of gender-inclusive language when referring to God as simply a politically correct rule. Lily responded, "No, not at all. Words cast the vision for what we hope to be and to become." Lily's standpoint better equipped her to understand the ways in which words serve as the building blocks for creating a more inclusive and equitable future; equitable and inclusive words play a part in disrupting a current order in pursuit of a new, more equitable one. Moreover, she recognized that being politically correct was not simply about hurting people's feelings, but rather about disrupting an inequitable power structure and reformulating language in a way that lays a foundation for a more inclusive, equitable world.

When referring to gender-inclusive language, almost all congregants in female-led congregations admitted that although they intellectually valued this approach to inclusion, they at first felt a little uncomfortable with the notion of referring to God in the feminine or as gender neutral. Despite these feelings, these congregants leaned into the discomfort until it no longer felt uncomfortable. I found this type of commitment key in cultivating allies in the pursuit of equality and, therefore, vital to undoing gender in congregations.

Steps Toward Change

- Work as a congregation to develop clearer understandings of the term *feminism*. Feminism comes in a variety of forms. Reflect on the specific components of feminism you find important. Reflect on issues you have with feminism and why you hold these issues.
- Listen to those who are more oppressed and marginalized than you; they are often able to see and understand oppressive systems more clearly.
- Plan and facilitate initiatives and education opportunities related to issues of sexism, gender inequality, and feminism.
- Hire a social worker qualified in leading and guiding you in all of these efforts.
- Social work educators: Integrate feminist perspectives and gender frames of analyses into educational curriculum.

Discussion Questions

- What is the argument behind standpoint theory? What are the implications of standpoint theory?
- What does feminism mean to you? What are some established definitions of feminism? What are previous missteps feminist movements have made in relation to queer and black feminisms?
- In what ways has the church shaped your understanding of feminism? What types of feminism have you observed in the church?
- There are dozens of versions of feminism. What type of feminist are you? (No, this is not a question only directed at women.)
- In what ways is progress toward gender equality opposed or resisted in dominant society? Why so?
- What types of organizational initiatives would be helpful in understanding and addressing issues of sexism and gender inequality?
- Do you understand women to be risk averse? Why? Identify a research study that speaks to this notion. Identify a research study that challenges this notion.

- Explain the concept of "undoing gender." What are ways gender is being undone and reimagined in more equitable ways in your world? Church? Classroom? Workplace? Family?
- Explain why words are important in changing gender structure.

Supplemental Readings

Collins, Patricia Hill. 2004. Feminist standpoint theory revisited": Where's the power?. In S. Harding (Ed.), *The feminist standpoint theory reader: Intellectual and political controversies*. p. 247. New York: Routledge.

Hartsock, Nancy C. 2019. *The feminist standpoint revisited, and other essays*. New York: Routledge.

Deutsch, F. M. 2007. Undoing gender. *Gender & Society, 21*(1), 106–127.

Djupe, Paul A., and Gilbert, Christopher P. 2002. The political voice of clergy. *The Journal of Politics, 64*(2), 596–609.

Knoll, Benjamin R., and Bolin, Cammie J. 2018. *She preached the word: Women's ordination in modern America*. Oxford University Press.

Maslach, C., and Jackson, S. E. 1981. The measurement of experienced burnout. *Journal of Organization Behavior, 2*(2), 99–113.

Nelson, Julie A. 2015. Are women really more risk-averse than men? A re-analysis of the literature using expanded methods. *Journal of Economic Surveys, 29*(3), 566–585.

Redfern, Catherine, and Aune, Kristin. 2010. *Reclaiming the F word: The new feminist movement*. London: Zed.

Solnit, Rebecca. 2014. *Men explain things to me*. Boston: Haymarket Books.

Stewart-Thomas, Michelle. 2010. Gendered congregations, gendered service: The impact of clergy gender on congregational social service participation. *Gender, Work & Organization, 17*(4), 406–432.

Conclusion

When people are committed to gender equality, what gets in their way of achieving it? Why do *well-intentioned* people reinforce sexist outcomes? In a country with at least some workplace equity laws in place and the vast majority of residents opposed to sexism, why do sexist outcomes persist? These questions are being asked in various workplaces, organizations, and institutions across the world with responses emerging in the form of diversity, equity, and inclusion initiatives, which often result in varying degrees of meaningful change. Thirty years ago, the Cooperative Baptist Fellowship (CBF) formed in large part to support women's equal leadership in the church; today Baptist women are enrolling in seminaries in rates almost equal to men, yet women pastors are leading only about 5% of CBF-affiliated congregations. This study critically examines the underlying organizational processes that contribute to the vast underrepresentation of women in top leadership positions within CBF-affiliated congregations. While the findings of this work cannot be generalized and assumed about other workplaces, organizations, or even other religious entities, my hope is that this work provides a critical lens for identifying and addressing implicitly gendered processes that reinforce structural sexism in other settings which maintain goals of equity and inclusion. Moreover, I intend for this book to serve as a way to initiate and inform conversations related to sexism, gender, and gender inequality as well as those aimed at creating methods of meaningful organizational change.

One key takeaway of this study proves to be that organizational efforts to understand and address sexism must extend well beyond simply enacting equitable policies (or establishing equitable theologies) and the good intentions of organizational actors. In fact, all of the congregations in this study had established inclusive theology in relation to gender and were filled with well-intentioned people who valued gender equality. Rather, gender inequality must be understood as embedded at every level of the organization, including policies, culture, symbols and images, division of labor, interactions, organizational logic, bodies, and individual internalizations, in ways that are mutually reinforcing and most often negatively impact women professionals and leaders. Moreover, organizations are intrinsically linked to and constrained by the unequal gender structure of broader society; organizations contribute to dominant gender structure and are consequences of the dominant gender structure (whether it be supporting it, resisting it, or both). Each chapter of this book draws on empirical data to

Preacher Woman. Katie Lauve-Moon, Oxford University Press (2021). © Oxford University Press.
DOI: 10.1093/oso/9780197527542.003.0009

illustrate specifically how these gendered processes are mutually reinforced in the context of CBF-affiliated congregations and in relation to broader society, thereby resulting in inequitable outcomes between men and women.

The chapters of this book demonstrate how gendered organizational processes mutually reinforce women's underrepresentation in top pastoral positions within CBF-affiliated congregations. Chapter 1 illustrates how the position of senior pastor conflates with leadership and authority and, therefore, is inherently masculinized despite some feminized pastoral expectations. This means that if congregants assume essential gender differences between men (e.g., masculinity) and women (e.g., femininity) beyond anatomy, then women will be less likely to secure these positions. Therefore, like other dominant masculinized images of leadership in dominant society, these normative masculine images of pastor function as a hurdle for women pursuing these positions despite maintaining inclusive theology. Chapter 2 shows how women ministers face gendered barriers on their professional paths from childhood to adolescence to college to seminary to securing pastoral positions and after. Gendered hurdles such as exclusionary theology or conservative interpretations of Scripture; negative or nonaffirming interactions with trusted family members, friends, and religious leaders; and the lack of women role models and mentors are *influenced by* established masculinized images of pastors and *further reinforce* these images and expectations. Moreover, these gendered hurdles influence women pastors' confidence levels in relation to their callings and (in some cases) delay their professional development, thereby resulting in *indirect* career paths. Additionally, men's complicit participation or employment at more conservative churches in order to gain professional experience further bolsters a sexist gender structure in Baptist life and provides an additional advantage on the pastoral job market.

Chapter 3 demonstrates how the gendered career trajectories exhibited in Chapter 2 produce negative consequences for women ministers on the job market *despite* congregants' intentions of equality in the hiring processes. Congregants' preferred hiring criteria, which were understood as *gender-neutral*, often maintained pre-existing inequitable gendered processes rather than eradicate sexism. For instance, most congregants preferred for senior pastor applicants to have previous senior pastor experience; this proved to be an advantageous criterion for male applicants who capitalized on the opportunities to serve in senior pastor roles that were offered to them even before they graduated seminary by more conservative churches that barred women from the pulpit. Additionally, congregants preferred a more direct career trajectory toward the position of senior pastor (e.g., youth pastor to associate pastor to senior pastor); women who demonstrated resourcefulness by pursuing alternative or nontraditional forms of ministry that proved more readily available to women than other more traditional positions were sometimes perceived as indecisive or lacking clarity in relation to their career goals and, therefore, penalized in the hiring process. Finally, most congregations preferred senior pastors in their thirties and forties; some women had aged out by the time they connected with inclusive theology that affirmed their callings and developed pastoral skills, thereby reinforcing unequal hiring outcomes between men and women pastors.

Moreover, Chapter 3 illustrates how previous gendered experiences in Baptist life (e.g., exclusionary theology, lack of exposure to women pastors or leaders more generally) influence hiring committees' (un)conscious gender biases during the hiring processes. While every congregant cognitively affirmed women's leadership in the church, it still *didn't feel right* for some congregants as they engaged women ministers. Additionally, while all congregants supported the concept of gender equality, many failed to recognize how their assumptions of essential gendered personality differences between men and women further reinforce an inequitable gender structure and men's advantage on the pastoral job market. In other words, if hiring committee members assume hegemonic masculinity (e.g., rationality, assertiveness, strength, leadership) to be the exclusive qualities of men, then only the *exceptional* women (if any) would be considered capable of effectively engaging the traditionally masculinized role of pastor, which is intertwined with expectations of authority and leadership. Such gendered assumptions do not merely form a gender structure of difference; they inherently reinforce a hierarchical gender structure by which men are assumed to possess the preferred qualities of masculinity that are most associated with positions of status and power.

Chapter 4 draws attention to the regulation of women pastors' bodies (including weight) and reveals how congregants' pre-existing images of the ideal senior pastor prove incongruent with women's bodies (e.g., voice, stature) and, therefore, congregants perceived women's bodies as incongruent with pastoral positions holding the most authority and power. Chapter 4 also highlights women's double bind as they engage the masculinized role of pastor. Congregants expected women to simultaneously conceal their femininity (including their feminine bodies) in order to maintain their authority and professionalism, which are conflated with masculinity, as pastors *and* accentuate their femininity in order to effectively fulfill dominant expectations of womanhood; these dual, conflicting gender expectations resulted in a double bind for women pastors to constantly negotiate *in addition* to their other official job duties. Male pastors rarely faced dual expectations in relation to their bodies or attire because normative male bodies and menswear are consistent with established images of senior pastors and, therefore, authority, leadership, and professionalism. This chapter also showed how women pastors who accentuated their femininity were consistently sexualized by male congregants as they engaged leadership tasks, thereby reinforcing dominant conceptions of female bodies as objects to be gazed upon and undermining the authority of women's pastoral positions; in these ways, normative images of pastors in Baptist life are reinforced rather than disrupted.

Chapter 5 presents the dual congregational expectations women pastors face in relation to their pastoral responsibilities at work and how they go about being a *wife* and *mother*, commonly referred to as the *second shift*.[1] Women pastors are often expected to take on the lion's share of household and childcare responsibilities. Therefore, congregants assume that they are pulled more between home and work than men, thus resulting in congregants doubting or being surprised by women's pastors' ability to *do it all*; this type of gendered assumption further bolsters images of the ideal pastor as a man with a wife at home caring for his children and taking care of household responsibilities. Chapter 5 also demonstrates the traditional role of *pastor's wife* and how some congregants implicitly assume that the work of pastors will be complemented by the unpaid work of their spouses. Pastors' wives typically face more congregational expectations than pastors' husbands in relation to this unpaid role, often leaving women pastors in heteronormative relationships to pick up some of the traditional pastor's wife responsibilities in addition to their own responsibilities both at home and work; I refer to this phenomenon as the "third shift." Congregational expectations of women pastors to fulfill their official job responsibilities at work *and* meet expectations of hegemonic femininity by effectively performing the majority (if not the entirety) of the second and third shifts presents an additional set of criteria not typically faced by male pastors, increases women pastors' potential for burnout, and further contributes to a sexist gender structure in Baptist life.

Chapter 6 focuses on the relationship between feminization and devaluation in the context of church work. In particular, it illustrates how more feminized church positions like children's pastors, office assistants, and office managers are often constrained by assumed subordinate characteristics of these positions; this chapter demonstrates how women are overrepresented in these feminized church positions, which are typically more overworked, underpaid, and underresourced than other pastoral positions. Furthermore, the role of children's pastor, overwhelmingly held by women, proved to be the only pastoral position not described by congregants as encompassing some element of leadership despite leading children, parents, and volunteers on a recurring basis. Chapter 6 also shows how relatively more masculinized positions like associate or senior pastor are perceived as more feminine when occupied by a woman and, therefore, subsequently carry less monetary status and overall value. For instance, sometimes women associate pastors are tasked with coordinating the children's ministry, which includes responsibilities that were nonexistent in the job description of the previous male associate pastor. Even in the cases when women associate pastors make the same salaries as male associate pastors, these additional job responsibilities decrease the value of their work compared to their male counterparts. The devaluing of feminized church positions and masculinized positions when occupied by women further contributes to an unequal gender structure by which people often disassociate leadership and professional skills from femininity, thereby diminishing its value and reinforcing the gender inequality.

Finally, Chapter 7 presents instances in which fellow church staff members fail to fully see or understand the effects of normative gender structure and, therefore, often simultaneously function as allies *as well as* additional hurdles faced by women ministers in Baptist life. For instance, women pastors' male colleagues fail to see the importance of being intentional about offering professional development opportunities to women and remain unaware of how few opportunities women preachers receive to develop their professional skills. This chapter also examines the particular standpoint of women pastors and how their experiences of exclusion and marginalization inform their social justice–oriented and riskier approaches to their jobs as compared to men pastors. While these approaches are often evaluated positively by social justice–minded congregants, some congregants described women pastors' leadership approaches as "agenda driven" or "biased." Some women ministers feared being labeled a *feminist* because of the stigma that this word often carries, particularly within religious circles. Consequently, very few congregational initiatives were directly aimed at eradicating sexism or gender inequality when compared to the extent to which churches sought to address issues of racism or homophobia. Silencing women pastors through the constructed stigma of feminism deters congregational efforts of gender equality and further reinforces sexism.

The multitude of gendered organizational processes presented in the chapters of this book effectively demonstrate how sexism manifests on the individual, interactional, organizational, and societal levels in ways that are mutually reinforcing. Therefore, sexism must be actively addressed at all of these levels in order for congregations (and other workplaces) to move closer to their goals of gender equality; addressing only one piece of the structure (e.g., biblical interpretation) fails to eradicate sexism. Figure C.1 provides a comprehensive visual of gender as a *social structure* within CBF-affiliate congregations where women face considerably more gendered barriers. It is important to note here the image below is not a neutral path in the case of men pastors. In fact, many of the hurdles women face on their professional paths (e.g., feminine voice and stature, theology exclusive of women's leadership, lack of female role models, the second and third shifts) most often work to men's advantage (e.g., masculine voice and stature, theology inclusive of male leadership, abundance of male role models and mentors, low or no expectations related to the second and third shifts). In other words, oppression is not positioned opposite of neutrality; it is positioned opposite of power, privilege, and advantage. Oppression does not exist without privilege. As

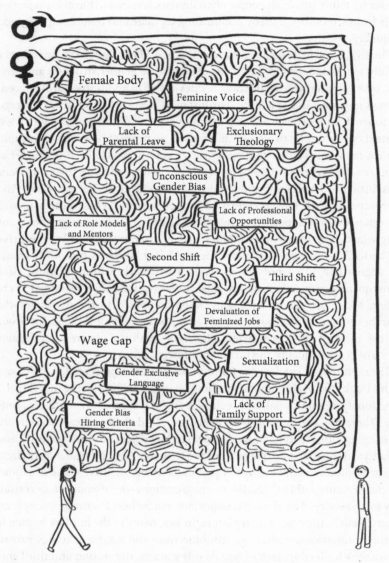

Figure C.1 Where ya been?: The Stained Glass Labyrinth

Courtesy of Dr. Amanda Wilson Harper. Image adapted from "What Took You So Long?" by Jumanah Zabaneh. Retrieved from https://twitter.com/j_zabaneh/status/1236530168505737217

demonstrated in Figure C.1, I build on Eagly and Carli's conceptual framework of a labyrinth and refer to women's path to the pulpit as the *stained-glass labyrinth* because women pastors' career trajectory includes numerous reinforcing hurdles, not simply one as suggested by the notion of the *stained-glass ceiling*.[2] I hope that future research applies this frame to analyze different types of gendered barriers (e.g., sexual harassment) in similar types of religious organizations or other types of workplaces.

It is also important to note that had the sample been more diverse, each side of the image would likely include considerably more barriers at the intersections of race, sexuality, gender identity, nationality, and/or able-bodiedness. For example, a black woman pastor seeking a job in the same context would likely face structural race hurdles in addition to gender hurdles. Likewise, a queer white male would likely be required to maneuver through considerably more barriers in the pursuit of pastoral positions than a cisgender, white, man in a heteronormative relationship. My hope is that future research builds on this study to identify the racialized and sexualized processes persisting in moderate-liberal congregations, particularly with a more diverse demographic composition, and how these organizational processes reinforce structural inequalities.

The overall findings of this project bring forth a few common misconceptions that stem from the lack of knowledge about how gender functions as a social structure. Some congregants conflated individual barriers and structural barriers. For example, losing a parent at an early age or dealing with clinical depression are individual adversities that any given human may unfortunately face over the life course. These types of challenges may certainly present situation-specific hurdles that make it more difficult to achieve professional goals. However, these types of adversities can potentially impact all people regardless of sex, race, economic status, sexuality or sexual orientation, gender identity, nationality, age, or physical ability. In other words, these kinds of hurdles do not *directly* function as components of a larger unequal power structure systematically impacting large groups of people with similar characteristics. Certainly, a man who lost a loved one while in seminary will struggle to stay on track in his pursuit of a senior pastor position; he may even put his professional goals on hold for a while, thereby delaying his career trajectory. However, the barriers he faces will be individual rather than structural; these barriers are not related to his identity. Meanwhile, a woman in the exact same situation will face similar personal barriers *in addition* to those resultant of her sex and an unequal gender structure.

Similar misunderstandings of gender structure emerged, for example, in a conversation about problematic words that are typically used when women embody masculinity (e.g., *bitch* when a woman is assertive; *slut* when a woman initiates sex outside of marriage). One male pastor expressed concerns about similar derogatory words being used when referring to men (e.g., *dick* when a man is arrogant or too authoritative). In this conversation, the pastor positioned the issue as one simply related to *disrespectful* language rather an unequal gender structure. In other words, when the aforementioned derogatory words are used when referring to women pastors, this language reinforces a larger gender structure by which women are systematically disadvantaged as they pursue positions of leadership and authority in the church (which require being assertive, for example). However, when men are referred to as *dicks*, it does not reinforce a larger gender structure by which men are socially, politically, or economically disenfranchised on the basis of sex. Here, this pastor failed to see the structural significance of being *politically correct* or the ways language can undergird and reinforce a larger unequal power structure. Instead, this pastor understood being politically correct as simply about being respectful or not hurting people's feelings or being unfair to individual personalities without seeing the larger implications of language as part of gender structure that most often disadvantages women in relation to power, resources, and status.

While the dominant gender structure in Baptist life (as well as larger society) often reinforces men's ascendance into positions of power and creates barriers for women, it is vital to acknowledge the ways in which this structure negatively impacts men. Some findings suggested that male pastors received messages of apprehension from family in their pursuit of pastoral ministry largely due to the lower economic status of the pastoral ministry when compared to more masculinized and higher paying fields like law, business, medicine, or engineering. Ultimately societal pressure for men to be masculine propels them toward positions of power and leadership. In this case, the critique is that men should pursue *more* powerful and economically secure positions. However, the lack of family support faced by women pastors was the critique of women pursuing positions with *too much* power and authority; as the dominant expectations of femininity are to support and care for others. There is a structural and hierarchical difference between these two gendered phenomena, but this does not mean men are not negatively impacted on more individual levels. Although not represented in this sample, the lack of familial support faced by men may contribute to their internal conflict when deciding whether or not becoming a pastor actually meets dominant expectations of masculinity, that is, securing a high-paying job that can support a family. Traditional expectations of masculinity are often characterized by phrases like "Man up!" because power is conflated with masculinity and masculinity is expected of men. These types of expectations position femininity and women at the lower end of the power structure in relationships, workplaces, and so on and *also* create an apparatus by which men are expected to be tough and powerful. While the position of senior pastor is masculinized, societal gender structures may influence or pressure men to pursue even more masculine positions so as to not appear weak or powerless in the context of broader society. Moreover, dominant expectations of masculinity often prohibit men from being emotional, sharing their feelings (which are so-cially constructed as feminine and weaker than thoughts), and communicating when they need help. Some research has even connected such expectations of masculinity with increased rates of suicide among white men.[3] These are im-portant issues that should be considered as congregations and other workplaces begin unpacking the concept of gender structure and reconstructing gender to-ward organizational equity and health.

Some pastors, church staff, and congregants underestimated the pervasiveness of gender structure in the context of these congregations. For instance, the pastor who stated, "Gender is something we don't address a lot, because that's something that we would say we've dealt with and we want gender equality especially in the church," provides the most succinct example of this pattern. Like others in the study, this pastor assumes that a completely equal organizational structure exists once theological and organizational rules shift from exclusionary to inclusive of women's leadership in the church. Moreover, this perspective assumes that not engaging in feminist initiatives, presumed to advantage women, presents a neu-tral stance when actually it reinforces a gender structure that advantages mas-culinity and men. While theology and biblical interpretation certainly proves to be the most rigid gendered barrier in churches,[4] this book illustrates that there are multiple other gendered processes constantly interacting and reinforcing each other in ways that deter women's advancement to pastoral positions. In other words, addressing one piece of the structure does not eradicate sexism. Moreover, this pastor fails to acknowledge the ways in which congregants may be impacted by an unequal gender structure *outside* of the church—in their fam-ilies, workplaces, classrooms, playgrounds, and so forth—and ways the church may act as an advocate on behalf of women congregants. Certainly, this study presents countless examples of congregants and church staff resisting dominant gender structure and progressing their congregations toward gender equality as evident by the adoption of inclusive theologies, the hiring of women in senior and associate pastor positions, relatively high rates of paid family leave policies, equal gender representation on pastoral search committees, and involvement in social justice initiatives. It also demonstrates the ways in which some women pastors have adopted effective strategies for clearing the gendered hurdles they face in their congregations. Despite all of this good work (and more), there re-mains a steady stream of inequitable gendered processes to be addressed within these congregations and society as a whole.

Seeing gender structure proves key to understanding and changing it for the purpose of gender equity. Gender structure proves difficult to see for those who do not experience it as discriminatory or oppressive. And some who *are* nega-tively impacted by gender structure may even accept it as normative or natural and never understand its inequitable effects on their lives; hence, its hegemonic significance. For those who are advantaged by dominant gender structure, it may be experienced as invisible because it may never actually create discomfort in their lives. Others may acknowledge certain forms of sexism but have yet to discover the various ways it manifests. For instance, some may acknowledge the injustice of sexist theology but fail to see or ignore how assuming fixed differences between men and women (beyond anatomy) inherently leads to inequality. Still some may see the injustice of structural sexism but fail to act because it may mean giving up their portion of power, security, and comfort. And, finally, there are those who explicitly oppose any resistance to the current gender structure and actively seek to reinforce it. The extent to which individuals *see* gender structure may vary by context or even by interaction; it is important to understand that we all exist on an infinite spectrum of seeing and knowing so that the work of structural change is ongoing.

Given that gender structure can be difficult to see and understand, it is important that congregations as well as other workplaces and organizations committed to gender equality prioritize *listening* as part of organizational culture. Listening is especially important for those who cannot *see* gender structure comprehensively yet. As the researcher of this study, I was often asked by pastors and congregants about the gendered themes that were emerging in congregations. In fact, after I completed data collection in a couple of congregations, I presented on the concepts of gender and gender structure as well as some general themes that were emerging in other congregations. After one of these presentations, a male senior pastor and I had a conversation about my presentation and study findings. After giving him more information about how sexism often manifests, he responded, "Have you ever considered that sometimes a cigar is just a cigar?" With this nod to Freud, this pastor was suggesting that perhaps there was no meaning behind the gendered processes I was identifying; perhaps the inequitable outcomes that persisted between men and women did not call for so complex of an explanation or analysis. I, who had received graduate training on the subject from some of the leading experts in the field, noted the gendered phenomenon of *mansplaining* that had occurred before me and responded, "Can I quote you on that?" A different male senior pastor began offering suggestions on ways I could make my study more compelling despite that he had never been formerly educated in sociology or gender studies or had been particularly involved in gender equality initiatives. I found interactions like these interesting because both of these pastors offered at least a couple meaningful examples of how they had worked toward gender equality in the past. However, they both missed (or failed to trust) how my academic knowledge as a gender researcher and my social positionality as a woman equipped me to analyze gender structure critically; they also missed how their efforts to centralize their own (uninformed) perspectives on the issue further reinforced a gender structure which centralizes the perspectives of men and diminishes the perspectives of women. For those who cannot see (usually those advantaged by the power structure), it is important to listen to those who can see. This is the first meaningful step toward change.

The process of seeing gender structure is ongoing because gender is constantly changing. The components of gender structure vary by time and place and, therefore, an organizational commitment to pursuing gender equality must be ongoing and indefinite. This type of commitment requires *openness* and *intentionality.* Most of the congregations in this study generally practiced openness and maintained postures of learning. I found that since all of the congregations *did not* approach biblical Scripture as a literal or inerrant text, it offered congregants more opportunities to think critically and creatively about new concepts and ideas. Moreover, these congregations were more often given tools to feel comfortable in the discomfort of not knowing it all or fully understanding. It is likely this very spirit of openness that led them to participating in this study and will carry them closer to reaching their goals of addressing issues of gender and inequality in their congregations. The primary intent of this book is to capitalize on these types of cultures of openness and provide pastors and churchgoers (and leaders of other workplaces) with helpful tools for identifying inequitable gender processes in their organizations.

The unequal gender structure that persists in Baptist life does not exist in a vacuum. This organizational gender structure is both a *component of* and a *product of* a larger gender structure that exists on the societal level; the two are intrinsically linked and mutually reinforcing. As mentioned in previous chapters, women represent only about a fourth of US Congressional positions and only 7% of Fortune 500 company chief executive officers. Even in the field of education in the United States, which is predominately female, only 67.7% of education administrators are women.[5] Moreover, women remain underrepresented in masculinized professions such as those of architects and engineers (15.7), lawyers (36.4), physicians and surgeons (40.8), and in math and computer occupations (25.8).[6] On a global scale, women are the world leaders of only 15 of 146 nations; eight current women world leaders are their country's first. Moreover, of 153 countries, the United States ranks 53rd in the Global Gender Gap Index, which examines women's economic participation and opportunity, educational attainment, health and survival, and political empowerment.[7] In order for congregations and other workplaces to effectively reach organizational goals of eradicating sexism and gender inequality, it is vital to recognize how organizational gendered processes are mutually reinforcing in ways that produce (or resist) inequitable outcomes between men and women *as well as* ways in which these organizations reinforce (or resist) a large gender structure on the societal level. Moderate-progressive congregations are morally situated to disrupt systems of sexism not only within the congregations themselves (internal ministry) but in their surrounding communities and society at large (external ministry); this type of disruption requires a critical analysis of gender structure, the undoing of gender structure, and redoing of gender structure in more equitable ways. Moreover, it requires the centralization of outcomes over *good intentions*. Each chapter presents detailed steps toward change related to the findings of the specific chapter. The following provides a summary of these steps for congregations and other organizations seeking gender equality.

- Put intentions aside. What are the organizational *outcomes* in relation to gender and other inequalities?
- Reflect on your own understandings of gender and who/what has influenced your conceptions of gender. Do you implicitly understand men and women to be essentially different? Do you implicitly value masculinity more than femininity? How do your understandings of gender influence your conceptions of *ideal leaders*? Consider further how these types of assumptions typically lead to inequitable outcomes between men and women.
- Attend unconscious bias trainings and workshops as an organization. It is particularly important that congregants in Baptist congregations engage in these types of educational opportunities since congregants hold a lot of power in the hiring of new church staff.
- Keep the conversation going after the trainings. Create process groups or book clubs for continued discussion related to the concept of gender and inequality. Continue to cultivate cultures of openness. Practice active listening. If you are in a more advantageous position in relation to gender structure, take a step back. Allow yourself to be led by others and figure out ways to support and partner.
- Critically examine organizational documents and protocols. For instance, even though job descriptions, hiring practices, and job evaluations may not be explicitly sexist, how may they implicitly produce sexist outcomes or other outcomes of inequality? Employ strategies for increasing diversity in the applicant pool and equity in the selection process. Create a committee charged with these types of tasks.
- Examine the more feminized positions in the organization. Who is doing the most invisible and underappreciated work? Is it adequately compensated and resourced?
- Practice applying your critical lens to gendered phenomena in broader society. How may the church work to address issues of gender inequality in broader society? What types of initiatives can it facilitate or be a part

of? How can the church design a community-driven ministry directed at achieving gender equality in the world?

- Hire a social worker to organize, facilitate, and lead all of the above! (But try not to fall into the trap of overworking and underpaying this feminized position.)
- For social work educators, include the critical theoretical content presented in the chapters of this book in social work curricula, particularly macro courses.

Most importantly, the aforementioned approaches to achieving organizational gender equality put the onus of change on the organization itself rather than on women pastors. Instead of exclusively expecting women pastors to adopt strategies to maneuver better through organizational gendered barriers and resist sexism, this work calls on organizations to change the gender structure itself so that women no longer have to clear unequal and sizeable hurdles on their paths to pastoral positions and in their positions as pastors. For it is only through structural change that gender equality can be fully realized.

A Note to the Readers

Pastors, Congregants, and Church Staff. One intention of this book is that church staff and congregants use it as a tool for working toward organizational gender equality. Every religious congregation is different. You may find gendered processes in your congregation that are very similar to the ones highlighted in this book. Or you may utilize the findings of this book as a guide for discovering completely different gendered phenomena in your church. The hope is that you will read, reflect, and discuss together as a congregation and develop strategies for organizational change.

Employees and Leaders in Other Workplaces and Organizations. This book ultimately provides insights into how sexism persists in workplaces despite the good intentions of organizational actors and the established organizational goals of gender equality. While the majority of workplaces do not include a religious component like the ones in this study, most workplaces with policies of diversity, equity, and inclusion are operating on a set of values that function similarly to the theological values of religious workplaces. Moreover, the underrepresentation of women pastors in leadership positions in the church parallels similar gendered trends in other fields such as politics, medicine, academia, law, engineering, technology, teaching, social work, and so on. This book provides a comprehensive look at how sexism may persist in implicit ways at all levels of the organization and presents a critical framework for identifying other types of gendered processes in workplaces of different fields.

Seminary Faculty and Religious Scholars. It is important that *all* seminarians regardless of sex understand the impact of gender structure within their congregations so that they can lead their congregations toward more equitable gender cultures and outcomes. This book provides important insights into various ways sexism manifests in the context of religious congregations. Moreover, this overview of gender structure may serve as a hermeneutical tool for identifying the role of dominant gender structure within biblical Scripture.

Sociologists of Gender, Work, and Religion. This book is particularly relevant to sociologists and gender scholars teaching and researching in the areas of gender inequality in labor, the workplace, and organizations. It offers one of the first sociological analyses of churches as gendered workplaces and demonstrates how even organizations comprised of actors with good intentions reinforce inequitable outcomes between women and men. This book could also serve as a textbook for gender courses because it adds new perspectives to the existing discourse on gendered organizations and work (e.g., the third shift) and covers key concepts such as hegemonic masculinities and femininities, complicit masculinities, pariah femininities, gendered socialization, gendered bodies, gender structure, feminization and devaluation of women's work, the glass ceiling, the glass escalator, the body and leadership, the second shift, and gender culture. Additionally, this book presents analyses on all five of Acker's organizational gendered processes, offering a comprehensive look at gendered organizations.

This book also offers a contribution to the field of sociology of religion as it illustrates the intersection of gendered theology and organizational processes. To date, very few studies examining inequality in religious organizations apply Acker's theoretical frames of gendered organizations. This work lays the groundwork for further research examining ways in which similar patterns play out in other types of religious organizations as well as other workplaces committed to equity and inclusion.

A major limitation of this work is that congregations included in this study were almost exclusively middle-upper class, highly educated, white, straight, and cisgender. It would be important to investigate ways in which some of the gendered patterns highlighted in this book manifest differently at the intersections of race and sexuality. Finally, drawing on Acker's theory of inequality regimes,[8] further research could be conducted investigating the extent to which congregations are racialized and sexualized organizations as well as gendered organizations.

Social Work Faculty & Organizational Social Workers. Social workers are inherently committed to social justice and are trained in creating sustainable models of change. Over the past 20 years, church social work has emerged as a significant area of research and practice. Social work faculty have established

associations, conferences, journals, and graduate programs focusing on social work practice in congregational settings. This book offers insight into ways
church social workers can reach their goals of social justice by creating methods
of change on the organizational level. It also presents theoretical frameworks that
prove relevant to macro social work curricula as well as opportunities to develop
best practices in relation to equity and inclusion initiatives in congregations and
to lead congregations in meeting their established goals of gender equality.

Discussion Questions

- Why is the concept of the stained-glass labyrinth important when considering the experiences of women pastors? More broadly, why is the concept of the labyrinth important when considering women's experiences in
workplaces?
- What is the difference between structural oppression and individual adver-
sity? Why is this distinction important when working toward social justice?
- What is meant by understanding the gendered processes internal and external to organizations as mutually reinforcing?
- Describe the process of undoing gender. What would this logistically
look like in your context? What are initial steps that you can take in your
congregations and workplaces toward undoing gender and eradicating
structural sexism?

Congregational Survey

Part C: Ministerial Roles

Please list 2–3 qualities/characteristics you generally associate with individuals in lead pastor positions:

_____

Please describe qualities or characteristics you value most in a lead pastor.

_____

_____

_____

_____

Please describe qualities or characteristics you <u>would</u> <u>not</u> <u>want</u> <u>in a</u> <u>lead</u> <u>pastor.</u>

_____

_____

_____

_____

Describe your preferred preaching style.

_____

_____

_____

Please list 2–3 personality characteristics or qualities you generally associate with individuals who hold the following church staff positions:

Associate Pastor:	Executive/Administrative Pastor:
Music/Worship Minister:	Missions/Outreach/Community Minister:
Teaching/Education Minister:	Spiritual Formation/Discipleship Minister:
Children's Minister:	Youth Minister:
Student/College Minister:	Older Adults Minister:
Office Manager/Church Administrator:	Church Secretary/Receptionist:

In your opinion, what are your current head pastor's strengths?

_____

_____

_____

_____

In your opinion, what are your current head pastor's limitations?

_____

_____

_____

_____

Do you think there are benefits AND/OR limitations of having co-head pastors?

_____

_____

_____

_____

Notes

Introduction

1. These words were delivered by *Nevertheless She Preached* (NSP) organizer Kyndall Rae Rothaus at the NSP 2017 conference.
2. This call-and-response reading was delivered by NSP organizers Elizabeth Amondi Ligawa and Kyndall Rae Rothaus at the 2017 NSP conference.
3. Rothaus, Kyndall R. 2018, January 16. "Nevertheless She Preached." Retrieved from https://www.workingpreacher.org/craft.aspx?post=5045.
4. Ibid.
5. Durso, P., & Pranato, K. 2015. "State of Women in Baptist Life." *Baptist Women in Ministry.* Retrieved from https://bwim.info/wp-content/uploads/2016/11/SWBL-2015-revised-7-11-16.pdf.
6. Ibid.
7. Chaves, Mark. 2019. *National Congregations Study—1998, 2006, 2012, and 2018–2019.* Ann Arbor, MI: Inter-university Consortium for Political and Social Research. Retrieved December 1, 2020. https://sites.duke.edu/ncsweb/explore-the-data/.
8. U.S. Census Bureau. 2019. "Labor Source Statistics from Current Population Survey: Employed Persons by Detailed Occupation, Sex, Race, and Hispanic or Latino Ethnicity." Retrieved from https://www.bls.gov/cps/cpsaat11.htm.
9. Chaves, 2019. https://sites.duke.edu/ncsweb/explore-the-data/.
10. U.S. Census Bureau, 2019.
11. Williams, Christine L. 1995. *Still a Man's World: Men Who Do Women's Work.* Vol. 1. Berkeley: University of California Press. Williams, Christine L. 2013. "The Glass Escalator, Revisited: Gender Inequality in Neoliberal Times, SWS Feminist Lecturer." *Gender & Society* 27(5):609–29.
12. Purvis, Sally B. 1995. *The Stained-Glass Ceiling: Churches and Their Women Pastors.* Louisville, KY: Westminster John Knox Press.
13. Adams, Jimi. 2007. "Stained Glass Makes the Ceiling Visible: Organizational Opposition to Women in Congregational Leadership." *Gender & Society* 21(1): 80–105.
14. Chaves, Mark. 1999. *Ordaining Women: Culture and Conflict in Religious Organizations.* Cambridge, MA: Harvard University Press.
15. Purvis, 1995.

    Schleifer, Cyrus, & Miller, Amy D. 2017. "Occupational Gender Inequality among American Clergy, 1976–2016: Revisiting the Stained-Glass Ceiling." *Sociology of Religion* 78(4):387–410.

Sullins, Paul. 2000. "The Stained Glass Ceiling: Career Attainment for Women Clergy." *Sociology of Religion* 61(3):243–66.

Chaves, 2019.

16. Nesbitt, Paula D. 1993. "Dual Ordination Tracks: Differential Benefits and Costs for Men and Women Clergy." *Sociology of Religion* 54(1):13–30.

Sullins, 2000.

Purvis, Sally. 1995.

Chang, Patricia M. Y. 1997. "Introduction to Symposium: Female Clergy in the Contemporary Protestant Church: A Current Assessment." *Journal for the Scientific Study of Religion* 36(4):565–73.

Finlay, B. 2003. *Facing the Stained Glass Ceiling: Gender in a Protestant Seminary.* Lanham, MD: University Press of America.

De Gasquet, Béatrice. 2010. "The Barrier and the Stained-Glass Ceiling. Analyzing Female Careers in Religious Organizations." *Sociologie du travail* 52:e22–e39.

17. Chang, 1997.

18. Manville, Julie. 1997. "The Gendered Organization of an Australian Anglican Parish." *Sociology of Religion* 58(1):25–38.

Zikmund, Barbara Brown, Lummis, Adair T., & Chang, Patricia M. Y. 1998. *Clergy Women: An Uphill Calling.* Louisville, KY: Westminster John Knox Press.

Finlay, 2003.

Frame, Marsha Wiggins, & Shehan, Constance L. 2004. "Care for the Caregiver: Clues for the Pastoral Care of Clergywomen." *Pastoral Psychology* 52(5):369–80.

Frame, Marsha Wiggins, & Shehan, Constance L. 2005. "The Relationship between Work and Well-Being in Clergywomen: Implications for Career Counseling." *Journal of Employment Counseling* 42(1):10–19.

Bagilhole, Barbara. 2006. "Not a Glass Ceiling, More a Lead Roof: Experiences of Pioneer Women Priests in the Church of England." *Equal Opportunities International* 25(2):109–25.

19. Smith, Christine A. 2013. *Beyond the Stained Glass Ceiling: Equipping & Encouraging Female Pastors.* Prussia, PA: Judson Press.

Wilkerson, Robyn. 2017. *Shattering the Stained Glass Ceiling: A Coaching Strategy for Women Leaders in Ministry.* Influence Resources.

Lewis, Karoline M. 2016. *She: Five Keys to Unlock the Power of Women in Ministry.* Nashville, TN: Abingdon Press.

20. Lillie, F. R. 1932. "Biological Introduction." Pp. 1-11 in E. Allen (ed.), *Sex and Internal Secretions*, 2nd ed. Baltimore, MD: Williams and Wilkins.

21. Zondek, Bernhard. 1934. "Mass Excretion of Oestrogenic Hormone in the Urine of the Stallion." *Nature* 133(3354), 209–10.

22. Evans, Herbert M. 1939. "Endocrine Glands: Gonads, Pituitary, and Adrenals." *Annual Review of Physiology* 1(1):577–652.

Frank, R. T. 1929. *The Female Sex Hormone.* Baltimore, MD: Charles C. Thomas.

Laqueur, Ernst, Dingemanse, Elisabeth, Hart, PC, & de Jongh, Samuel E. 1927. "Female Sex Hormone in Urine of Men." *Klinische Wochenschrift* 6(1):859.

Parkes, Alan S. 1938. "Terminology of Sex Hormones." *Nature* 141(3557):36.

Siebke, Harald. 1931. "Presence of Androkinin in Female Organism." *Archiv für Gynaekologie* 146:417–62.

23. Phoenix, Charles H., Goy, Robert W., Gerall, Arnold A., & Young, William C. 1959. "Organizing Action of Prenatally Administered Testosterone Propionate on the Tissues Mediating Mating Behavior in the Female Guinea Pig." *Endocrinology* 65(3): 369–82.

24. Phoenix, Charles H., Goy, Robert W., Gerall, Arnold A., & Young, William C. 1959. "Organizing Action of Prenatally Administered Testosterone Propionate on the Tissues Mediating Mating Behavior in the Female Guinea Pig." *Endocrinology* 65(3):369–82.

25. Arnold, Arthur P., & Gorski, Roger A. 1984. "Gonadal Steroid Induction of Structural Sex Differences in the Central Nervous System." *Annual Review of Neuroscience* 7(1):413–42.

Brizendine, Louann. 2006. *The Female Brain*. New York: Broadway Books.

Cahill, Larry. 2003. "Sex-Related Influences on the Neurobiology of Emotionally Influenced Memory." *Annals of the New York Academy of Sciences* 985(1):163–73.

Collaer, Marcia L., & Hines, Melissa. 1995. "Human Behavioral Sex Differences: A Role for Gonadal Hormones During Early Development?" *Psychological Bulletin* 118(1):55.

Cooke, Bradley, Hegstrom, Carol D., Villeneuve, Loic S., & Breedlove, Marc S. 1998. "Sexual Differentiation of the Vertebrate Brain: Principles and Mechanisms." *Frontiers in Neuroendocrinology* 19(4):323–62.

Holterhus, Paul-Martin, Bebermeier, Jan-Hendrik, Werner, Ralf, Demeter, Janos, Richter-Unruh, Annette, Cario, Gunnar, Appari, Mahesh, Siebert, Reiner, Riepe, Felix, & Brooks, James D. 2009. "Disorders of Sex Development Expose Transcriptional Autonomy of Genetic Sex and Androgen-Programmed Hormonal Sex in Human Blood Leukocytes." *BMC Genomics* 10(1):292

Lippa, Richard A. 2005. *Gender, Nature, and Nurture*. Milton Park, UK: Routledge.

26. Jordan-Young, Rebecca M. 2011. *Brain Storm: The Flaws in the Science of Sex Differences*. Cambridge, MA: Harvard University Press.

27. Epstein, Cynthia Fuchs. 1988. *Deceptive Distinctions: Sex, Gender, and the Social Order*. New Haven, CT: Yale University Press.

Fausto-Sterling, Anne. 2000. *Sexing the Body: Gender Politics and the Construction of Sexuality*. New York: Basic Books.

Jordan-Young, 2010.

Oudshoorn, Nelly. 2003. *Beyond the Natural Body: An Archaeology of Sex Hormones*. Abingdon, UK: Routledge

28. Joel, Daphna, Berman, Zohar, Tavor, Ido, Wexler, Nadav, Gaber, Olga, Stein, Yaniv, Shefi, Nisan, Pool, Jared, Urchs, Sebastian, & Margulies, Daniel S. 2015. "Sex Beyond the Genitalia: The Human Brain Mosaic." *Proceedings of the National Academy of Sciences* 112(50):15468–73.

29. See Bem, S. L. 1981. "Gender Schema Theory: A Cognitive Account of Sex Typing." *Psychological Review* 88:354–64.

30. Edwards, Allen L., & Ashworth, Clark D. 1977. "A Replication Study of Item Selection for the Bem Sex Role Inventory." *Applied Psychological Measurement* 1(4):501–507.

    Locksley, Anne, & Colten, Mary Ellen. 1979. "Psychological Androgyny: A Case of Mistaken Identity?" *Journal of Personality and Social Psychology* 37(6):1017.

31. Bem, Sandra Lipsitz. 1981. "Gender Schema Theory: A Cognitive Account of Sex Typing." *Psychological Review* 88(4):354.

    Bem, Sandra L. 1993. *The Lenses of Gender: Transforming the Debate on Sexual Inequality.* New Haven, CT: Yale University Press.

32. Choi, N., Fuqua, D., & Newman, J. 2008. "The Bem Sex-Role Inventory. A Summary Report of 23 Validation Studies." *Educational and Psychological Measurement* 63:872–87.

33. Gill, Sandra, Stockard, Jean, Johnson, Miriam, & Williams, Suzanne. 1987. "Measuring Gender Differences: The Expressive Dimension and Critique of Androgyny Scales." *Sex Roles* 17(7–8):375–400.

34. Thomas, Jerry R., & French, Karen E. 1985. "Gender Differences across Age in Motor Performance: A Meta-Analysis." *Psychological Bulletin* 98(2):260.

    Butterfield, Stephen A., & Loovis, E. Michael. 1993. "Influence of Age, Sex, Balance, and Sport Participation on Development of Throwing by Children in Grades K-8." *Perceptual and Motor Skills* 76(2):459–64.

    Plimpton, Carol E., & Regimbal, Celia. 1992. "Differences in Motor Proficiency According to Gender and Race." *Perceptual and Motor Skills* 74(2):399–402.

    Smoll, Frank L., & Schutz, Robert W. 1990. "Quantifying Gender Differences in Physical Performance: A Developmental Perspective." *Developmental Psychology* 26(3):360.

    Martin, Karin A. 1998. "Becoming a Gendered Body: Practices of Preschools." *American Sociological Review* 63(4):494–511.

35. See Risman, Barbara J. 1998. *Gender Vertigo: American Families in Transition.* New Haven, CT: Yale University Press.

36. See Chodorow, Nancy J. 1999. *The Reproduction of Mothering: Psychoanalysis and the Sociology of Gender.* Berkeley: University of California Press.

37. Martin, Karin A. 1998. "Becoming a Gendered Body: Practices of Preschools." *American Sociological Review* 63(4):494–511.

    Kane, Emily W. 2012. *The Gender Trap: Parents and the Pitfalls of Raising Boys and Girls.* New York City: NYU Press.

38. Martin, 1998.

39. Powlishta, K. K., Sen, M. G., Serbin, L. A., Poulin-Dubois, D., & Eichstedt, J. A. 2001. "From infancy through middle childhood: The role of cognitive and social factors in becoming gendered." Pp. 116–132 in R. K. Unger (ed.), *Handbook of the Psychology of Women and Gender.* Hoboken, NJ: John Wiley & Sons, Inc. Pp. 116–32.

40. Risman, 1998, p. 15.

41. Kane, 2012.

42. Risman, 1999.

43. West, Candace, & Zimmerman, Don H. 1987. "Doing Gender." *Gender & Society* 1(2):125–51.

Butler, Judith. 2006. "Performative Acts and Gender Constitution: An Essay in Phenomenology and Feminist Theory." Pp. 73–83 in *The Routledgefalmer Reader in Gender & Education*. Abingdon, UK: Routledge.

Butler, J. 1999. *Gender Trouble*. New York: Routledge.

44. West, Candace, & Zimmerman, Don H. 1987. "Doing Gender." *Gender & Society* 1(2):127.

45. Lorber, Judith. 1994. *Paradoxes of Gender*: New Haven, CT: Yale University Press.

West & Zimmerman, 1987.

46. Kanter, Rosabeth Moss. 2008. *Men and Women of the Corporation: New Edition*. New York: Basic Books.

47. Acker, Joan. 1990. "Hierarchies, Jobs, Bodies: A Theory of Gendered Organizations." *Gender & Society* 4(2):139–58.

Acker, Joan. 1992. "From Sex Roles to Gendered Institutions." *Contemporary Sociology* 21(5):565–69.

48. Britton, Dana M. 1997. "Gendered Organizational Logic: Policy and Practice in Men's and Women's Prisons." *Gender & Society* 11(6):796–818.

Britton, Dana M. 2003. *At Work in the Iron Cage: The Prison as Gendered Organization*. New York: NYU Press.

49. Acker, 1990, p. 561.

50. Martin, Patricia Yancey. 2004. "Gender as Social Institution." *Social Forces* 82(4): 1249–73.

Lorber, Judith, & Farrell, Susan A. 1991. *The Social Construction of Gender*. Newbury Park, CA: Sage

Lorber, Judith. 1994. *Paradoxes of Gender*. New Haven, CT: Yale University Press.

51. Acker, 1992, p. 567.

52. Britton, 1997.

Wingfield, Adia Harvey. 2009. "Racializing the Glass Escalator: Reconsidering Men's Experiences with Women's Work." *Gender & Society* 23(1):5–26.

Manchester, Colleen Flaherty, Leslie, Lisa M., & Kramer, Amit. 2013. "Is the Clock Still Ticking? An Evaluation of the Consequences of Stopping the Tenure Clock." *ILR Review* 66(1):3–31.

Purcell, David. 2013. "Baseball, Beer, and Bulgari: Examining Cultural Capital and Gender Inequality in a Retail Fashion Corporation." *Journal of Contemporary Ethnography* 42(3):291–319.

Paap, Kris. 2018. *Working Construction: Why White Working-Class Men Put Themselves—and the Labor Movement—in Harm's Way*. Ithaca, NY: Cornell University Press.

53. Irvine, Leslie, & Vermilya, Jenny R. 2010. "Gender Work in a Feminized Profession: The Case of Veterinary Medicine." *Gender & Society* 24(1):56–82.

Kurtz, Don L., Linnemann, Travis, & Williams, L. Susan. 2012. "Reinventing the Matron: The Continued Importance of Gendered Images and Division of Labor in Modern Policing." *Women & Criminal Justice* 22(3):239–63.

54. Snyder, Karrie Ann, & and Green, Adam Isaiah. 2008. "Revisiting the Glass Escalator: The Case of Gender Segregation in a Female Dominated Occupation." *Social Problems* 55(2):271–99.

Leahey, Erin. 2007. "Not by Productivity Alone: How Visibility and Specialization Contribute to Academic Earnings." *American Sociological Review* 72(4):533–61.

Kenney, Sally J. 2000. "Beyond Principals and Agents: Seeing Courts as Organizations by Comparing Référendaires at the European Court of Justice and Law Clerks at the US Supreme Court." *Comparative Political Studies* 33(5):593–625.

Kenney, Sally J. 2004. "Equal Employment Opportunity and Representation: Extending the Frame to Courts." *Social Politics: International Studies in Gender, State & Society* 11(1):86–116.

55. Davies, Karen. 2003. "The Body and Doing Gender: The Relations between Doctors and Nurses in Hospital Work." *Sociology of Health & Illness* 25(7):720–42.

Kelan, Elisabeth K. 2010. "Gender Logic and (Un) Doing Gender at Work." *Gender, Work & Organization* 17(2):174–9

Britton, 1997.

56. Rhoton, Laura A. 2011. "Distancing as a Gendered Barrier: Understanding Women Scientists' Gender Practices." *Gender & Society* 25(6):696–716.

Britton, Dana M., & Williams, Christine L. 1995. " 'Don't Ask, Don't Tell, Don't Pursue': Military Policy and the Construction of Heterosexual Masculinity." *Journal of Homosexuality* 30(1):1–21.

Lester, Jaime. 2008. "Performing Gender in the Workplace: Gender Socialization, Power, and Identity among Women Faculty Members." *Community College Review* 35(4):277–305.

Dellinger, Kirsten, & Williams, Christine L. 1997. "Makeup at Work: Negotiating Appearance Rules in the Workplace." *Gender & Society* 11(2):151–77.

57. Eagly, Alice Hendrickson, Carli, Linda L., Eagly, Alice H., & Carli, Linda Lorene. 2007. *Through the Labyrinth: The Truth About How Women Become Leaders*. Cambridge, MA: Harvard Business Press.

58. Acker, Joan. 2006. "Inequality Regimes: Gender, Class, and Race in Organizations." *Gender & Society* 20(4):441–64.

59. Risman, Barbara J. 2004. "Gender as a Social Structure: Theory Wrestling with Activism." *Gender & Society* 18(4):429–50.

60. Risman, 2004, p. 432.

61. Rosenthal, Lisa, Levy, Sheri R., London, Bonita, Lobel, Marci, & and Bazile, Cartney. 2013. "In Pursuit of the Md: The Impact of Role Models, Identity Compatibility, and Belonging among Undergraduate Women." *Sex Roles* 68(7–8):464–73.

Sealy, Ruth, & Singh, Val. 2006. "Role Models, Work Identity and Senior Women's Career Progression-Why Are Role Models Important?" Pp. E1–E6 in *Academy of Management Proceedings*, Vol. 2006. Briarcliff Manor, NY: Academy of Management.

62. Jolls, Christine, & Sunstein, Cass R. 2006. "The Law of Implicit Bias." *California Law Review* 94:969.

Greenwald, Anthony G., & Krieger, Linda Hamilton. 2006. "Implicit Bias: Scientific Foundations." *California Law Review* 94(4):945–67.

Ridgeway, Cecilia L. 2009. "Framed before We Know It: How Gender Shapes Social Relations." *Gender & Society* 23(2):145–60.

63. Jolls & Sunstein, 2006.

64. Bem, Sandra L. 1993. *The Lenses of Gender: Transforming the Debate on Sexual Inequality.* New Haven, CT: Yale University Press.

65. See Appendix A for Part C of the Congregational Survey, which examines congregants' expectations pertaining to different church staff positions. This is the only portion of the survey that is reported in this book.

Chapter 1

1. Southern Baptist Convention. 2020. "Fast Facts about the SBC." Retrieved from http://www.sbc.net/becomingsouthernbaptist/fastfacts.asp.

2. Southern Baptist Convention. 2012. *Encyclopedia Britannica.* https://www.britannica.com/topic/Southern-Baptist-Convention. Accessed October 24, 2020.

3. Ammerman, Nancy Tatom. 1990. *Baptist Battles: Social Change and Religious Conflict in the Southern Baptist Convention.* New Brunswick, NJ: Rutgers University Press.

4. Ibid., p. 31.

5. Carter, James. 2009. "Losing My Religion for Equality." *The Sydney Morning Herald.* Retrieved from https://www.smh.com.au/politics/federal/losing-my-religion-for-equality-20090714-dk0v.html.

6. Freedman, David. 1983. "Woman, a Power Equal to a Man." *Biblical Archaeology Review* 9:56–58.

7. Ibid.

8. Ammerman, Nancy Tatom. 1990. *Baptist Battles: Social Change and Religious Conflict in the Southern Baptist Convention.* New Brunswick, NJ: Rutgers University Press.

9. Lauve-Moon, K. 2016. "The Case of Dean Diana Garland: Taking a Stand at Southern Baptist Theological Seminary." *Women Leading Change: Case Studies on Women, Gender, and Feminism* 1(2):19.

10. Garland, Diana. Telephone interview with author, December 9, 2013.

   James, R. B., Jackson, B., Shepherd, R., & Showalter, C. 2006. *The Fundamentalist Takeover in the Southern Baptist Convention.* Missouri: Impact Media (pp. 14).

   Steinfels, Peter. 1994. "Baptists Dismiss Seminary Head in Surprise Move." *New York Times.* Retrieved October 24, 2020. https://www.nytimes.com/1994/03/11/us/baptists-dismiss-seminary-head-in-surprise-move.html.

11. Lauve-Moon, 2016, p. 20.

12. Baptist Faith and Message. 2000. In *Report to SBC Convention. Adrian Rogers.* Nashville: SBC. https://bfm.sbc.net/bfm2000/. Retrieved December 7, 2020.

13. Lauve-Moon, 2016, p. 20.

14. Acker, Joan. 1990. "Hierarchies, Jobs, Bodies: A Theory of Gendered Organizations." *Gender & Society* 4(2):139–58.

15. Blair-Loy, Mary. 2001. "It's Not Just What You Know It's Who You Know: Technical Knowledge, Rainmaking, and Gender Among." *Research in the Sociology of Work* 10:51–83.

16. Gorman, Elizabeth H. 2005. "Gender Stereotypes, Same-Gender Preferences, and Organizational Variation in the Hiring of Women: Evidence from Law Firms." *American Sociological Review* 70(4):702–28.

17. Davies, Karen. 2003. "The Body and Doing Gender: The Relations between Doctors and Nurses in Hospital Work." *Sociology of Health & Illness* 25(7):720–42.

18. Hatmaker, Deneen M. 2013. "Engineering Identity: Gender and Professional Identity Negotiation among Women Engineers." *Gender, Work & Organization* 20(4):382–96.

19. Kenney, Sally Jane. 2013. *Gender and Justice: Why Women in the Judiciary Really Matter*. Abingdon, UK: Routledge.

20. Manchester, Colleen Flaherty, Leslie, Lisa M., & Kramer, Amit. 2013. "Is the Clock Still Ticking? An Evaluation of the Consequences of Stopping the Tenure Clock." *ILR Review* 66(1):3–31.

21. Rhoton, Laura A. 2011. "Distancing as a Gendered Barrier: Understanding Women Scientists' Gender Practices." *Gender & Society* 25(6):696–716.

22. U.S. Census Bureau. 2019. "Labor Source Statistics from Current Population Survey. Employed Persons by Detailed Occupation, Sex, Race, and Hispanic or Latino Ethnicity." Retrieved from https://www.bls.gov/cps/cpsaat11.htm.

23. Williams, Christine L. 1995. *Still a Man's World: Men Who Do Women's Work*, Vol. 1. Berkeley: University of California Press.

    Wingfield, Adia Harvey. 2009. "Racializing the Glass Escalator: Reconsidering Men's Experiences with Women's Work." *Gender & Society* 23(1):5–26.

    Williams, Christine L. 2013. "The Glass Escalator, Revisited: Gender Inequality in Neoliberal Times, SWS Feminist Lecturer." *Gender & Society* 27(5):609–29.

24. Williams, 1995; Wingfield, 2009; Williams, 2013.

25. Lupton, Deborah. 1997. "Doctors on the Medical Profession." *Sociology of Health & Illness* 19(4):480–97.

    Jones, Lorelei, & Green, Judith. 2006. "Shifting Discourses of Professionalism: A Case Study of General Practitioners in the United Kingdom." *Sociology of Health & Illness* 28(7):927–50.

    Riska, Elianne. 2008. "The Feminization Thesis: Discourses on Gender and Medicine." *NORA—Nordic Journal of Feminist and Gender Research* 16(1):3–18.

26. Lupton, 1997, p. 488.

27. Ibid., p. 489.

28. Ibid., p. 485.

29. Freidson, E. 1993. "How Dominant Are the Professions?" Pp. 54–66 in Hafferty, F. and McKinlay, J. (eds.), *The Changing Medical Profession: An International Perspective*. New York: Oxford University Press.

    Light, D. 1993. "Countervailing Power: The Changing Character of the Medical Profession in the United States." Pp. 69–79 in Hafferty, F., and McKinlay, J. (eds.), *The Changing Medical Profession: An International Perspective*. New York: Oxford University Press. Lupton, 1997.

30. Willis, E. 1993. "The Medical Profession in Australia." Pp. 104–15 in Hafferty, F., and McKinlay, J. (eds.), *The Changing Medical Profession: An International Perspective*. New York: Oxford University Press.

31. U.S. Census Bureau of Labor Statistics. "Median Usual Weekly Earnings of Full-time Wage and Salary Workers, by Detailed Occupation, 2017 Annual Averages." 2017. Retrieved from https://www.bls.gov/opub/reports/womens-earnings/2017/pdf/home.pdf.

    U.S. Census Bureau of Labor Statistics. 2019. "Employed Persons by Detailed Occupation, Sex, Race, and Hispanic or Latino Ethnicity." Retrieved from https://www.bls.gov/cps/cpsaat11.htm.

32. Davies, Karen. 2003. "The Body and Doing Gender: The Relations between Doctors and Nurses in Hospital Work." *Sociology of Health & Illness* 25(7):720–42.

33. Eagly, Alice Hendrickson, Carli, Linda L., Eagly, Alice H., & Carli, Linda Lorene. 2007. *Through the Labyrinth: The Truth about How Women Become Leaders*. Cambridge, MA: Harvard Business Press.

Chapter 2

1. Purvis, Sally B. 1995. *The Stained-Glass Ceiling: Churches and Their Women Pastors*. Louisville, KY: Westminster John Knox Press.

2. Eagly, Alice Hendrickson, Carli, Linda L., Eagly, Alice H., & Carli, Linda Lorene. 2007. *Through the Labyrinth: The Truth about How Women Become Leaders*. Cambridge, MA: Harvard Business Press.

Chapter 3

1. Clegg, Stewart, & Dunkerley, David. 2013. *Organization, Class and Control. (Rle: Organizations)*. Abingdon, UK: Routledge.

2. Acker, Joan. 1990. "Hierarchies, Jobs, Bodies: A Theory of Gendered Organizations." *Gender & Society* 4(2):139–58.

3. Ibid., p. 147.

4. Fobes, Catherine. 2001. "Searching for a Priest . . . Or a Man? Using Gender as a Cultural Resource in an Episcopal Campus Chapel." *Journal for the Scientific Study of Religion* 40(1):87–98.

    Britton, Dana M. 1997. "Gendered Organizational Logic: Policy and Practice in Men's and Women's Prisons." *Gender & Society* 11(6):796–818.

5. Banaji, Mahzarin R., & Greenwald, Anthony G. 2016. *Blindspot: Hidden Biases of Good People*. London: Bantam.

6. Correll, Shelley J. 2017. "SWS 2016 Feminist Lecture: Reducing Gender Biases in Modern Workplaces: A Small Wins Approach to Organizational Change." *Gender & Society* 31(6):725–50.

Easterly, Debra M., & Ricard, Cynthia S. 2011. "Conscious Efforts to End Unconscious Bias: Why Women Leave Academic Research." *Journal of Research Administration* 42(1):61–73.

7. Girod, Sabine, Fassiotto, Magali, Grewal, Daisy, Ku, Manwai Candy, Sriram, Natarajan, Nosek, Brian A., & Valantine, Hannah. 2016. "Reducing Implicit Gender Leadership Bias in Academic Medicine with an Educational Intervention." *Academic Medicine* 91(8):1143–50.

8. Acker, 1990.

9. Joel, Daphna, Berman, Zohar, Tavor, Ido, Wexler, Nadav, Gaber, Olga, Stein, Yaniv, Shefi, Nisan, Pool, Jared, Urchs, Sebastian, & Margulies, Daniel S. 2015. "Sex Beyond the Genitalia: The Human Brain Mosaic." *Proceedings of the National Academy of Sciences* 112(50):15468–73.

Jordan-Young, Rebecca M. 2011. *Brain Storm: The Flaws in the Science of Sex Differences*. Cambridge, MA: Harvard University Press.

Fine, C. 2017. *Testosterone Rex: Myths of Sex, Science, and Society*. New York: WW Norton & Company.

10. Schippers, Mimi. 2007. "Recovering the Feminine Other: Masculinity, Femininity, and Gender Hegemony." *Theory and Society*, 36(1), 85–102.

11. For a comprehensive understanding of the term "complicit masculinities," see Connell, R. W. 2005. *Masculinities*. Cambridge, UK: Polity.

12. Yoder, Janice D. 1991. "Rethinking Tokenism: Looking Beyond Numbers." *Gender & Society* 5(2):178–92.

Chapter 4

1. Acker, Joan. 1990. "Hierarchies, Jobs, Bodies: A Theory of Gendered Organizations." *Gender & Society* 4(2):139–58.

2. Schippers, Mimi. 2007. "Recovering the Feminine Other: Masculinity, Femininity, and Gender Hegemony." *Theory and Society* 36(1):85–102.

3. Ibid.

4. Acker, 1990.

5. Kenny, Kate, & Bell, Emma. 2011. "Representing the Successful Managerial Body." Pp. 163–76 in E. Jeanes, D. Knights, P. Y. Martin (eds.), *Handbook of Gender, Work and Organization*. West Sussex, United Kingdom: Wiley & Sons.

Kerfoot, Deborah, & Knights, David. 1993. "Management, Masculinity and Manipulation: From Paternalism to Corporate Strategy in Financial Services in Britain." *Journal of Management Studies* 30(4):659–77.

Connell, R. W., & Wood, Julian. 2005. "Globalization and Business Masculinities." *Men and Masculinities* 7(4):347–64.

Schilt, Kristen. 2006. "Just One of the Guys? How Transmen Make Gender Visible at Work." *Gender & Society* 20(4):465–90.

6. Case, Anne, & Paxson, Christina. 2008. "Stature and Status: Height, Ability, and Labor Market Outcomes." *Journal of Political Economy* 116(3):499–532.

Lindqvist, Erik. 2012. "Height and Leadership." *Review of Economics and Statistics* 94(4):1191–96.

Hamstra, Melvyn R. W. 2014. "'Big' Men: Male Leaders' Height Positively Relates to Followers' Perception of Charisma." *Personality and Individual Differences* 56:190–92.

Davies, Karen. 2003. "The Body and Doing Gender: The Relations between Doctors and Nurses in Hospital Work." *Sociology of Health & Illness* 25(7):720–42.

Sinclair, Amanda. 2011. "Leading with Body." Pp. 117–30 in E. Jeanes, D, Knights, & P. Y. Martin (Eds.), *Handbook of Gender, Work and Organization*. West Sussex, United Kingdom: John Wiley & Sons, Ltd.

7. Gladwell, Malcolm. 2005. *Blink: The Power of Thinking Without Thinking*. New York: Little, Brown and Co..

8. Persico, Nicola, Postlewaite, Andrew, & Silverman, Dan. 2004. "The Effect of Adolescent Experience on Labor Market Outcomes: The Case of Height." *Journal of Political Economy* 112(5):1019–53.

9. CDC/National Center for Health Statistics. Retrieved from https://www.cdc.gov/nchs/fastats/body-measurements.htm.

10. Schippers, Mimi. 2007. "Recovering the Feminine Other: Masculinity, Femininity, and Gender Hegemony." *Theory and Society* 36(1):85–102.

11. Ibid.

12. Ibid.

13. Ridgeway, Cecilia L. 2011. *Framed by Gender: How Gender Inequality Persists in the Modern World*. Oxford: Oxford University Press.

14. Glass, Christy M., Haas, Steven A., & Reither, Eric N. 2010. "The Skinny on Success: Body Mass, Gender and Occupational Standing across the Life Course." *Social Forces* 88(4):1777–806.

Dellinger, Kirsten, & Williams, Christine L. 1997. "Makeup at Work: Negotiating Appearance Rules in the Workplace." *Gender & Society* 11(2):151–77.

15. Frevert, T. K., & Walker, L. S. 2014. "Physical Attractiveness and Social Status." *Sociology Compass*, 8(3), 313–23.

16. Haynes, Kathryn. 2012. "Body Beautiful? Gender, Identity and the Body in Professional Services Firms." *Gender, Work & Organization* 19(5):489–507.

Weitz, Rose. 2001. "Women and Their Hair: Seeking Power through Resistance and Accommodation." *Gender & Society* 15(5):667–86.

Kaslow, Florence W., & Schwartz, Lita L. 1978. "Self-Perceptions of the Attractive, Successful Female Professional." *Intellect* 106(2393):313–15.

Chapter 5

1. Boushey, Heather. 2009. "The New Breadwinners." Pp. 30–67 in *The Shriver Report. A Woman's Nation Changes Everything*.

2. Milkie, Melissa A., Raley, Sara B., & Bianchi, Suzanne M. 2009. "Taking on the Second Shift: Time Allocations and Time Pressures of US Parents with Preschoolers." *Social Forces* 88(2):487–517.

3. Raley, S., Bianchi, S. M., & Wang, W. 2012. "When Do Fathers Care? Mothers' Economic Contribution and Fathers' Involvement in Child Care." *American Journal of Sociology* 117(5):1422–59.

4. Crittenden, Ann. 2002. *The Price of Motherhood: Why the Most Important Job in the World Is Still the Least Valued*. New York: Macmillan.

5. Maume, David J. 2008. "Gender Differences in Providing Urgent Childcare among Dual-Earner Parents." *Social Forces* 87(1):273–97.

6. Frame, Marsha W., & Shehan, Constance L. 2004. "Care for the Caregiver: Clues for the Pastoral Care of Clergywomen." *Pastoral Psychology* 52(5):369–80.

7. Schleifer, Cyrus, & Miller, Amy D. 2017. "Occupational Gender Inequality among American Clergy, 1976–2016: Revisiting the Stained-Glass Ceiling." *Sociology of Religion* 78(4):387–410.

   For a review of marriage penalties, see Killewald, Alexandra, & Gough, Margaret. 2013. "Does Specialization Explain Marriage Penalties and Premiums?" *American Sociological Review* 78(3):477–502.

8. Barreto, Manuela, & Ellemers, Naomi. 2005. "The Burden of Benevolent Sexism: How It Contributes to the Maintenance of Gender Inequalities." *European Journal of Social Psychology* 35(5):633–42.

9. Acker, Joan. 1990. "Hierarchies, Jobs, Bodies: A Theory of Gendered Organizations." *Gender & Society* 4(2):139–58.

10. Bort, Julie, Pflock, Aviva, & Renner, Devra. 2005. *Mommy Guilt: Learn to Worry Less, Focus on What Matters Most, and Raise Happier Kids*. New York: AMACOM/ American Management Association.

11. Horowitz, Julianna. 2019. "Despite Challenges at Home and Work, Most Working Moms and Dads Say Being Employed Is What's Best for Them." Pew Research Center. Retrieved from https://www.pewsocialtrends.org/2007/07/12/fewer-mothers-prefer-full-time-work/.

12. Bettinger, E., Hægeland, T., & Rege, M. 2014. "Home with Mom: The Effects of Stay-at-Home Parents on Children's Long-Run Educational Outcomes." *Journal of Labor Economics* 32(3):443–67.

13. England, Paula, Allison, Paul, & Wu, Yuxiao. 2007. "Does Bad Pay Cause Occupations to Feminize, Does Feminization Reduce Pay, and How Can We Tell with Longitudinal Data?" *Social Science Research* 36(3):1237–56.

   Levanon, Asaf, England, Paula, and Allison, Paul. 2009. "Occupational Feminization and Pay: Assessing Causal Dynamics Using 1950–2000 US Census Data." *Social Forces* 88(2):865–91.

14. Perl, P. 2002. "Gender and Mainline Protestant Pastors' Allocation of Time to Work Tasks." *Journal for the Scientific Study of Religion* 41(1):169–78.

   For a detailed description of the motherhood penalty more generally, see

   Budig, M. J., & England, P. 2001. "The Wage Penalty for Motherhood." *American Sociological Review* 66(2):204–25.

   Budig, M. J., & Hodges, M. J. 2010. "Differences in Disadvantage: Variation in the Motherhood Penalty across White Women's Earnings Distribution." *American Sociological Review* 75(5):705–28.

15. Hochschild, Arlie, and Machung, Anne. 2012. *The Second Shift: Working Families and the Revolution at Home*. New York: Penguin.

16. Bureau of Labor Statistics. 2018. "Employment Characteristics of Families Summary." Retrieved from https://www.bls.gov/news.release/famee.nr0.htm.

17. Boushey, H. 2009. "The New Breadwinners." Pp. 30–67 in *The Shriver Report. A Woman's Nation Changes Everything*.

18. Organization for Economic Cooperation. 2019. "Parental Leave Systems." Retrieved from http://www.oecd.org/els/soc/PF2_1_Parental_leave_systems.pdf.

19. Acker, Joan. 1990. "Hierarchies, Jobs, Bodies: A Theory of Gendered Organizations." *Gender & Society* 4(2):139–58.

20. UNICEF Office of Research. 2013. "Child Well-Being in Rich Countries: A Comparative Overview." Retrieved from https://www.unicef-irc.org/publications/pdf/rc11_eng.pdf.

21. Barnes, Riché Jeneen Daniel. 2008. "Black Women Have Always Worked." Pp. 189–209 in *The Changing Landscape of Work and Family in the American Middle Class: Reports from the Field*. Lanham, MD: Lexington Books.

22. Organization for Economic Cooperation. 2019. "Parental Leave Systems." Retrieved from http://www.oecd.org/els/soc/PF2_1_Parental_leave_systems.pdf.

   Hochschild, Arlie, and Machung, Anne. 2012. *The Second Shift: Working Families and the Revolution at Home*. New York: Penguin.

23. Murphy-Geiss, Gail E. 2011. "Married to the Minister: The Status of the Clergy Spouse as Part of a Two-Person Single Career." *Journal of Family Issues* 32(7):932–55.

24. Southwestern Theological Seminary Website. "Seminary Studies for Student Wives." Retrieved March 24, 2020. http://catalog.swbts.edu/womens-programs/seminary-studies-for-student-wives/.

25. Deutsch, Francine M. 2007. "Undoing Gender." *Gender & Society* 21(1):106–27.

Chapter 6

1. England, Paula, Allison, Paul, and Wu, Yuxiao. 2007. "Does Bad Pay Cause Occupations to Feminize, Does Feminization Reduce Pay, and How Can We Tell with Longitudinal Data?" *Social Science Research* 36(3):1237–56.

   Levanon, Asaf, England, Paula, and Allison, Paul. 2009. "Occupational Feminization and Pay: Assessing Causal Dynamics Using 1950–2000 US Census Data." *Social Forces* 88(2):865–91.

2. Davies, Margery. 2010. *Woman's Place Is at the Typewriter*. Philadelphia: Temple University Press.

   England, Allison, & Wu, 2007.

   Levanon, England, & Allison, 2009.

3. Irvine, Leslie, & Vermilya, Jenny R. 2010. "Gender Work in a Feminized Profession: The Case of Veterinary Medicine." *Gender & Society* 24(1):56–82.

4. Parts of this section are derived from a detailed literature review of feminized jobs and women's work from: Williams, C. L. 1995. *Still a Man's World: Men Who Do Women's*

Work (Vol. 1). Berkeley: University of California Press. Please review her work for a more in-depth understanding of feminized jobs, devaluation, and the glass escalator.

5. Rhoton, Laura A. 2011. "Distancing as a Gendered Barrier: Understanding Women Scientists' Gender Practices." *Gender & Society* 25(6):696–716.

6. Secretaries and administrative assistants are understood as interchangeable. I used the term *church secretary* in the text and survey because it still seemed to be a term commonly used by congregants.

7. Gribskov, Margaret. 1987. "Adelaide Pollock and the Founding of the NCAWE." P. 121 in *Women Educators: Employees of Schools in Western World Countries*.

8. Williams, 1995.

9. Quoted in ibid., p. 32. Also quoted in Grumet, M. R. 1988. *Bitter Milk: Women and Teaching*. Amherst: University of Massachusetts Press, p. 39.

10. Quoted in Williams, 1995, p. 27. Also quoted in Rothman, Sheila M. 1980. *Woman's Proper Place: A History of Changing Ideals and Practices, 1870 to the Present* (Vol. 5053). New York: Basic Books, p. 57.

11. Florence, N. (1860). Notes on Nursing. What it is and what it is not. *D. Appleton and Company, New York*. p. 3.

12. Fairchild, S. C. 1904. "Women in American Libraries." *Library Journal* 29:157–62. Quoted in Williams, 1995, p. 37.

13. Simpson, R. L., & Simpson, I. H. 1969. "Women and Bureaucracy in the Semi-Professions." Pp. in 199–200, *The Semi-Professions and Their Organization*. Also quoted in quoted in Williams, 1995, p. 41.

14. Schleifer, Cyrus, & Miller, Amy D. 2017. "Occupational Gender Inequality among American Clergy, 1976–2016: Revisiting the Stained-Glass Ceiling." *Sociology of Religion* 78(4):387–410.

15. For a review, see Killewald, Alexandra, & Gough, Margaret. 2013. "Does Specialization Explain Marriage Penalties and Premiums?" *American Sociological Review* 78(3):477–502.

16. England, Allison, and Wu, 2007.

17. Jordan-Young, Rebecca M. 2011. *Brain Storm: The Flaws in the Science of Sex Differences*. Cambridge, MA: Harvard University Press.

18. U.S. Census Bureau. 2019. "Labor Source Statistics from Current Population Survey. Employed Persons by Detailed Occupation, Sex, Race, and Hispanic or Latino Ethnicity." Retrieved from https://www.bls.gov/cps/cpsaat11.htm.

19. Williams, 1995.

20. Benevolent sexism refers to the idea that certain gendered behaviors or decisions as positive (e.g., decision to give a children's pastor an assistant because of her inability to balance demands of being a wife and mother with her job) but actually reinforces an unequal gender structure.

    Glick, Peter, & Fiske, Susan T. 2018. "The Ambivalent Sexism Inventory: Differentiating Hostile and Benevolent Sexism." Pp. 116–60 in *Social Cognition*. New York: Routledge.

21. Acker, Joan. 1990. "Hierarchies, Jobs, Bodies: A Theory of Gendered Organizations." *Gender & Society* 4(2):139–58.

22. Schleifer, Cyrus, & Miller, 2017.
23. England, Allison, & Wu, 2007.
24. Levanon, England, & Allison, 2009.
25. Lummis, A. T., & Nesbitt, Paula D. 2000. "Women Clergy Research and the Sociology of Religion." *Sociology of Religion* 61(4):443–53.
    Nesbitt, Paula D. 1997. "Clergy Feminization: Controlled Labor or Transformative Change?" *Journal for the Scientific Study of Religion*, 36(4):585–98.
    Nesbitt, Paula D. 1997. *Feminization of the Clergy in America: Occupational and Organizational Perspectives*. Oxford University Press on Demand.
26. Blau, Francine D., & Kahn, Lawrence M. 2007. "The Gender Pay Gap: Have Women Gone as Far as They Can? *Academy of Management Perspectives* 21(1):7–23.
27. Chamberlain, Andrew. 2019. "Progress on the Gender Pay Gap." Glassdoor Economic Research. Retrieved from https://www.glassdoor.com/research/gender-pay-gap-2019/.
28. Purvis, Sally B. 1995. *The Stained-Glass Ceiling: Churches and Their Women Pastors*. Louisville, KY: Westminster John Knox Press.

Chapter 7

1. Hartsock, Nancy C. 2019. *The Feminist Standpoint Revisited, and Other Essays.* New York: Routledge, Collins, Patricia Hill. 2004. "'Feminist Standpoint Theory Revisited': Where's the Power?" in S. Harding (Ed.), *The Feminist Standpoint Theory Reader: Intellectual and Political Controversie*, p. 247. New York: Routledge.
2. Harris, C. R., & Jenkins, M. 2006. "Gender Differences in Risk Assessment: Why Do Women Take Fewer Risks Than Men?" *Judgement and Decision-Making* 1(1):48–63.
3. Nelson, Julie A. 2015. "Are Women Really More Risk-Averse Than Men? A Re-analysis of the Literature Using Expanded Methods." *Journal of Economic Surveys* 29(3):566–85.
    Fine, C. 2017. *Testosterone Rex: Unmaking the Myths of Our Gendered Minds.* New York: Icon Books.
4. Djupe, Paul A., & Gilbert, Christopher P. 2002. "The Political Voice of Clergy." *The Journal of Politics* 64(2):596–609. Stewart-Thomas, Michelle. 2010. "Gendered Congregations, Gendered Service: The Impact of Clergy Gender on Congregational Social Service Participation." *Gender, Work & Organization* 17(4):406–32.
5. Gault, Barbara A., & Sabini, John. 2000. "The Roles of Empathy, Anger, and Gender in Predicting Attitudes toward Punitive, Reparative, and Preventative Public Policies." *Cognition & Emotion* 14(4):495–520.
6. Djupe, Paul A., & Gilbert, Christopher P. 2002. "The Political Voice of Clergy." *The Journal of Politics* 64(2):596–609. Stewart-Thomas, Michelle. 2010. "Gendered Congregations, Gendered Service: The Impact of Clergy Gender on Congregational Social Service Participation. *Gender, Work & Organization* 17(4):406–32.

7. Social positionality refers to one's relationship to power; to one's relationship to privilege and oppression.

8. Solnit, Rebecca. 2014. *Men Explain Things to Me*. Boston: Haymarket Books.

9. Redfern, Catherine, & Aune, Kristin. 2010. "Politics & Religion Transformed." In *Reclaiming the F Word: The New Feminist Movement*. London: Zed.

10. Maslach, C., & Jackson, S. E. 1981. "The Measurement of Experienced Burnout." *Journal of Organization Behavior* 2(2):99–113.

11. Deutsch, F. M. 2007. "Undoing Gender." *Gender & Society* 21(1):106–27.

Conclusion

1. Hochschild, A., & Machung, A. 2012. *The Second Shift: Working Families and the Revolution at Home*. New York: Penguin.

2. Purvis, Sally B. 1995. *The Stained-Glass Ceiling: Churches and Their Women Pastors*. Louisville, KY: Westminster John Knox Press.

3. Mac an Ghaill, Mairtin, & Haywood, Chris. 2012. "'Understanding Boys': Thinking through Boys, Masculinity and Suicide." *Social Science & Medicine* 74(4):482–89.

4. Adams, J. 2007. "Stained Glass Makes the Ceiling Visible: Organizational Opposition to Women in Congregational Leadership." *Gender & Society* 21(1):80–105.

5. U.S. Census Bureau. 2019. "Labor Source Statistics from Current Population Survey: Employed Persons by Detailed Occupation, Sex, Race, and Hispanic or Latino Ethnicity." Retrieved from https://www.bls.gov/cps/cpsaat11.htm.

6. Ibid.

7. Global Gender Gap Report. 2020. World Economic Forum. http://www3.weforum.org/docs/WEF_GGGR_2020.pdf.

8. Acker, Joan. 2006. "Inequality Regimes: Gender, Class, and Race in Organizations." *Gender & Society* 20(4):441–64.

Bibliography

Acker, Joan. 1990. Hierarchies, jobs, bodies: A theory of gendered organizations. *Gender & Society*, 4(2), 139–158.

Acker, Joan. 1992. From sex roles to gendered institutions. *Contemporary Sociology*, 21(5), 565–569.

Acker, Joan. 2006. Inequality regimes: Gender, class, and race in organizations. *Gender & Society*, 20(4), 441–464.

Adams, Jimi. 2007. Stained glass makes the ceiling visible: Organizational opposition to women in congregational leadership. *Gender & Society*, 21(1), 80–105.

Ammerman, Nancy Tatom. 1990. *Baptist battles: Social change and religious conflict in the Southern Baptist Convention*. New Brunswick, NJ: Rutgers University Press.

Arnold, Arthur P., and Gorski, Roger A. 1984. Gonadal steroid induction of structural sex differences in the central nervous system. *Annual Review of Neuroscience*, 7(1), 413–442.

Bagilhole, Barbara. 2006. Not a glass ceiling, more a lead roof: Experiences of pioneer women priests in the Church of England. *Equal Opportunities International*, 25(2), 109–125.

Banaji, Mahzarin R., and Greenwald, Anthony G. 2016. *Blindspot: Hidden biases of good people*. London: Bantam.

Barnes, Riché Jeneen Daniel. 2008. Black Women Have Always Worked. In *The changing landscape of work and family in the American middle class: Reports from the field* (pp. 189–209). Lanhan, MD: Lexington Books.

Barreto, Manuela, and Ellemers, Naomi. 2005. The burden of benevolent sexism: How it contributes to the maintenance of gender inequalities. *European Journal of Social Psychology*, 35(5), 633–642.

Bem, Sandra Lipsitz. 1981. Gender schema theory: A cognitive account of sex typing. *Psychological Review*, 88(4), 354.

Bem, Sandra Lipsitz. 1993. *The lenses of gender: Transforming the debate on sexual inequality*. New Haven, CT: Yale University Press.

Bettinger, E., Hægeland, T., and Rege, M. 2014. Home with mom: The effects of stay-at-home parents on children's long-run educational outcomes. *Journal of Labor Economics*, 32(3), 443–467.

Blair-Loy, Mary. 2001. It's not just what you know, it's who you know: Technical knowledge, rainmaking, and gender among finance executives. *Research in the Sociology of Work*, 10, 51–83.

Blau, Francine D., and Kahn, Lawrence M. 2007. The gender pay gap: Have women gone as far as they can? *Academy of Management Perspectives*, 21(1), 7–23.

Bort, Julie, Pflock, Aviva, and Renner, Devra. 2005. *Mommy guilt: Learn to worry less, focus on what matters most, and raise happier kids*. New York: AMACOM/American Management Association.

Boushey, H. 2009. The new breadwinners. In *The Shriver Report: A woman's nation changes everything* (pp. 30–67). New York: Free Press.

Britton, Dana M. 1997. Gendered organizational logic: Policy and practice in men's and women's prisons. *Gender & Society, 11*(6), 796–818.

Britton, Dana M. 2003. *At work in the iron cage: The prison as gendered organization.* New York: NYU Press.

Britton, Dana M., and Williams, Christine L. 1995. Don't ask, don't tell, don't pursue: Military policy and the construction of heterosexual masculinity. *Journal of Homosexuality, 30*(1), 1–21.

Brizendine, Louann. 2006. *The female brain.* New York: Broadway Books.

Budig, M. J., and England, P. 2001. The wage penalty for motherhood. *American Sociological Review, 66* (2), 204–225.

Budig, M. J., and Hodges, M. J. 2010. Differences in disadvantage: Variation in the motherhood penalty across white women's earnings distribution. *American Sociological Review, 75*(5), 705–728.

Bureau of Labor Statistics. 2018. Employment characteristics of families summary. Retrieved from https://www.bls.gov/news.release/famee.nr0.htm

Butler, Judith. 1999. *Gender trouble.* New York: Routledge.

Butler, Judith. 2006. Performative acts and gender constitution: An essay in phenomenology and feminist theory. In *The Routledgefalmer reader in gender & education* (pp. 73–83). Abingdon, UK: Routledge.

Butterfield, Stephen A., and Loovis, E. Michael. 1993. Influence of age, sex, balance, and sport participation on development of throwing by children in grades K–8. *Perceptual and Motor Skills, 76*(2), 459–464.

Cahill, Larry. 2003. Sex-related influences on the neurobiology of emotionally influenced memory. *Annals of the New York Academy of Sciences, 985*(1), 163–173.

Case, Anne, and Paxson, Christina. 2008. Stature and status: Height, ability, and labor market outcomes. *Journal of Political Economy, 116*(3), 499–532.

CDC/National Center for Health Statistics. https://www.cdc.gov/nchs/fastats/body-measurements.htm

Chamberlain, Andrew. 2019. Progress on the gender pay gap. Glassdoor Economic Research. https://www.glassdoor.com/research/gender-pay-gap-2019/

Chang, Patricia M. Y. 1997. Introduction to symposium: Female clergy in the contemporary Protestant church: A current assessment. *Journal for the Scientific Study of Religion, 36*(4), 565–573.

Chaves, Mark. 1999. *Ordaining women: Culture and conflict in religious organizations.* Cambridge, MA: Harvard University Press.

Chaves, Mark. *National Congregations Study—1998, 2006, and 2012.* Ann Arbor, MI: Inter-university Consortium for Political and Social Research, Retrieved May 6, 2015, from https://doi.org/10.3886/ICPSR03471.v3

Chodorow, Nancy J. 1999. *The reproduction of mothering: Psychoanalysis and the sociology of gender.* Berkeley: University of California Press.

Choi N., Fuqua, D., and Newman, J. 2008. The BEM sex-role inventory. A summary report of 23 validation studies. *Educational and Psychological Measurement, 63*, 872–887.

Clegg, Stewart, and Dunkerley, David. 2013. *Organization, class and control (Rle: Organizations).* Abingdon, UK: Routledge.

Collaer, Marcia L., and Hines, Melissa. 1995. Human behavioral sex differences: A role for gonadal hormones during early development?. *Psychological Bulletin, 118*(1), 55.

Collins, Patricia Hill. 2004. Feminist standpoint theory revisited: Where's the power? In *The feminist standpoint theory reader: Intellectual and political controversies*, p. 247. New York: Routledge.

Connell, R. W., and Julian Wood. 2005. Globalization and business masculinities. *Men and Masculinities*, *7*(4), 347–364.

Connell, R. W. 2005. *Masculinities*. Cambridge, UK: Polity.

Cooke, Bradley, Hegstrom, Carol D., Villeneuve, Loic S., and Breedlove, S. Marc. 1998. Sexual differentiation of the vertebrate brain: Principles and mechanisms. *Frontiers in Neuroendocrinology*, *19*(4), 323–362.

Correll, Shelley J. 2017. SWS 2016 feminist lecture: Reducing gender biases in modern workplaces: A small wins approach to organizational change. *Gender & Society*, *31*(6), 725–750.

Crittenden, Ann. 2002. *The price of motherhood: Why the most important job in the world is still the least valued*. New York: Macmillan.

Davies, Karen. 2003. The body and doing gender: The relations between doctors and nurses in hospital work. *Sociology of Health & Illness*, *25*(7), 720–742.

Davies, Margery. 2010. *Woman's place is at the typewriter*. Philadelphia: Temple University Press.

De Gasquet, Béatrice. 2010. The barrier and the stained-glass ceiling. Analyzing female careers in religious organizations. *Sociologie du travail*, *52*, e22–e39.

Dellinger, Kirsten, and Williams, Christine L. 1997. Makeup at work: Negotiating appearance rules in the workplace. *Gender & Society*, *11*(2), 151–177.

Deutsch, Francine M. 2007. Undoing gender. *Gender & Society*, *21*(1), 106–127.

Djupe, Paul A., and Gilbert, Christopher P. 2002. The political voice of clergy. *The Journal of Politics*, *64*(2), 596–609.

Durso, P., and Pranato, K. 2015. State of women in Baptist life. *Baptist Women in Ministry*. Retrieved from https://bwim.info/wp-content/uploads/2016/11/SWBL-2015-revised-7-11-16.pdf

Eagly, Alice Hendrickson, and Carli, Linda Lorene. 2007. *Through the labyrinth: The truth about how women become leaders*. Cambridge, MA: Harvard Business Press.

Easterly, Debra M., and Ricard, Cynthia S. 2011. Conscious efforts to end unconscious bias: Why women leave academic research. *Journal of Research Administration*, *42*(1), 61–73.

Eberhardt, J. L. 2020. *Biased: Uncovering the hidden prejudice that shapes what we see, think, and do*. New York: Penguin Books.

Edwards, Allen L., and Ashworth, Clark D. 1977. A replication study of item selection for the BEM Sex Role Inventory. *Applied Psychological Measurement*, *1*(4), 501–507.

England, Paula, Allison, Paul, and Wu, Yuxiao. 2007. Does bad pay cause occupations to feminize, does feminization reduce pay, and how can we tell with longitudinal data? *Social Science Research*, *36*(3), 1237–1256.

Epstein, Cynthia Fuchs. 1988. *Deceptive distinctions: Sex, gender, and the social order*. New Haven, CT: Yale University Press.

Evans, Herbert M. 1939. Endocrine glands: Gonads, pituitary, and adrenals. *Annual Review of Physiology*, *1*(1), 577–652.

Fairchild, S. C. 1904. Women in American libraries. *Library Journal*, *29*, 157–162.

Fausto-Sterling, Anne. 2000. *Sexing the body: Gender politics and the construction of sexuality*. New York: Basic Books.

Finlay, B. 2003. *Facing the stained glass ceiling: Gender in a Protestant seminary.* Lanham, MD: University Press of America.

Fine, C. 2017. *Testosterone rex: Unmaking the myths of our gendered minds.* New York: Icon.

Fobes, Catherine. 2001. Searching for a priest . . . or a man? Using gender as a cultural resource in an Episcopal campus chapel. *Journal for the Scientific Study of Religion,* 40(1), 87–98.

Frame, Marsha Wiggins, and Shehan, Constance L. 2004. Care for the caregiver: Clues for the pastoral care of clergywomen. *Pastoral Psychology,* 52(5), 369–380.

Frame, Marsha Wiggins, and Shehan, Constance L. 2005. The relationship between work and well-being in clergywomen: Implications for career counseling. *Journal of Employment Counseling,* 42(1), 10–19.

Frank, R. T. 1929. *The female sex hormone.* Baltimore, MD: Charles C. Thomas.

Freedman, David. 1983. Woman, a power equal to a man. *Biblical Archaeology Review,* 9, 56–58.

Freidson, E. 1993. How dominant are the professions? In F. Hafferty and J. McKinlay (Eds.), *The changing medical profession: An international perspective.* New York: Oxford University Press.

Frevert, T. K., and Walker, L. S. 2014. Physical attractiveness and social status. *Sociology Compass,* 8(3), 313–323.

Gault, Barbara A., and Sabini, John. 2000. The roles of empathy, anger, and gender in predicting attitudes toward punitive, reparative, and preventative public policies. *Cognition & Emotion,* 14(4), 495–520.

Gill, Sandra, Stockard, Jean, Johnson, Miriam, and Williams, Suzanne. 1987. Measuring gender differences: The expressive dimension and critique of androgyny scales. *Sex Roles,* 17(7–8), 375–400.

Girod, Sabine, Fassiotto, Magali, Grewal, Daisy, Ku, Manwai Candy, Sriram, Natarajan, Nosek, Brian A., and Valantine, Hannah. 2016. Reducing implicit gender leadership bias in academic medicine with an educational intervention. *Academic Medicine,* 91(8), 1143–1150.

Gladwell, Malcolm. 2005. *Blink: The power of thinking without thinking.* New York: Little, Brown and Co.

Glass, Christy M., Haas, Steven A., and Reither, Eric N. 2010. The skinny on success: Body mass, gender and occupational standing across the life course. *Social Forces,* 88(4), 1777–1806.

Glick, Peter, and Fiske, Susan T. 2018. The ambivalent sexism inventory: Differentiating hostile and benevolent sexism (1996). *Social Cognition* (pp. 116–160). New York: Routledge.

Gorman, Elizabeth H. 2005. Gender stereotypes, same-gender preferences, and organizational variation in the hiring of women: Evidence from law firms. *American Sociological Review,* 70(4), 702–728.

Greenwald, Anthony G., and Krieger, Linda Hamilton. 2006. Implicit bias: Scientific foundations. *California Law Review,* 94(4), 945–967.

Gribskov, Margaret. 1987. Adelaide Pollock and the founding of the NCAWE. In P. Schmuck (Ed.), *Women Educators: Employees of Schools in Western World Countries* (p. 121). Albany, New York: State University of New York Press.

Grumet, M. R. 1988. *Bitter milk: Women and teaching.* Amherst: University of Massachusetts Press.

Hamstra, Melvyn R. W. 2014. "Big" men: Male leaders' height positively relates to followers' perception of charisma. *Personality and Individual Differences*, *56*, 190–192.

Harris, C. R., and Jenkins, M. 2006. Gender differences in risk assessment: Why do women take fewer risks than men? *Judgement and Decision-Making*, *1*(1), 48–63.

Hartsock, Nancy C. 2019. *The feminist standpoint revisited, and other essays*. New York: Routledge.

Hatmaker, Deneen M. 2013. Engineering identity: Gender and professional identity negotiation among women engineers. *Gender, Work & Organization*, *20*(4), 382–396.

Haynes, Kathryn. 2012. Body beautiful? Gender, identity and the body in professional services firms. *Gender, Work & Organization*, *19*(5), 489–507.

Hochschild, Arlie, and Machung, Anne. 2012. *The second shift: Working families and the revolution at home*. New York: Penguin.

Holterhus, Paul-Martin, Bebermeier, Jan-Hendrik, Werner, Ralf, Demeter, Janos, Richter-Unruh, Annette, Cario, Gunnar, Appari, Mahesh, Siebert, Reiner, Riepe, Felix, and Brooks, James D. 2009. Disorders of sex development expose transcriptional autonomy of genetic sex and androgen-programmed hormonal sex in human blood leukocytes. *BMC Genomics*, *10*(1), 292.

Horowitz, Julianna. 2019. Despite challenges at home and work, most working moms and dads say being employed is what's best for them. Pew Research Center. https://www.pewsocialtrends.org/2007/07/12/fewer-mothers-prefer-full-time-work/

Irvine, Leslie, and Vermilya, Jenny R. 2010. Gender work in a feminized profession: The case of veterinary medicine. *Gender & Society*, *24*(1), 56–82.

James, R. B., Jackson, B., Shepherd, R., and Showalter, C. 2006. *The Fundamentalist Takeover in the Southern Baptist Convention*, p. 14. Missouri: Impact Media.

Joel, Daphna, Berman, Zohar, Tavor, Ido, Wexler, Nadav, Gaber, Olga, Stein, Yaniv, Shefi, Nisan, Pool, Jared, Urchs, Sebastian, and Margulies, Daniel S. 2015. Sex beyond the genitalia: The human brain mosaic. *Proceedings of the National Academy of Sciences*, *112*(50), 15468–15473.

Jolls, Christine, and Sunstein, Cass R. 2006. The law of implicit bias. *California Law Review*, *94*, 969.

Jones, Lorelei, and Green, Judith. 2006. Shifting discourses of professionalism: A case study of general practitioners in the United Kingdom. *Sociology of Health & Illness*, *28*(7), 927–950.

Jordan-Young, Rebecca M. 2011. *Brain storm: The flaws in the science of sex differences*. Cambridge, MA: Harvard University Press.

Kane, Emily W. 2012. *The gender trap: Parents and the pitfalls of raising boys and girls*. New York: NYU Press.

Kanter, Rosabeth Moss. 2008. *Men and women of the corporation: New edition*. New York: Basic Books.

Kaslow, Florence W., and Schwartz, Lita L. 1978. Self-perceptions of the attractive, successful female professional. *Intellect*, *106*(2393), 313–315.

Kelan, Elisabeth K. 2010. Gender logic and (un) doing gender at work. *Gender, Work & Organization*, *17*(2), 174–179.

Kenney, Sally J. 2000. Beyond principals and agents: Seeing courts as organizations by comparing référendaires at the European court of justice and law clerks at the US Supreme Court. *Comparative Political Studies*, *33*(5), 593–625.

Kenney, Sally J. 2004. Equal employment opportunity and representation: Extending the frame to courts. *Social Politics: International Studies in Gender, State & Society*, *11*(1), 86–116.

Kenney, Sally J. 2013. *Gender and justice: Why women in the judiciary really matter.* Abingdon, UK: Routledge.

Kenny, Kate, and Bell, Emma. 2011. Representing the successful managerial body. In E. Jeanes, D. Knights, P. Y. Martin (Eds.), *Handbook of gender, work and organization* (pp. 163–176). West Sussex, United Kingdom: Wiley & Sons.

Kerfoot, Deborah, and Knights, David. 1993. Management, masculinity and manipulation: From paternalism to corporate strategy in financial services in Britain. *Journal of Management Studies, 30*(4), 659–677.

Killewald, Alexandra, and Gough, Margaret. 2013. Does specialization explain marriage penalties and premiums? *American Sociological Review, 78*(3), 477–502.

Knoll, Benjamin R., and Bolin, Cammie J. 2018. *She preached the word: Women's ordination in modern America.* New York: Oxford University Press.

Kurtz, Don L., Linnemann, Travis, and Williams, L. Susan. 2012. Reinventing the matron: The continued importance of gendered images and division of labor in modern policing. *Women & Criminal Justice, 22*(3), 239–263.

Laqueur, Ernst, Dingemanse, Elisabeth, Hart, P. C., and de Jongh, Samuel E. 1927. Female sex hormone in urine of men. *Klinische Wochenschrift, 6*(1), 859.

Lauve-Moon, K. 2016. The case of Dean Diana Garland: Taking a stand at Southern Baptist Theological Seminary. *Women Leading Change: Case Studies on Women, Gender, and Feminism, 1*(2), 19.

Leahey, Erin. 2007. Not by productivity alone: How visibility and specialization contribute to academic earnings. *American Sociological Review, 72*(4), 533–561.

Lester, Jaime. 2008. Performing gender in the workplace: Gender socialization, power, and identity among women faculty members. *Community College Review, 35*(4), 277–305.

Levanon, Asaf, England, Paula, and Allison, Paul. 2009. Occupational feminization and pay: Assessing causal dynamics using 1950–2000 US census data. *Social Forces, 88*(2), 865–891.

Lewis, Karoline M. 2016. *She: Five keys to unlock the power of women in ministry.* Nashville, TN: Abingdon Press.

Light, D. 1993. Countervailing power: The changing character of the medical profession in the United States. In F. Hafferty & J. McKinlay (Eds.), *The changing medical profession: An international perspective,* (pp. 69–79). New York: Oxford University Press.

Lillie, F. R. 1939. Biological introduction. In Allen E (Ed.), *Sex and internal secretions,* 2nd ed (pp. 1–11). Baltimore, MD: Williams and Wilkins.

Lindqvist, Erik. 2012. Height and leadership. *Review of Economics and Statistics, 94*(4), 1191–1196.

Lippa, Richard A. 2005. *Gender, nature, and nurture.* Milton Park, UK: Routledge.

Locksley, Anne, and Colten, Mary Ellen. 1979. Psychological androgyny: A case of mistaken identity? *Journal of Personality and Social Psychology, 37*(6), 1017.

Lorber, Judith, and Farrell, Susan A. 1991. *The social construction of gender.* Newbury Park, CA: Sage.

Lorber, Judith. 1994. *Paradoxes of gender.* New Haven, CT: Yale University Press.

Lummis, A. T., and Nesbitt, Paula D. 2000. Women clergy research and the sociology of religion. *Sociology of Religion, 61*(4), 443–453.

Lupton, Deborah. 1997. Doctors on the medical profession. *Sociology of Health & Illness, 19*(4), 480–497.

Mac an Ghaill, Mairtin, and Haywood, Chris. 2012. Understanding boys': Thinking through boys, masculinity and suicide. *Social Science & Medicine, 74*(4), 482–489.

Manchester, Colleen Flaherty, Leslie, Lisa M., and Kramer, Amit. 2013. Is the clock still ticking? An evaluation of the consequences of stopping the tenure clock. *ILR Review*, 66(1), 3–31.

Manville, Julie. 1997. The gendered organization of an Australian Anglican parish. *Sociology of Religion*, 58(1), 25–38.

Martin, Karin A. 1998. Becoming a gendered body: Practices of preschools. *American Sociological Review*, 63(4), 494–511.

Martin, Patricia Yancey. 2004. Gender as social institution. *Social Forces*, 82(4), 1249–1273.

Maume, David J. 2008. Gender differences in providing urgent childcare among dual-earner parents. *Social Forces*, 87(1), 273–297.

Milkie, Melissa A., Raley, Sara B., and Bianchi, Suzanne M. 2009. Taking on the second shift: Time allocations and time pressures of US parents with preschoolers. *Social Forces*, 88(2), 487–517.

Murphy-Geiss, Gail E. 2011. Married to the minister: The status of the clergy spouse as part of a two-person single career. *Journal of Family Issues*, 32(7), 932–955.

Nelson, Julie A. 2015. Are women really more risk-averse than men? A re-analysis of the literature using expanded methods. *Journal of Economic Surveys*, 29(3), 566–585.

Nesbitt, Paula D. 1993. Dual ordination tracks: Differential benefits and costs for men and women clergy. *Sociology of Religion*, 54(1), 13–30.

Nesbitt, Paula D. 1997. Clergy feminization: Controlled labor or transformative change? *Journal for the Scientific Study of Religion*, 36(4), 585–598.

Nesbitt, Paula D. 1997. *Feminization of the clergy in America: Occupational and organizational perspectives*. Oxford University Press on Demand.

Florence, N. 1860. Notes on Nursing. What it is and what it is not. *D. Appleton and Company, New York*.

Organization for Economic Cooperation. 2019. Parental leave systems. http://www.oecd.org/els/soc/PF2_1_Parental_leave_systems.pdf

Oudshoorn, Nelly. 2003. *Beyond the natural body: An archaeology of sex hormones*. Abingdon, UK: Routledge.

Paap, Kris. 2018. *Working construction: Why white working-class men put themselves—and the labor movement—in harm's way*. Ithaca, NY: Cornell University Press.

Parkes, Alan S. 1938. Terminology of sex hormones. *Nature*, 141(3557), 36.

Perl, P. 2002. Gender and mainline Protestant pastors' allocation of time to work tasks. *Journal for the Scientific Study of Religion*, 41(1), 169–178.

Persico, Nicola, Postlewaite, Andrew, and Silverman, Dan. 2004. The effect of adolescent experience on labor market outcomes: The case of height. *Journal of political Economy*, 112(5), 1019–1053.

Phoenix, Charles H., Goy, Robert W., Gerall, Arnold A., and Young, William C. 1959. Organizing action of prenatally administered testosterone propionate on the tissues mediating mating behavior in the female guinea pig. *Endocrinology*, 65(3), 369–382.

Plimpton, Carol E., and Regimbal, Celia. 1992. Differences in motor proficiency according to gender and race. *Perceptual and Motor Skills*, 74(2), 399–402.

Powlishta, K. K., Sen, M. G., Serbin, L. A., Poulin-Dubois, D., and Eichstedt, J. A. 2001. "From infancy through middle childhood: The role of cognitive and social factors in becoming gendered." In R. K. Unger (Ed.), *Handbook of the psychology of women and gender* (p. 116–132). New Jersey: John Wiley & Sons, Inc.

Purcell, David. 2013. Baseball, beer, and bulgari: Examining cultural capital and gender inequality in a retail fashion corporation. *Journal of Contemporary Ethnography*, *42*(3), 291–319.

Purvis, Sally B. 1995. *The stained-glass ceiling: Churches and their women pastors.* Louisville, KY: Westminster John Knox Press.

Raley, S., Bianchi, S. M., and Wang, W. 2012. When do fathers care? Mothers' economic contribution and fathers' involvement in child care. *American Journal of Sociology*, *117*(5), 1422–1459.

Redfern, Catherine, and Aune, Kristin. 2010. *Reclaiming the F word: The new feminist movement.* London: Zed.

Rhoton, Laura A. 2011. Distancing as a gendered barrier: Understanding women scientists' gender practices. *Gender & Society*, *25*(6), 696–716.

Ridgeway, Cecilia L. 2009. Framed before we know it: How gender shapes social relations. *Gender & Society*, *23*(2), 145–160.

Ridgeway, Cecilia L. 2011. *Framed by gender: How gender inequality persists in the modern world.* Oxford: Oxford University Press.

Riska, Elianne. 2008. The feminization thesis: Discourses on gender and medicine. *NORA—Nordic Journal of Feminist and Gender Research*, *16*(1), 3–18.

Risman, Barbara J. 1998. *Gender vertigo: American families in transition.* New Haven, CT: Yale University Press.

Risman, Barbara J. 2004. Gender as a social structure: Theory wrestling with activism. *Gender & Society*, *18*(4), 429–450.

Risman, Barbara J., and Davis, Georgiann. 2013. From sex roles to gender structure. *Current Sociology*, *61*(5–6), 733–755.

Rosenthal, Lisa, Levy, Sheri R., London, Bonita, Lobel, Marci, and Bazile, Cartney. 2013. In pursuit of the MD: The impact of role models, identity compatibility, and belonging among undergraduate women. *Sex Roles*, *68*(7–8), 464–473.

Rothaus, Kyndall R. 2018, January 16. Nevertheless she preached. Retrieved from https://www.workingpreacher.org/craft.aspx?post=5045

Rothman, Sheila M. 1980. *Woman's proper place: A history of changing ideals and practices, 1870 to the present* (Vol. 5053). New York: Basic Books.

Sayce, S., and Acker, J. 2012. Gendered organizations and intersectionality: Problems and possibilities. *Equality, Diversity and Inclusion: An International Journal*, *31*(3): 214–224.

Schilt, Kristen. 2006. Just one of the guys? How transmen make gender visible at work. *Gender & Society*, *20*(4), 465–490.

Schippers, Mimi. 2007. Recovering the feminine other: Masculinity, femininity, and gender hegemony. *Theory and Society*, *36*(1), 85–102.

Schleifer, Cyrus, and Miller, Amy D. 2017. Occupational gender inequality among American clergy, 1976–2016: Revisiting the stained-glass ceiling. *Sociology of Religion*, *78*(4), 387–410.

Sealy, Ruth, and Singh, Val. 2006. Role models, work identity and senior women's career progression—Why are role models important? In *Academy of Management Proceedings*, Vol. 2006 (pp. E1–E6). Briarcliff Manor, NY: Academy of Management.

Siebke, Harald. 1931. Presence of androkinin in female organism. *Archiv für Gynaekologie*, *146*, 417–462.

Simpson, R. L., and Simpson, I. H. 1969. Women and bureaucracy in the semi-professions. In *The semi-professions and their organization* (pp. 199–200). New York: Free Press.

Sinclair, Amanda. 2011. "Leading with Body." In E. Jeanes, D. Knights, and P. Y. Martin (Eds.), *Handbook of Gender, Work and Organization,* (pp. 117–30). West Sussex, United Kingdom: John Wiley & Sons.

Smith, Christine A. 2013. *Beyond the stained glass ceiling: Equipping and encouraging female pastors.* Prussia, PA: Judson Press.

Smoll, Frank L., and Schutz, Robert W. 1990. Quantifying gender differences in physical performance: A developmental perspective. *Developmental Psychology, 26*(3), 360.

Snyder, Karrie Ann, and Green, Adam Isaiah. 2008. Revisiting the glass escalator: The case of gender segregation in a female dominated occupation. *Social Problems, 55*(2), 271–299.

Solnit, Rebecca. 2014. *Men explain things to me.* Boston: Haymarket Books.

Southwestern Theological Seminary Website. Seminary studies for student wives. Retrieved March 24, 2020, from http://catalog.swbts.edu/womens-programs/seminary-studies-for-student-wives/

Stewart-Thomas, Michelle. 2010. Gendered congregations, gendered service: The impact of clergy gender on congregational social service participation. *Gender, Work & Organization, 17*(4), 406–432.

Sullins, Paul. 2000. The stained glass ceiling: Career attainment for women clergy. *Sociology of Religion, 61*(3), 243–266.

Thomas, Jerry R., and French, Karen E. 1985. Gender differences across age in motor performance: A meta-analysis. *Psychological Bulletin, 98*(2), 260.

UNICEF Office of Research. 2013. Child well-being in rich countries: A comparative overview. Retrieved from https://www.unicef-irc.org/publications/pdf/rc11_eng.pdf

U.S. Census Bureau. 2019. Labor source statistics from current population survey. Employed persons by detailed occupation, sex, race, and Hispanic or Latino ethnicity. Retrieved from https://www.bls.gov/cps/cpsaat11.htm.

U.S. Census Bureau of Labor Statistics. 2017. Retrieved from https://www.bls.gov/opub/reports/womens-earnings/2017/pdf/home.pdf

Weitz, Rose. 2001. Women and their hair: Seeking power through resistance and accommodation. *Gender & Society, 15*(5), 667–686.

West, Candace, and Zimmerman, Don H. 1987. Doing gender. *Gender & Society, 1*(2), 125–151.

Wilkerson, Robyn. 2017. *Shattering the stained glass ceiling: A coaching strategy for women leaders in ministry.* Springfield, Missouri: Influence Resources.

Williams, Christine L. 1995. *Still a man's world: Men who do women's work.* Vol. 1. Berkeley: University of California Press.

Williams, Christine L. 2013. The glass escalator, revisited: Gender inequality in neoliberal times, SWS feminist lecturer. *Gender & Society, 27*(5), 609–629.

Willis, E. 1993. "The Medical Profession in Australia." In Hafferty, F., and J. McKinlay (Eds.), *The Changing Medical Profession: An International Perspective,* (pp. 104–115). New York: Oxford University Press.

Wingfield, Adia Harvey. 2009. Racializing the glass escalator: Reconsidering men's experiences with women's work. *Gender & Society, 23*(1), 5–26.

Yoder, Janice D. 1991. Rethinking tokenism: Looking beyond numbers. *Gender & Society, 5*(2), 178–192.

Zikmund, Barbara Brown, Lummis, Adair T., and Chang, Patricia M. Y. 1998. *Clergy women: An uphill calling.* Louisville, KY: Westminster John Knox Press.

Zondek, Bernhard. 1934. Mass excretion of oestrogenic hormone in the urine of the stallion. *Nature, 133*(3354), 209–210.

Index